Walking Together Through Life

Walking Together Through Life

A LIVINGSTON FAMILY MEMOIRS

G. HERBERT LIVINGSTON

authorHOUSE®

AuthorHouse™
1663 Liberty Drive
Bloomington, IN 47403
www.authorhouse.com
Phone: 1-800-839-8640

First published by AuthorHouse   09/16/2011

ISBN: 978-1-4634-0557-1 (sc)
ISBN: 978-1-4634-0556-4 (hc)
ISBN: 978-1-4634-1282-1 (ebk)

Library of Congress Control Number: 2011908066

Printed in the United States of America

CONTENTS

ACKNOWLEDGMENTS

To my daughter Nellie and her husband Ralph Kester, and my granddaughter Karen Crites who edited this volume, and to others who advised and encouraged me concerning this project, many thanks. Even through these efforts I know there will be still some errors. I take sole responsibility for all the writing.

FORWARD

I am ninety-four years of age, and I have begun looking back over seventy-four years of being an ordained minister. I decided I should write a testimony of what God has done in the combined lives of my wife Maria and myself. We were married for almost seventy-two years when she died in 2009. This volume has the history of a long successful marriage.

At the beginning of the Great Depression, both of our parents lost control of their farms and had to depend on the government for income. Both of us were penniless farm teenagers. Taking a clue from the Scriptures that often refers to the experiences of life as a walk; we have used that term for our life together. We started lives in the valley of poverty and moved uphill from one achievement to another. This book is the story of that journey.

The main part of this book is a record of being a minister, a professor and over two decades of retirement. Without the expert assistance and encouragement of Maria, this goal would not have happened.

CHAPTER 1

THE BIG EVENT

June 6, 1955 was a balmy day on the beautiful campus of Drew University, Madison, New Jersey. Tall hardwood trees shaded the ground. The occasion was the annual commencement service for the graduates of the University, one of the most famous institutions of the United Methodist Church. That afternoon over one thousand people were seated on folding chairs lined up row on row behind the graduates and facing the long pillared porch at the rear of Meade Hall. Administrative officers and other dignitaries were seated on the porch.

I was seated with my wife and three children in one of the rows reserved for the graduates. I wore a long black robe trimmed with blue velvet with three blue stripes on each sleeve. At the very end of the ceremony of presenting diplomas to the college and seminary graduates, President Fred G. Hollaway turned to Dr. John Paterson and requested him to bring George Herbert Livingston to the platform. Within a few moments, Dr. Paterson was escorting me to the platform, presenting me to the President and Dean Stanley R. Hopper. Dr. Hopper announced to the audience that I had successfully completed and defended before a committee of three faculty members a dissertation entitled, "The Hebrew Prophetic Consciousness," thus earning the right to possess the degree of Doctor of Philosophy. The two men then lifted a hood bearing the colors of Drew University over my head and on my shoulders. Next, they placed a black, flat academic hat with a shiny golden tassel on my head. The Dean announced I was henceforth Doctor George Herbert

Livingston. Dr. Paterson then took my arm and escorted me from the porch to my seat.

I embraced and kissed my lovely, loyal wife, Maria, and hugged our three children while the audience clapped and clapped. It was a climactic moment in my life and the life of my family, for this event was the completion of years of pastoral ministry and tedious academic study.

After the commencement service, friends celebrated with us for a brief time the accomplishment of earning a doctoral degree. We then drove about a hundred miles north to Callicoon, NY to visit friends related to a four church United Methodist charge I had served as pastor from June 1948 to May 1951. A celebration party was held for us and we rejoiced together. Several days later we returned by car to our home at 511 North Lexington Ave., Wilmore, KY. Close friends hosted another celebration party. It was a thrilling time, but soon we had to return to our academic duties at Asbury Theological Seminary where I had already served as Professor of Old Testament for two years.

CHAPTER 2

GROWING UP

Maria and I now had a few moments to search our memories and wonder: How was it that both of us had arisen from the poverty of the depression years to the positions of responsibility we both held? How had the Lord Jesus Christ been our Savior, Helper and Guide through those difficult years? What had been the steps of personal growth and professional service that marked our journey through life? What did the future hold? Answers to these questions may be found in the following narrative.

I was born July 27, 1916 on a small farm near Russell, Lucas Co. Iowa, son of George Wendell Livingston and Clara Lutheria Baker, grandson of Thomas M. Livingston and Aurilla Johnson and Joseph Baker and Miranda Andrews.

In 1918, my family moved to a hundred and eight acre farm five miles east of Cameron, Barron County, Wisconsin. My parents had heard about the availability of cheap land, which lumber companies were selling after cutting down huge white pine trees and supplying rapidly growing Chicago, Illinois, Milwaukee and Madison, Wisconsin, as well as the twin cities of Minnesota, St. Paul and Minneapolis, with lumber for houses.

Our farm had two buildings: One was a shack with two rooms, unfit for a family to live in, and, the other a poorly constructed barn that could house two horses and a few cows. Much of the land still had large white pine stumps that Dad had to remove. I was too young to remember this momentous move. As a boy, I learned that the family had lived in a rented house in Cameron during the fall of 1918 and the winter of 1919. Uncle Frank came to help my Dad and my brothers construct a 26 ft by 28 ft house made of cement blocks and lumber. The house had a full basement, with a dirt floor, and four rooms on the main floor. The family of nine somehow squeezed into these limited quarters. The situation was relieved somewhat when the older boys found places where they could work for board and room while attending Cameron High School.

During the winter months, when temperatures often plummeted well below zero, the wood-burning kitchen stove and the large, pot-bellied heating stove in the combined living room/bedroom were strained to the limit to keep the house warm. Neither the walls nor the ceiling had insulation, and the windows had no storm windows. The kind of insulation used in modern times was unknown. We wore plenty of warm, woolen clothes, even in the house.

My sister Vera, who was entering her teens, was assigned the task of looking after her baby brother. She watched over me with tender care. As I became four and five years of age, she enjoyed teaching me the ABC's, colors and simple math. I soon could read simple sentences and write the name the family favored, "Herbie". My mother later told me she wanted to name me Herbert Everett when I was born, but my older brothers soon put the three initials together and called me their little hel. That sounded like "hell", so mother quickly dropped Everett and proposed George Herbert. That stopped a lot of fun. I have been Herbert ever since.

On the morning of November 24, 1921, there was excitement and unusual activity around the house. At sunrise, Dad quickly fed us breakfast and explained that mother was ill. He said we three boys needed to go to the barn with him while he milked the cows and fed all the animals. Vera kept us busy in the barn with games and by reading stories. When Dad disappeared with the milk and took some time returning to the barn, we paid no attention. When he disappeared repeatedly, we began to ask questions but Vera did not explain. She increased her efforts to keep us busy with games.

About noon Dad returned from the house and told us to put on our warm clothes and come with him, for he had a surprise. As we crowded into the house, we heard strange noises and began to ask questions. We were soon ushered into our parents' bedroom, and in our mother's arms was the cause of the crying, a little baby. We soon learned the baby was a girl and her name was Dorothy Louise.

We were excited and we boys began to ask, "Where did she come from? How did she get here? How long would she stay?" Dad simply said, "A doctor came from Cameron and delivered the baby." Our united response was, "Where did he get the baby? How did he bring her safely in the cold? How much did he charge for her?" Dad didn't bother to explain the situation, and managed to interest us in how pretty the baby was and that she would grow up to be a wonderful playmate for us. Nothing was said about a stork.

At age six I entered the first grade at Sumner elementary (aka grade school) in a small community of six families. The wood framed building had one large main room where classes were held. Three small rooms were side by side along the back of a large room. One was a kitchenette, one the teacher's room and one was equipped for hanging clothes and storing lunch boxes. The building had a full basement with a concrete floor. Back of a large room, there was a room large enough for a big wood-burning furnace and a storage area for blocks of wood. During the winter, the large room was used for recreation and games during recess and time for lunch.

Children in grades one through eight were seated in rows of old style school desks in the large upper room. In a radius of two miles of the school there were a number of large farm families, so the enrollment usually numbered more than thirty students. One lady teacher was in charge of the school and keeping classes running smoothly, and keeping some fun-loving boys under control was a constant challenge.

The school was a mile from our home and my brothers and I always walked to school and back home each day. This walk became rather frightening when the winter winds blew snow blizzards out of the northwest. The snow often came down so heavily it was difficult to follow the pathway, and the strong wind was so cold it often chilled us through and through.

When I entered first grade, I quickly found that my sister Vera had given me a "head start" that the other first graders lacked. I often spent my spare time listening to students in the other grades recite their lessons to the teacher in segments of fifteen minutes. I learned a lot just listening, but Vera, on weekends, enjoyed giving me more instruction. She wanted to become a teacher, and after completing the necessary training, she taught in a school with only one room for several years before she married in February of 1929.

As a result of Vera's help, I was always ahead of my grade level, so in the middle of the fourth grade year, my teacher announced she was advancing me to the fifth grade level. I found my classes more of a challenge, but Vera was at home from high school on weekends to help me.

I remember when I was in sixth grade; Vera was in the Rice Lake Normal School for teachers twelve miles from home. She would bring her textbooks home on weekends. I was attracted immediately to a rather thick book entitled World History. During the time she took that course, I read the book from cover to cover.

I enjoyed school and because I had been advanced a full grade. I was a year younger that others when I graduated from grade school and entered Cameron High School five miles from home. There were no school buses, so walking continued to be the necessary mode of travel. My brother Ralph was also attending Cameron High School so we would often test each other's walking speed. Now and then a neighbor would pick us up and take us to town, or in the afternoon, as far as they could toward our home. Several of the winters I was able to work for my board and room at a farm close to Cameron. I graduated from the high school in May 1933, two months before my seventeenth birthday.

To this point I have described the educational influences that helped shape my childhood. There was another factor in my growing up that cannot be ignored. That factor was the impact of the religious convictions and the disciplined, gentle nurture that my mother bestowed upon her children. Mother was raised in a Christian home related to the small Methodist Episcopal (aka M. E.) church in Russell, Iowa. Faithful attendance at Sunday school and worship services marked the religious devotion of her parents and all their children. Revival services were frequent and at one of these services mother yielded her life to Jesus Christ.

Mother received her education at the village elementary school and during those years she became acquainted with my Dad. There was no high school in Russell, so the education of both Dad and Mom ended with the eighth grade. Since both families had limited financial resources, Mom and Dad, not yet married, began immediately earning what money they could to meet their needs.

Dad's father had a Quaker and Methodist background, and his mother's father had been a Methodist lay preacher, besides being a wheelwright (a carpenter who made wagon wheels). Because of his parent's upbringing, they insisted their children go to the Methodist Sunday school, though they rarely went to worship services. As a result, Dad had some religious training but no serious interest in living a Christian life. Yet, he was a hard worker, had a pleasant personality and fairly high ethical standards.

On the farm in Wisconsin, mother felt very isolated. Several other families had moved from Russell, Iowa to Barron County also, but they were too far away for frequent visits. The farm neighbors to the west were all recent immigrants from Norway and though friendly were not very religious Lutherans. Our neighbors to the east of us were more than a mile away and in those days a mile was a long way for a busy mother.

During the summer months, when it wasn't raining on Sunday, Dad would hitch the team to the wagon so the entire family could attend the morning service of the M. E. Church in the small village of Canton, three miles to the north. In the winter months, occasionally the weather was mild enough so we could attend the Christmas Sunday service and in the spring the Easter service. This situation meant we children grew up unable to attend very many Sunday school sessions.

The lack of Sunday school instruction for her children was a heavy burden for mother, so she tried to instruct us by reading from a tattered Bible Story book and a half dozen or so other religious books, in the limited family library. Early on, she taught us how to read the King James Bible. When I was eight, she gave me a new Bible that she urged me to read. I still have this Bible that has lost its back cover and some its leaves. I read many pages of this Bible at an early age.

Mother had a set of ethical rules that she repeatedly set before us and tried her best to enforce, though Dad thought she was too strict. We must not swear or use bad words of any kind. We must treat all girls and women with respect. We could not call any female neighbor a woman. She was a lady. We could not smoke, chew tobacco, or drink any alcoholic beverage. She even forbade Root Beer, because the word beer was in its name. We could not be mean to each other and Sunday was definitely a day when work, except feeding and milking the cows, could not be done or athletic games played. She wanted to have family prayers, but Dad objected. He did not favor being too religious, though he did not object to her moral standards

Four events that made a religious impact on me while young are still vivid in my memory. One event happened when I was six years old, the second just before my twelfth birthday, the third when I had just turned fourteen, and the fourth just before my seventeenth birthday.

In the first instance, everyone was in the fields except mother, baby Dorothy and myself. It was a pleasant, sunny morning in August. I was sitting in a sand pile near the house playing. I could sense that mother was under a good deal of stress. She was trying to care for a very fussy baby and do the family washing only a few yards from where I was playing.

The washing machine was different from modern types. Basically, it was a wooden tub that could hold about fifteen gallons of water and had beneath it four sturdy wooden legs and several steel, cogged wheels which were moved by an upright wooden handle about eighteen inches long. By moving the handle back and forth, mother could cause a spindle, with fan shaped projections, to rotate back and forth inside the tub to cleanse the clothes placed in it. On the upper edge of the tub was a wringer with a crank. This gadget squeezed water out of the clothes.

The entire process was hard work, and on that morning mother had to care for a sick baby too. I could see the stress and pain on her face. While this was happening, I noticed a man dressed in black clothes, walking from the south on the graveled road that passed our house. In a few moments he appeared in the yard and quickly sized up the situation.

He introduced himself as Rev. F. F. Wolfe, pastor of the Free Methodist Church in Chetek, six miles to the south. He asked whether he could hold the baby. Mother readily agreed. While walking back and forth, Rev. Wolfe explained how the Free Methodist Church was different from the M. E. Church. He also asked about the possibility of starting Sunday afternoon services in the Sumner schoolhouse. Mother expressed interest and suggested she and her family probably would be interested in attending such services.

Dorothy soon fell asleep in the pastor's arms and was laid in a nearby crib. He asked whether he could pray with mother and for her family. She quickly gave her assent and thanked him profusely as he left the yard.

As she looked at the departing figure, she murmured under her breath. "There goes a man of God." I took in every move and word of the event and have never forgotten it. This was the first contact of the family with the Free Methodist Church, a church that has played a major role in my religious life.

The second event happened six years later in the summer of 1928. My father, mother and seven children had driven seven miles to visit a Johnson family that my parents had known in Iowa. Returning home that Sunday evening, our route took us through Canton where earlier in the day my mother had noticed a sign. It advertised that the Free Methodists in the area were holding a camp meeting in a grove of trees beside the road. On the way home, Mother insisted we stop for the evening service, held under a large tent. The tent was almost full of people, but our family found seats on a front row.

Typical of the Free Methodists at that time, no instruments were used during the congregational singing. After prayer, the preacher of the evening was introduced. I don't remember his name but his figure and his voice are still quite vivid in my memory. He was tall and awkward in his actions but his voice was clear and strong. He used no notes and he was almost constantly moving about the wooden, plank platform. His sermon was based on the life and death of Samson preserved in the book of Judges of the Old Testament. He dramatically acted out the crucial events of Samson's life, using backwoods English. Nevertheless, the entire congregation, including myself, listened spellbound. I had heard about Samson before, but this presentation impressed me deeply.

The Free Methodists always concluded their services with an altar call for sinners to come to a plank altar and pray for salvation from their sins. A few people knelt at the altar to pray , but none of my family did. On the way home my mother remarked how much the service was like the revival meetings held in the Methodist Church in Russell, Iowa, which she attended as a girl. She was very impressed.

The next morning was a beautiful, sunny day. My mother often asked me to help about the house, since Vera was not at home and Dorothy was not old enough to help very much. My older brothers helped Dad in the fields. Early in the forenoon, mother asked me to take a small bucket to a growth of choke cherry trees about seven hundred feet from the house. Choke cherries were a dark purple berry about the size of small garden peas. They grew in abundance along the twigs and small branches of the tree. They were sour to the taste but when the juice was mixed with fruits like strawberries, raspberries or blackberries, which grew wild and in abundance on the farm, the result was a wonderfully tasteful jam or jelly.

I climbed the tree, which was about twenty feet high, and stretched out on limb after limb stripping the small cherries from their stems and dumping them into my pail. As I was doing so, my mind began to replay the sermon I had heard the night before. I saw a comparison between Samson's early training and mine, especially the religious sensitivity of the mother, and the corrupting influence of the people around him and in our community.

I realized that in spite of my mother's ban on swearing, I had picked up many swear words from my older brothers and from my school pals. Away from my mother's presence, my quick temper and swear words mixed together all too often. I also picked up "dirty" words. I knew what they meant and used them in jokes frequently. Lying and cheating were also part of my behavior. For the first time, a sense of shame and guilt began to trouble my conscience. Then fear began to grip me as I thought about how Samson's sins brought violence, betrayal and death into his life.

As conflicting thoughts and emotions boiled within me, I became aware of words coming into my mind, "Herbie, I want you to be a preacher." Those words have never left my memory. My immediate reaction was shock and disbelief. Why should I think of such a thing? Then I thought, "Someone is close by and trying to make fun of me." I looked around carefully and called out several names of my pals, but no response. I asked myself, "Who would use 'I want' in such a sentence." Then it came to me, God had spoken directly to Samson's mother and father. Could it be that God had just spoken to me? Fear really gripped my heart then. I grabbed my nearly full bucket and ran back to the house, I put the bucket on the table and dashed outside and found a hiding place in the barn.

Confusion gripped my mind and emotions. I could see no way I could ever be a preacher. It just wasn't possible. I concluded my imagination had gotten the better of me and that I should never tell anyone, even mother, about the incident, and for years I never did. Nevertheless, several changes came into my life. I swore less often and when I did, I felt a sense of guilt. The same guilt was associated with lying, and cheating and stealing. I didn't do these things as often, but shame followed each act.

The third incident of religious significance to me happened in the summer of 1930. Several years before, Dad had purchased a fairly reliable, used car and we were able to attend the M. E. church services more often in the summer months. Mother was excited, for the new pastor, Rev. Lockhart, was more evangelical and revival oriented than many of the other pastors who had preceded him. She felt spiritually challenged by his preaching. It was the kind of preaching she remembered from her girlhood days.

Rev. Lockhart had announced that during August an evangelist from Milwaukee, Wisconsin would hold a revival meeting for ten days at the Canton church. Mother was determined to attend with the family as many evening services as possible. I found it difficult to enjoy the evangelist's messages, because when he talked about the consequences of sin and how Jesus could save a person and deliver from guilt, I felt very uncomfortable. The evangelist wanted people to come to the altar and pray and I felt I could never do such a thing in public.

I remember it was the last Sunday evening service of the revival and Dad and Mom, Dorothy and I were sitting in a church pew. The church was packed with people and the singing was lively. I don't remember anything about the sermon, but when the altar call began, almost immediately Mother rose from her seat and walked to the altar to pray. I was amazed. Why would my wonderful mother do such a thing? She couldn't be a sinner.

After a few minutes, she came back to the pew and insisted that Dad, Dorothy and I come to the altar also. Reluctantly, we did so, and I remember wondering how I could possibly be saved from my sins. Soon a minister was kneeling in front of me asking whether I believed in Jesus Christ, I replied I did. He asked whether I wanted to be forgiven of my sins and I said I did. He asked me to repeat after him, "Lord, be merciful to me a sinner" and somehow I mumbled the words. He then declared I was saved from my sins.

The thing I especially remember about that evening was how radiant, how happy my mother was. Dad didn't say much. In the days to come that radiance remained in my mother's face and expressions. I knew I did not experience such happiness and sense of freedom. I was puzzled but said little about it. Mostly, I was overwhelmed by the change that had taken place in my mother's life.

Looking back and evaluating the incident, I have concluded I was not yet converted to Christ; rather spiritual sensitivities had been awakened to my need for conversion so I could truly obey Christ in all I did. In particular, I had a renewed realization that God was calling me to his ministry. I did not say a "No" to this kind of future for my life; neither did I say "Yes" to the possibility. I sensed I was not ready to obey the Lord in this matter. I could see no way I was qualified for ministry.

I had always found it difficult to recite or give oral reports in class and I knew speaking in public was an essential aspect of ministry. I began to read in earnest the Bible, Mother had given me, and I studied Sunday school lessons carefully. The person in charge of the Sunday school held at the Sumner grade school by the Free Methodists asked me to teach a half dozen young boys and girls. Very reluctantly, I agreed to do so and I found the task enjoyable and challenging.

The Great Depression had swept into northwestern Wisconsin and farm income plummeted so low that farmers, including Dad, found it almost impossible to make ends meet. Dad found he could not meet the annual payments to one of my uncles who held the mortgage. At the same time, an injury to the back of the head, which happened when he fell on ice as a young man, was increasingly causing severe headaches. He was also feeling a loss of energy. Several years later, a doctor discovered Dad had diabetes and needed insulin shots. My brother Ralph had to quit high school in his sophomore year to work full time on the farm. My parents did their best to keep me in high school and fortunately, I was able to graduate in May 1933.

There were other events taking place. My oldest brother married in 1927 and found a job in a neighboring city. My oldest sister Vera married, and moved to Eau Claire, Wisconsin where her husband Clel got a job in a dairy that processed milk and sold it in bottles from house to house. Brother Ray got a job at the same dairy and finished high school in Eau Claire.

Brother Floyd, in his late twenties, quit a job at a dairy farm in central Illinois. He arranged with Uncle Percy to take responsibility for the mortgage and become the operator of the home farm. Soon he was living in our home taking charge of the farm, much to the displeasure of my father.

The family atmosphere was tense and I was tense inside. The future looked bleak. Where in Wisconsin or elsewhere could I ever find a job and a future? Going to college seemed out of the question. There was no money to pay tuition. When not working for my board and room at a small farm near Cameron during the school year, I would milk three cows in the morning and in the evening, help keep the barn clean and work in the fields. Floyd needed our help but could not pay Ralph or myself wages, except for board and room.

During those three years, I was trying to work through my personal problems about which I told no one. In the school curriculum, I found a class on public speaking and enrolled. Secretly, I thought I would need this training some time. I tried to live a decent life but I discovered I still had a quick, hot temper and quite capable of spilling out a string of curse words. Remorse and depression would seize me and I would suffer in silence. The summer of 1933 arrived and I was fresh out of Cameron High School. I faced what seemed to me was a very bleak future.

Early in July, word got out that the Free Methodists were going to have a revival meeting in Sumner. Several nearby pastors, led by a Rev. Carl Olsen, had arranged for a young evangelist named Walter Kendall to come as the preacher. This event was the setting for the fourth and climatic spiritual incident of my life.

A tent capable of holding forty to fifty people was set up on the grounds of the Sumner elementary school. The thought crossed my mind that this could be an opportunity for me to get my spiritual problems cleared up. Perhaps I could go to the plank altar and ask Jesus to save me from my sins and help me settle this call to ministry business, but the thought of doing this in public terrified me.

While working in the fields, I would try praying: repenting of my sins and begging for forgiveness, but I was evading saying yes to a future in the ministry. Why say yes to a future that was impossible? Why couldn't these matters be settled in private before the Lord, instead of having to do it publicly?

Ten days slipped by. Floyd and Ralph refused to go to the meetings so only Dorothy and I went with Dad and Mom almost every night. The evangelist was a good preacher and conviction rested heavily upon me. There was good attendance at each service but no one responded to the altar calls.

On the last Sunday of the revival meeting, after the Sunday school and worship service, I told my parents I wanted to walk home alone. My mother gripped my hand and murmured, "I am praying for you." There were trees and brush along the road, and I soon pushed my way through the brush to an open area and sat down. My mind was full of confusion. I wanted to go to the altar but couldn't bring myself to do so.

While berating my cowardice, I began reading a four-page pamphlet I had received during the Sunday school lesson. One short article described an object lesson that could illustrate why some people found it difficult to yield themselves to the Lord. The lesson used a small box with an open side. In view was an iron nail hovering in mid-air with a string tied it to the bottom of the box.

The question was, "Why didn't the nail fall to the bottom of the box, for no string was tying it to the top of the box?" The answer was that a magnet was attached on the inside to the top of the box, and was trying to draw the nail to itself. Application: The nail is a person (me) wanting to yield to Christ but could not because fear was holding me back. By cutting the string (renouncing fear) a person would be drawn by the power of the Holy Spirit to come to Jesus for salvation. I uttered a short prayer, "Lord, if you will help me take a front seat near the altar and give me special strength I will go to the altar tonight." I went home and had a good afternoon with my family.

Before the evening service, I was chatting with some boys my age, who, had come to the service. They wanted to sit in the back row. I sat down with them and suddenly realized I had prayed for a front seat. The tent was filling rapidly and soon an usher came and requested that all of us boys move up front. My heart jumped. The Lord was answering my prayer and I was soon only a few feet from the altar.

I remember little about the service, except when the altar call was given, I immediately went to it and knelt to pray. I didn't know how to pray a true prayer of repentance, but I tried. In a few moments, I felt an arm around my shoulders and it was Mother. She told me how to pray but my biggest problem was saying yes to the call to ministry that was pressing on me. I became desperate and silently yielded myself to the call. Immediately peace flooded my soul.

The next Sunday at worship service, I discovered that a young man from a Free Methodist college in South Dakota had stopped and spoken a few moments to the congregation at one of the evening services of the revival meeting we had missed. He had left a catalog and literature about the school with the pastor. I asked permission to read this literature and took it home.

I quickly found that the school was a combined academy (high school) and a two-year junior college, specializing in teacher training and ministerial training. The literature informed me many of its students worked their way through school by doing custodial and kitchen work on the campus. I immediately wrote a letter to the president of the school about my interest in college studies, that my parents had no money to help me and that I would like to work my way through college.

A week later a letter came from President Ansted encouraging me to enroll and that indeed I could work on the campus. Enrollment forms were in the letter and I showed them to my parents. They were impressed but made it clear they did not have money to help me with the college expenses nor with train fare to the school. Yet, they did not object to my returning the completed enrollment forms, along with my high school records. I soon received word that I was accepted as a student.

The question, other than money, was how I would I travel the four hundred and fifty miles to the school in South Dakota? I began to argue that I had hitch hiked to Cameron many times to attend high school, why couldn't I hitch hike to South Dakota. I had heard a number of young men were traveling this way around the country, and it would cost very little. Dad and mother finally agreed. A box was packed with clothes; it wasn't a very large box. It would be shipped by parcel post.

Dad had picked up a military knapsack of World War I vintage at an auction. We packed it with things I would need on the trip, such as a sack of sandwiches for lunch. With a strap attached, the pack could be carried on my shoulder. Maps were obtained and a route was chosen. I would swing south of the Twin Cities to Rochester, Minnesota and go straight west. I thought I could complete the trip, for I had five dollars and eighty-five cents in my pocketbook.

Looking back to my growing up years, I am humbled to realize how God watched over my family and me during perilous times. I was born in the middle of World War I and after it ended my family moved from southern Iowa to northwestern Wisconsin to create a farm out of a parcel of a destroyed pine forest. I was the seventh of eight children of a poverty stricken father and mother. With borrowed money and hard work a house was built and stumps pulled up for crops of potatoes and grain. Slowly, a dairy herd was formed but farm income was limited. We had enough to eat and a place to sleep but we were short of almost everything else. Suddenly, the national financial structure collapsed and many farms and businesses became bankrupt in 1929.

Did extreme poverty cause crimes and riots in our area? No! Neighbor helped neighbor, the fine art of pinching pennies became a skill, and resourceful hope filled planning pulled us through. Our farm-oriented society in northwestern Wisconsin had its flaws, but it was not devastated.

My Dad grew up in a non-religious home, though his grandparents were devoted Methodists. Dad's views about religion affected the attitude of my older siblings. Mother was quite the opposite of Dad. She had been a devoted Methodist since childhood and by precept and example witnessed to the vitality of her faith.

She made a public recommitment of her life to the Lord in a Methodist revival meeting in 1930 positively impacted Dad, my youngest sister and myself. Our older siblings seemed to be unimpressed at the time but in later years all became Christians.

Mother's nurture of my religious life between 1930 and the summer of 1933 came to a climax in my conversion and acceptance of a call to ministry. She was overjoyed and strongly supported my going to a South Dakota religious college to train for a ministerial career. Her prayers never ceased to follow me till the end of her life.

Being a penniless, farm boy caused me problems during my growing years. I wanted things but there was no money to buy them. All of my siblings and I had to use scraps of this or that to make toys and do our farm jobs. All of our friends had to do the same. We quarreled about it some but never engaged in serious unlawful behavior. We improvised and survived successfully. Yes, we got into mischief, learned to curse and engaged in some immoral activities.

Alcoholism was rare in our community but smoking home-rolled cigarettes was common. I almost got addicted to it, but at my conversion I was delivered from this behavior, and never returned to it throughout my life. I thank the Lord for what he has done for me.

Livingston Family, 1920
Front l-r Raymond, Herbert, Ralph
Back l-r George W., Vera, Harold, Floyd, Clara

Our Farm Home, c. 1926

Dad and Mom Livingston 1951

My Grade School

CHAPTER 3

COLLEGE DAYS

To the surprise of everyone, Vera and Clel came for a visit the second Sunday of August. At the time, their home was at Mondovi, Wisconsin, located about twenty miles southwest of Eau Claire and directly on the way to Rochester, Minnesota. I told them about my desire to attend Wessington Springs Junior College in South Dakota and would they let me ride home with them and start my trip from Mondovi. I was excited when they agreed to take me with them.

The next morning Clel took me to a junction in the road and explained which way to go to get to the bridge that crossed the Mississippi River to Kellogg, Minnesota. I arrived there shortly after noon. I bought a bottle of Orange Crush for five cents and ate a sandwich. I headed south on state highway # 34 and connected with US 14 just west of Dover. I managed to get to Kasson, twenty or so miles west of Rochester, shortly before dark. That night I slept under a spirea bush with low spreading branches.

The car drivers who had given me rides were mostly friendly farmers who were all going short distances. The traffic was limited and sometimes I walked, (I wasn't experienced enough in hitch-hiking to know I should stay at the edge of town or at a crossroads and wait for a ride) for three or four miles between rides. As a result I was very tired at the end of the day.

When I neared Mankato, a farmer told me I should go southwest on state highway # 60 to US 16. I did so but made slow progress. About five in the afternoon, a carpenter stopped for me and took me to his home

(I believe it was in Windom) and invited me to eat dinner at his home. Did I ever eat! As it neared bedtime, he informed me that because of the size of his family, there was no extra room in the house, but suggested I could sleep on the front seat of his pickup truck. My feet stuck out the open door window. No matter, I slept soundly.

After breakfast the next morning, the carpenter told me that a freight train would be stopping in town shortly. He knew the brakeman and thought he could get him to allow me to ride on top a boxcar to Pipestone, Minnesota, which was not far from the South Dakota border. At that town, the road that went west to Wessington Springs became SD state road # 34. The brakeman agreed to let me ride and promised to watch me carefully. The train was not fast and jiggled quite a bit. The sun was hot but I was so glad to make this kind of progress I didn't mind.

It was noon when I got off the train; I bought something to drink and ate my last sandwich. By this time it was quite dry and tasteless. The traffic was almost nonexistent and I walked in the heat to almost the state border. I noticed to the left a nice farmhouse with a few almost dried up trees. I noticed also a hand pump in the middle of the yard. My throat was dry with thirst, so I walked to the house and found a middle-aged lady working in a sad looking flowerbed. I introduced myself and asked whether I could have a cup of water from the well. The lady looked me over and said she would get a clean cup from the kitchen.

When the lady returned, she had in her hand a large plate with two sandwiches of thick, home-baked bread spread with real butter, and also a clean tin cup. She even pumped till the water was cool and filled the cup. She asked me to inform her when I was finished. What a wonderful meal. I thanked her profusely when I returned the cup and plate. As I left the yard, I said to myself, "I think I have met an angel."

As I traveled west through South Dakota, I noticed the fields were very brown and the trees were fewer and fewer. As I traveled again with a series of short rides with friendly farmers, I noticed no crops in the fields. The countryside looked like a desert. A hot wind blew constantly and dust filled the air.

After ten hours on the road, I arrived in Wessington Springs and made my way to the small college campus. I was tired, very thirsty and famished. As I entered a door on the ground floor of a building, I heard the six o'clock whistle blow downtown. I stepped into what appeared to be a dining room and saw at the far side of the room a table at which people were eating. A man arose and came toward me; I introduced myself and informed him I had come from Wisconsin to enroll as a student. The man, whom I discovered was the Dean of the school, invited me to the table and told me to eat all I wanted. What a load was off my shoulders. After three days of difficult travel, I had arrived safely at my destination. I bowed my head and thanked God for His mercies.

A young man introduced himself as a sophomore who had returned early to help prepare the campus and buildings for classes. He informed me there was plenty of work to do. He gave me a short tour of the campus, and since I had not washed in three days, I suggested I should take a bath. He took me to the fourth floor, which was the boy's dormitory and showed me the bathroom. He said he had an extra cot with sheets in his room and invited me to use them.

When back in the room, I counted the money I still had in my pocketbook and discovered I had made the three-day trip on less than a dollar. While doing this, I heard strange sounds coming from an area about four blocks away. I was well acquainted with cows mooing, but these sounds were more like cows bawling, mixed with pigs squealing.

My friend explained the drought had been so terrible the cattle were starving in the fields. The national government was buying these cattle from farmers, bringing them to town overnight and the next day killing them, dumping their bodies into ditches and covering them with dirt. Many of the farmers were declaring bankruptcy and moving to the far west to search for jobs. My heart sank. I had come to a state facing a major disaster.

The next morning I began working in the kitchen helping the chef clean it before the influx of students the day after Labor Day. The wage was ten cents an hour, which was what young men and women were earning in the area, if they could find a job. I was ready to enroll in Wessington Springs Junior College, Wessington Springs, Jerauld County, South Dakota. By enrollment day, I had decided to take the liberal arts curriculum. I would major in religion and minor in teacher training.

The President assured me I could work throughout the school year. There would be construction projects on the campus during the summer. I quickly wrote my second letter home, informing my parents for the first time that I felt a call to the ministry and this course of study was the beginning of preparation for that vocation. I found out afterwards that the news came as a shock to everyone in the family and community, except Mother.

About 125 students enrolled. About half of the students who were in the high school classes came from Wessington Springs or nearby farms, but most came from other states. The remaining students were in the freshman and sophomore years of college. The teacher training courses were popular and drew a number of high school graduates, mostly young ladies, from the town and surrounding farms. South Dakota was dotted with small, one-room grade schools and demand for teachers with a junior college degree was strong.

Other college students were young men preparing for the ministry. They came from several states and from several provinces of Canada. About fifty students lived in the dormitory, the young ladies on the second and third floors and the young men on the fourth floor. The stairway doors between the ladies and men's floors were securely locked.

As the classes got under way, I discovered I had joined a community different than any I had ever known or heard about. During the enrollment process, the students were given a document regulating life on and off campus. We were required to sign this document. Though the rules were strict, very few students objected to them. About one-third of the students were Free Methodists, the others came from families that belonged to several other denominations. No problem and bickering over differences of belief were rare.

The first surprise came when I ate in the dining hall. Seven students and one professor sat at each table. Occasionally at breakfast, which was at seven a.m., a verse of a hymn was sung, and always at each meal a professor offered a prayer of thanksgiving. On the first day, the professor often a woman, explained why the plates and cutlery were placed as they were, it was the correct way. Next was an explanation of how the knife, fork and spoon should be held in the hand. To more than one this was news. The food, which was placed on the table in bowls and platters, were passed a certain way and moderate amounts of food were taken at each serving. Second helpings were available. All students should chew the food with lips closed. After the meal was finished, all those at a table would rise as a unit and exit the room. That also was new to many of us.

The second surprise came when we went to our classes, for each class was opened with a prayer by the professor, by a ministerial student or a young lady of spiritual reputation. Back home, most teachers in the grade school began each school day with a verse or two from a hymn and a memorized prayer, but never did this happen in high school.

The professors were competent, presented the lessons clearly and answered questions from the students. Some would offer tutoring to the students having a difficult time, also from seven to nine p. m. each school day; the students who lived on campus were required to meet in a large room for study. The high school and college students met in separate rooms. The professors took turns monitoring the rooms.

The third surprise was the overall spiritual atmosphere of the school community. Almost all the students in the dormitories were committed Christians or came from Christian homes. A few from the town or farms had little Christian training and were interested primarily in obtaining their degree. All the faculty and staff were devoted Christians and soon became close friends with the students. All did more than their teaching or administrative jobs. They spent hours each day counseling the students or supervising group activities. They were with students when they gathered, sometimes for small group prayer meetings, for the Thursday evening, student body meetings or church worship services. The emphasis of the teachers was on spiritual growth and inner transformation by the Holy Spirit.

A uniform regulation was the observance of a "quiet hour" each Sunday afternoon 2 to 3 p.m. in our dorm rooms. All resident students must be quiet during this time, unless they were off campus on a ministry assignment. A student could take a nap, study or pray. Roommates could converse quietly but with no one else. I mostly took a nap and wrote a letter to my parents. Most students appreciated this quiet time, but some did not.

Normally, the students related well with each other, but there were times when problems occurred. For new students, there were homesickness problems and financial problems. Soon there were work problems and study problems. Some students didn't like each other and arguments would produce some sharp words. To counter homesickness, friendships were promoted. To help the poor students, others would pool their small gifts to help in emergencies. The upper classmen would tutor those needing help and bring about reconciliation between students quarreling, or contending with the administrators about their displeasure with the rules. For me it was a learning experience and I felt I was making spiritual progress from day to day. My quick temper had almost disappeared, and swearing had completely stopped. I no longer was prone to lie, cheat, steal or be mean to others. What a blessing.

I didn't expect to go home for Christmas, but a ride most of the way prompted me to take the trip. I arrived home to the surprise and joy of the family. I was questioned closely about my college experiences and the prospect of continuing my studies. I was glad I could give a good report. Mother especially was happy I was preparing to be a minister. I talked to Ralph about coming out in August to earn his high school diploma. He was uncertain he would like a school with a strong religious emphasis. I stressed this route was the only one that held a future for him. He said he would think about it.

I stayed a week and left on a Monday morning. I was in Sleepy Eye, Minnesota that evening. It had been a bitterly cold day. I asked several people and discovered there was no lodging available and the only place open all night was the constable's office. Going there I discovered a friendly fellow, who on hearing my story, offered to provide some blankets for me to sleep on a bunk, for this building was also the town jail. He also offered me some milk and part of his ample lunch. I slept soundly that night and arrived in Wessington Springs late in the afternoon of the next day. On later trips I found that small town jails were a good place to sleep.

One day in the middle of the winter, President Ansted requested an interview with me. I wondered, "What have I done wrong," but my fears were unnecessary. He had good news. Congress had passed a law to financially aid needy college students. The President had selected me and a few other students to apply for this aid. The government would pay qualified students for working twenty hours a week around the college campus. Because the school was church related no work could be done in any of the college buildings or as assistance with any phase of the school program. The President told me the wage would be thirty cents an hour. "Wow," I thought, "that is three times as much as the school paid, I would have time to study more." I made out the application and the next week I began working for the US government!

During the summer of 1934, I worked on a construction project on the campus. The government program was only for the school year so I was again in the employ of the college, but at the wage of twenty cents an hour. The main project was the construction of a stage connected to the large room on the third floor of the Administration building.

As a lad on the farm, I had learned how to use a hammer, a saw and a framing square, but on these jobs I improved my skills under the tutelage of experienced carpenters. In the years ahead, I was to value this training greatly.

My earnings that summer paid off the first year of college and provided a small amount for the second year. The tuition, board and room, per school year was a bit less than four hundred dollars.

During that summer, a milestone toward a future ministerial career happened. The pastor had asked Bob Short and me to each give a fifteen-minute devotional at the Wednesday night prayer meeting. This was my first presentation of a biblical message. I was scared but did my best. Unknown to either of us, the congregation wanted to hear us in order to decide whether to grant us an Exhorters license and then recommend us to the conference for a Local Preachers license. In short order an Exhorters license was handed to us and in July the Free Methodist conference in South Dakota granted us the Local Preachers license. We were now officially recognized as candidates for the ministry. That event was an important confirmation of my call to preach. The license was renewed in the summers of 1935 and 1936.

My brother Ralph arrived at Wessington Springs late in August 1934 and we both enrolled. Ralph entered the sophomore class of the high school on campus and I enrolled as a sophomore in the junior college. To my delight, Ralph fit in well with the men in the dormitory and before the fall semester was over, he went to the altar in a church service and accepted Jesus Christ into his life. He was an earnest Christian throughout his life.

Through the fall semester of 1934, I carried a full class load. One of the new classes that challenged me was Greek. A great deal of memorization was required and my workload of 25 to 30 hours per week left little time for that kind of study. Much of my work was now at the Ansted home. The spring government subsidy was no longer available so my wage was the new wage for college work, twenty cents per hour.

When the weather cooled down and heat was needed in the buildings, I took on the job of keeping coal in the furnace of one of the buildings. The colder it got the more time the job required. I fired the furnace early in the morning and banked the fire late at night. Shoveling coal and the resulting ash was hard work. I was fast getting behind in my sleeping time.

In the middle of November, I became exhausted and my health failed. I awoke one morning early in the week but could not get out of bed. I had a bad cold. I got another fellow to tend my furnace and as soon as possible managed to go to the college clinic in the dormitory. A nurse, Helen Stuve, from Wisconsin, had enrolled in Bible courses and was in charge of the clinic. She put me to bed at the clinic and called the town doctor.

I had congestion in my left lung and a high fever. The next day the doctor was concerned for he noted the initial signs of pneumonia. He and the nurse prepared a poultice and bound it to my back behind my left lung and gave the nurse several kinds of medicine. Penicillin was not yet available.

By the fourth day, the doctor was very concerned, for the spot on my lung was getting larger and I wasn't responding to the medicine. He notified President Ansted I was in real danger of not recovering. The President sent out a call for prayer for my recovery. I was later told the kitchen chef, Larry Cartwright, and his wife went with another couple to the President's home and requested that they join together for a special period of prayer.

The next morning I was feeling some better. The nurse was puzzled and called the doctor. My temperature was down and the spot on my lung was a bit smaller. He had never known his medicines to check pneumonia like that, so feared a setback. He ordered the nurse to keep a close watch on me. The next morning I was feeling even better and the doctor noted the spot on the lung had decreased some more. He allowed me to sit up at the edge of the bed for a while. The next day I was permitted to walk a bit, and the next day I walked from one end of the hall to the other. The old doctor had never seen anything like it.

In a few more days he allowed me to obtain assignments from my instructors and catch up on my classes while still in the clinic. Two weeks after I became ill, I returned to my classes and in another week I could work short periods each day. I did not return to the job of firing a furnace. The conclusion of the college community was that I had been healed by the Lord. I must say in fifty years of ministry I never had more than brief periods of flu or colds. In that time period, I was never in a hospital bed due to illness.

I did not go home for Christmas, or in the spring semester of 1935. I continued my studies and worked on the average of twenty-five hours per week. I worked more and more at the Ansted home. I took voice lessons and learned how to read music and sing bass in a four-part harmony. I also took speech lessons and took part in several declamation contests. I felt a preacher needed to know how to speak before an audience. On some weekends, I would go with other fellows preparing for the ministry, to school houses in the countryside and help conduct Sunday services for people who lived in the neighborhood. Occasionally, I would give short devotionals.

During the month of May 1935, I was busy with sophomore activities leading up to the commencement exercises. The class took a "Skip" trip to Big Stone Lake, which lies on the border between Minnesota and South Dakota, the weekend of May 15th-19th. The Baccalaureate service was at the local Methodist Church on May 26th and the Commencement was on May 28th. I was awarded the Associate of Arts degree and the Associate in Religion degree. It was a great day. I had graduated!

During the spring, I learned that President Ansted was negotiating with the Department of Education of South Dakota concerning setting up a curriculum of religious studies for a junior and senior year. The degree for this extension of studies would be Bachelor of Arts in Religion. President Ansted's request was granted and I became excited about entering this program. I felt comfortable at the college and did not have money to transfer to a regular four-year liberal arts college. I decided to stay another two years, 1935-37.

I remained on campus aiding in several remodeling projects. I had one brief break at the beginning of July. Helen Stuve, the nurse, of Humbird, Wisconsin had become very interested in Bob Short who lived in Wessington Springs and attended the college. Her younger brother brought a pick-up truck loaded with ripe strawberries to sell in Wessington Springs and take Bob back to Humbird so Bob could visit Helen and her family. Bob asked me to go with them so I could visit my home 100 miles north at Cameron, Wisconsin.

I obtained permission to leave work for a week to make this trip. Mrs. Ansted's parents were living with President and Mrs. Ansted, and her father drew me aside and asked whether I had money to buy food on the trip. I told him I had less than a dollar. He gave me a wad of green paper and said I could pay him back as soon as I could. I discovered the wad was a dollar bill.

We arrived at Humbird, WI on the day before the Fourth of July. I learned the Stuve boy was going on July 6th to northwestern Wisconsin with a load of ripe strawberries and planned to sell them in a town where a relative lived. He said he would route his return trip through Cameron and leave me at my parent's home. I got there in the evening of Saturday. Everyone was overjoyed about my surprise visit, for I did not have time to send a message I was coming. My folks did not have a telephone. I spent Sunday visiting and had a great time, but half of my week was already gone. I left home on Monday morning to return to Wessington Springs. I paused in Cameron to mail a card to the Ansteds informing them I would be back in three days. I had with me a bag of clothes and a brown sack of sandwiches and cookies.

Putting into practice some tips about hitch hiking I had obtained from students who also traveled by this method, (i.e. ask in towns about rides, or stay at edge of town.) I arrived at the north side of St. Paul in three hours. In just a few minutes I had a ride to Fargo, North Dakota. This was out of the way, but at least it was going west. On the way, my benefactor treated me to an excellent lunch. From Fargo I cut across country toward Aberdeen, South Dakota. About eight o'clock I arrived in Oakes, ND, tired and ready for some sleep, but where?

Checking out the small town, I found it was located on a railroad line. I stopped at the train station and asked the clerk if he could recommend a place to sleep. After getting acquainted with me, he suggested an answer to my problem. He took me to a passenger coach located on a sidetrack, unlocked the door and showed me how the nicely cushioned seats could be folded down and made into a soft bed. He said he would have to lock me in overnight, but he would return at six in the morning to unlock the door. That was fine with me and I quickly fell asleep.

The next forenoon, I quickly reached Aberdeen and continued south to Woonsocket. On the west edge of the town, who should pick me up but the man who transported mail for the government to Wessington Springs and beyond. He recognized me as one of the students who carried mail from the college to the post office and back to the college. Later the Ansteds told me they had just received the card I had sent from Cameron. I still had the wadded dollar bill.

The college purchased a fairly nice brick building two blocks from the school, for an increase of enrollment of men was expected and more dormitory space was needed. I spent much of July and August working as a carpenter and painter on the remodeling that was needed. I preached several times also.

The Ansteds had fixed up their basement for summer living, for air conditioners were unknown. One evening I was invited for dinner. More and more, I was becoming a part of the family. An interesting thing happened just before the meal. I was washing my face and hands at the sink and the ladies, including a sixteen-year-old daughter, Eva Marie, were rushing back and forth. At one point, Eva Marie called out to her grandmother, who was in a back room, "Precious, you may come to the table now."

President Ansted spoke up, "Ho, Ho, so you are now calling this young man 'Precious'". Eva strongly protested this interpretation of her call to grandmother, but to no avail. From then on, President Ansted always called me Precious, whether I was at his home or at the school. The girls in the dormitory never called me that!

Another interesting incident happened that summer. President Ansted's wife and children needed to drive to Oklahoma to visit some of her relatives. The President's office secretary also lived in a room on the main floor of the home, so the President asked me to stay several nights in a large basement room where he and his wife were sleeping during the hot summer. He set up a cot at one side of the room. During the night, I began walking in my sleep. Suddenly I found myself standing at the foot of the President's bed. He was awake and asked what I was doing. I mumbled I had to go to the bathroom. He pointed across the room to the door of that room and said I should go in that direction. Then he added, "Next time don't try to open that door by twisting my big toe." Was I embarrassed!

In 1935, among the new students was a young lady who was born in the Netherlands, and at the time lived with her family in Timber Lake, SD. Because she had worked as a waitress for several years, she was placed in charge of other students who worked during mealtime in the dining room. One evening just before the dinner, I was working in the kitchen. Suddenly the swinging, double doors opened and there was a beautiful young lady with wavy black hair, clear blue eyes and a stunning smile. I'm afraid I stared at her for a moment.

The thought flashed through my mind, "Someday, I would like to date that young lady." I knew that would not likely happen because of my heavy study and work schedule. Now and then, our paths crossed, especially after she also began working at the Ansted residence.

One of the new developments of the new fall semester was the organization of the Gospel Tidings Mixed Quartet. Bob Short was the tenor, Leona Kingery, the soprano, Vlera Warner, the alto and myself the bass. Since Bob's Dad owned the Variety Store downtown, Bob had access to an old Chevrolet sedan. This meant the quartet could travel some distance to sing at churches. We received additional training from one of the lady music professors.

Soon we were busy on Sundays singing at services held in schoolhouses near Wessington Springs. Bob and I would take turns preaching. Within a few weeks we were going as far as Kimball, where the girls lived, also, to Corsica, Kennebec, Bates, Brookings and a few times we sang on the college weekly radio program at Huron. The offerings we received barely paid for the gas and oil of the car. However, we enjoyed ourselves immensely, though we were not earning as much as we should, to apply on our school bill.

One interesting event of the semester was the arrival in December of a railroad car loaded with 1,200 bushels of beautiful apples from Washington State. Everyone was canning apples in half-gallon, glass jars. The town, and farm community for miles around, was enlisted to help on a fifty-fifty basis. The college provided the glass jars for its share of the canned apples. We had no problem with desserts the rest of the year. It was apples, apples and apples!

About the middle of December, the weather became bitterly cold with a fair amount of snow. Maybe the Dust Bowl days were coming to an end. Because of the cold weather the opening of school was delayed until the end of January. I took a job firing one of the furnaces again, but they needed almost constant attention, even at night. I soon found I was losing too much sleep and was starting to have colds. Fearing I might have a bad illness such as I had in the fall of 1934, I had to quit the furnace job. The severe cold and blizzards continued until February 22nd when, for the first time in 35 days, the temperature climbed above 32 degrees.

Late in February, our quartette was able to travel to schools and to churches to sing in Mitchell, Sioux Falls, Revillo and Ortley. I took my turn preaching. At times, we would sing at various services at the college.

One of my classes was Debate and often we would hold debates among the class members before various town organizations and at a state debate contest in Mitchell, SD. I enjoyed those events.

The big event of the semester took place on March 20th. A few of us male students were chatting late in the afternoon. One fellow spoke up, "Do you know the girl who is hard to date here, the Dutch girl Maria. I've tried twice and she has turned me down. I can usually get a date from other girls whenever I want one." I replied, "Maybe your method is getting rusty." He retorted. "I don't see you dating anyone. I dare you to get a date from Maria." I thought a moment and said, "OK I will give it a try." He said, "I mean tonight for the student meeting." I gulped and mumbled, "OK."

That evening study hall was from 7:00 to 7:50. Maria was sitting as usual in a row of seats to my right and the third seat back. My brother, Ralph, was seated behind me. I had a hard time studying. I knew I had to ask Maria soon or I would be the laughing stock among the fellows. Finally, I tore a sheet from my notebook and scribbled, "Maria, would you go to the student meeting with me at 8:00 p.m.?" I folded the sheet, put her name on it and turning to my brother, asked him to pass it over to Maria. I hunched over my books with my heart in my throat. In just a few moments, Ralph tapped me on the shoulder and handed me the note. Breathlessly, I opened the note and saw one word, "Yes." Wow, did I strut a bit when we walked into the student meeting together. I located the student who had dared me. He sat dejected with his head down!

From that night on, Maria and I frequently went to student gatherings together and some evenings we found time to chat a few moments in the fellowship room, called the parlor, of the girls' dormitory. Some evenings we were able to obtain permission to walk a bit around town, or to join with another couple or more to go to a picnic area in the hills back of the college, for a wiener roast. We were rapidly falling in love.

At the end of April another student, Orville Hepler, and I were asked by President Ansted to build a trailer house for his family. He had plans for one that would be seven feet wide and eighteen feet long. It would be made entirely of wood framing and of quarter inch plywood sheeting. This project occupied our spare time for six weeks. It also cut into the time Maria and I could be together, we managed to get in quality time.

At Commencement, Maria was granted a First Grade Certificate, a form of a diploma. She was now qualified to teach in any rural grade school in South Dakota: An achievement that created some problems during the next school year.

Maria decided to spend two months on campus during the summer, working on various jobs and also helping in the Ansted home. For my part, Orville and I would work long days completing the trailer house by June 15th. For the remainder of the summer, I was to be one of a team of three students who would contact a number of Free Methodist Churches, seeking prospective students for the fall semester. We were to travel by hitchhiking. A certain amount would be applied to our bill each week and we were to receive five dollars a week for expenses. My area was to be southern Minnesota and all of Wisconsin. I was to leave on June 19th.

Maria and I treasured the few hours we squeezed out of the end of each day. On June 2nd, I kissed Maria for the first time. On June 6th I told her I loved her and she told me she loved me. Wow, what an evening! It was hard to part company on June 19th when I left for southern Minnesota.

We have a diary I filled out each day during that summer as well as the letters we wrote to each other. Maria had a schedule of where I would be each day and addresses of a number of pastors with whom I would be staying a day or two. We kept the US mail system busy. The pastors I met put a great deal of pressure on me to join the Wisconsin conference the next summer and become a pastor of a Free Methodist church. I was not ready to make a decision for I had interest in the Iowa conference as well.

I had a break in my schedule during the last week of July that I had planned to spend with my parents at Eau Claire, Wisconsin, but a desire to see Maria became too great. I had to get back to Wessington Springs. I hitchhiked for two days and surprised Maria, for I had not told her I was coming. We had a great reunion. The big moment of our lives happened the evening of July 25, 1936. We had walked to the city park, about half a mile from the campus, and were sitting at a picnic table. I was tense and my heart was beating wildly. Suddenly I blurted out, "Maria, would you consent to being a Free Methodist preacher's wife?" I heard her gasp, but the reply came quickly, "Yes, I would."

Parting was painful a few days later, when Maria returned home as she had planned, and I returned to Wisconsin for three more weeks of visiting churches and contacting prospective students. At the end of that August, a number of the students I talked to that summer enrolled in the high school or college courses of study. By common consent, both of us kept secret our commitment to each other until early in the spring of 1937. We also agreed I would visit her home in Timber Lake, South Dakota when I had completed my summer's work in August.

On August 10th I headed toward Timber Lake and after two days of hitchhiking I arrived in the little village of Trail City about 12 miles from Timber Lake. It was getting near sundown and no traffic was on the road. I phoned Maria's home to tell them where I was and they agreed to come get me. It was a great moment for me when the car arrived and Maria introduced me to her parents: Burt and Nellie; her sisters, Lucy, Tillie, Jeanette and Fanny; and her little brother William. It was the beginning of a long and wonderful relationship with her family. I spent a week in the drought devastated village of Timber Lake. There were no crops, grass or live trees anywhere. Burt's small income working on a WPA project near Timber Lake barely kept the family in food. This was true of almost all the other families in the village and surrounding communities.

I arrived back in Wessington Springs August 22nd and Maria arrived by train the evening of the 24th and we enrolled for the fall semester on the 26th. Two new professors arrived also: George Turner and Curry Mavis. Prof. Mavis would teach courses in Christian ministry and behavior as well as serve as the pastor of the local Free Methodist Church. Prof. Turner would teach Greek, Church History and several Bible courses. Unknown to us then, these two men were to have a close association with us over a number of decades.

Several shocks came to us close together. On the day after registration, President Ansted announced he was resigning and was moving his family to California, where he had a new position. They were leaving in a few days. It was with sad hearts that Maria and I helped other students load the Ansted's belongings in a truck and say good-bye. Both of us had worked in their home and regarded them as substitute parents. The pastor of the local Free Methodist Church, Rev. Harden, immediately became the new president of the school. He was a godly man and well liked by staff and students. The transition went smoothly.

On September 2nd, Maria's folks called saying a rural school board near Timber Lake needed a teacher and had asked whether Maria would take the position. They thought she should take the job and were driving to Wessington Springs on the 4th. Maria's parents arrived and the new president requested an interview with them. We had told him about the situation and he assured us he would do everything possible to keep Maria in school. President Harden told them Maria was at the top of a list for a music scholarship, which would pay for a good deal of her tuition. The president wanted Maria to continue singing in a ladies quartette for his weekly program on the Huron radio program. This information pleased Maria's folks so much they consented for her to stay in school. Were we relieved and happy.

Maria had a beautiful voice and loved to sing. The three young ladies who sang with her in the trio were Ruth Upton, and Adelaine Baughman. Besides singing regularly in the radio program, the quartette sang in a number of nearby churches and in many college academic affairs and college worship services. She would sing in trios or duets with one or two of these young ladies at various meetings. She was especially close to Adelaine who was her roommate. Often Maria and I would team up with Adelaine and Jon Carlton on double dates and informal songfests. We had a great time together.

Several other new developments marked the beginning of the fall semester. I had not completed the course requirements for a teaching certificate during my first two years, so I signed up for a needed course and for practice teaching. The college also had a private elementary school on campus, which was called a Model School, at which potential teachers could fulfill this requirement. Several afternoons each week, I taught at this school for the first half of the semester. I took private speech (academically called expression) lessons. I was elected president of the student ministerial association, also known as the Oxford Club. I began a new job at the college assisting another student, Jon Carlton, baking bread, buns and rolls two or three nights each week. I also squeezed in time to work five to ten hours per week at the Mavis residence.

Most importantly, Maria and I were able to find a half hour or so chatting in the girl's parlor or walking around campus. It all added up to a very busy semester, which ended December 22nd.

Two days later, my brother Ralph and I hitchhiked to our parent's home in Eau Claire, Wisconsin. Dad was feeling better physically and now had a job as a janitor at the Baptist Church in the city. Part of his salary was free use of the old parsonage located just behind the church. Ralph and I began searching for short term jobs, because the college had announced there would be no school until the beginning of February. Unemployment was high, so no jobs.

After two weeks, I decided to hitchhike to southern Iowa to visit my relatives who still lived in or near my birth town, Russell. On the way, I stopped in Mason City, Iowa to visit a couple that had graduated from Wessington Springs College in May 1935. The husband, Larry Cartwright, was serving as pastor of the local Free Methodist Church. I wanted to talk to Larry and his wife about taking a pastorate near them in the fall of 1937. I then went on to Des Moines, Iowa to visit with another graduate of the college, Elliott Hollister, who was serving the local Free Methodist Church. I had the same agenda, to explore possibilities of being a pastor in that part of Iowa.

I arrived in Russell in the afternoon of Jan. 14th and made contact with my mother's widowed, younger sister, Aunt Maude Zimmer. She made sure I visited all my cousins in the area, only one of whom I had met before. I saw the graves of my grandparents and my sister Leta who had died as a baby. I worshipped at the Methodist Church that had been so important to my mother in the early years of her life. The visit was important to me, for it moved my second-hand knowledge of the place to a real bonding with my mother's family. None of my father's family lived in the small town, though the graves of his parents and one of his grandmothers were in the local cemetery. I was glad I made the trip.

After several days I returned to Des Moines to visit the Hollister's and then on to Mason City to visit the Cartwright's. I wanted to ask more questions about the possibility of being a pastor in Iowa and weigh their opinions against the invitation I had received to take a pastoral assignment in Wisconsin. In the forenoon of January 20th I renewed my journey westward. So far on this trip the weather had been pleasant. Things would soon change.

As I traveled, I noticed clouds gathering in the west. They became more dense and threatening throughout the afternoon. During my last ride of the day, which would take me to Sioux Falls, SD, snowflakes began to fill the air and by the time we were approaching the city a blinding blizzard was swirling about us, and the temperature was falling rapidly. We safely made it to the city, but I was faced with a problem.

Where would I stay during the night? Fortunately, one of the students I had become acquainted with at the college lived in the city and by searching the telephone directory I located his family and soon had an invitation to stay with them overnight. They provided a hearty supper, a warm bed and a bountiful breakfast.

By morning, the blizzard had stopped but the temperature was well below zero. That didn't stop me from going out to US highway # 16 and try to get to Wessington Springs, 125 miles away. Very soon after taking a position by the side of the highway, a young man stopped and said he was going to Mitchell and would I like to ride in his warm car. With delight, I said yes. Travel was not easy however; snowplows were busy clearing the road of hard, drifted snow. It was slow going, with more standing still than going forward. As a result, we were barely able to arrive in Mitchell before dark. I knew the Free Methodist pastor in the city, and after contacting him by phone, I had an invitation to stay overnight. The next morning I started out again. By that time, the roads were cleared, so I arrived at the college soon after noon. The temperature had remained well below zero while I traveled.

I had kept Maria informed of my travels with a series of letters. In those days it cost three cents to send a letter. I found several letters from her awaiting me at the college post office. One letter did not make me happy. She informed me that another school was begging her to teach its children, and her parents felt she should accept the request. That meant she would not return for classes during the second semester. Emotions gripped me. Of course, I wanted her near me in school. That night before I fell asleep, I had made a decision.

The next morning I packed a small bag with clothes and started for Timber Lake. Snow was in the air and it was moderately cold. I managed to get to Roscoe, a short distance west of Aberdeen on US highway # 12. Where would I spend the cold night? I thought of the city jail and in a few moments, I was safely and warmly settled down for the night. The constable in charge was a very kind man, he allowed me to phone Maria and tell her where I was and why. The next morning I managed to get a ride with a man who hauled mail to Mobridge. I thought I would surely get to Timber Lake by nightfall, but I was disappointed. Just east of Selby, a blinding blizzard suddenly hit us. By driving slowly, and carefully, the driver was able to get to Selby. Snowdrifts blocked the highway to the west. We found a hotel room for the night.

The blizzard had stopped by morning but huge and very hard drifts of snow two to three feet thick blocked the road wherever the highway cut through a slight rise of the land. We had a very slow trip to Mobridge, having to stop repeatedly for snowplows to clear a way through the drifts. We arrived in town about dark. The driver advised that I meet a train from the west that was due to arrive soon. Perhaps I could find a car or truck with a Dewey county license plate. If so, I should inquire at the station about the owner of the vehicle and whether I could ride with them to Timber Lake, the main town in the county.

Fortunately, I found such a license plate, located the owners and obtained a ride to Timber Lake. I knew where the Saarloos home was located so I started down a street. I noticed the figure of a lady a short ways in front of me who I thought walked like Maria, it was she. We had a big, wonderful kiss and soon were in her warm home. What a trip!

I spent a week with Maria's family and appreciated her parents and siblings more and more as the days passed. We discussed in detail the impact the drought had on their farm animals and the crops. That previous summer they were forced to sell everything and move to town. The only job available was on the government sponsored WPA. The job at the rural school seemed attractive though the pay was very low. I left knowing Maria's parents had not fully made up their minds, so I was fearful Maria might not come back to school.

I hitchhiked back to Wessington Springs in sub-zero temperatures, strong winds and snow often in the air. I had to stay overnight with a pastor in Aberdeen, but made it back to school safely the next day. President Harden was concerned with Maria's problem and phoned and wrote her parents, giving them encouraging promises. Throughout the semester, he would provide Maria with scholarships and work on the campus.

Two weeks after enrollment, Maria arrived on campus by train. What a happy reunion! We gave God the glory for answering prayer. My baking schedule interfered too often with our hope for a few minutes together at the end of each day, but notes back and forth helped fill the gaps. Maria worked quite a bit in the college laundry, starching and ironing shirts. Drip-dry and no-iron clothes were unknown in those days. Custom required that boys wear nice shirts to class and white shirts were preferred on Sundays. Pullover shirts and denim pants were for work only.

Up to the middle of the semester, Maria and I had told no one, including our parents of our commitment to each other. We decided to break the news to our parents and no one else. From my school studies, I learned that in an earlier period in U. S. history, it was the custom in cultured circles for the young man to formally request permission of the parents of a young lady to marry her. I thought that was a nice way of breaking the news, so I wrote a rather formal letter to Maria's parents requesting such permission. I remember the surprised tone of their reply but also their pleasure in granting such permission. I also wrote my parents of our engagement. They too were pleased, though they had not yet met Maria.

Late in April, Maria began to have trouble with a very sore big toe, and then a rash broke out on one of her hands. The problem was so serious she was assigned to the school clinic in the girls' dormitory. This situation persisted for several weeks and many a note (still in our possession) were passed back and forth, carried by helpful students. Her instructors came and tutored her in regards to her class assignments and her roommate and other girls helped with writing reports and essays. At one point, Maria became so depressed she suggested in a note that perhaps she would be more of a hindrance than a help to me in ministry and wondered whether she ought not to take back her promise to me. I quickly wrote a note stating I was against such a notion and persuaded her to never consider such a thought again. She took my advice seriously.

Maria recovered soon due to the medications applied to her hand and toe. Several years later we learned from a friend with some medical experience that strong soaps used in laundries and in some homes would cause the rash and suggested some brands of soap that were easy on the skin. She has been careful ever since, with good results. The big toe also healed properly.

My expression classes began to produce results. On April 30th I gave a humorous reading in a declamation contest (such was the college's name for the event) and won first place. I also won first place in a conference-wide contest among young people in the conference. Maria wanted to attend those contests but her illness prevented it. Early in May I was told the college administration had decided to grant me a graduation night in which an important part of the program, on May 27th, would be a reading delivered by me. For me that was a big event.

When my parents heard about this occasion, they sent me a new suit, a white shirt, new stockings and new shoes. I was overwhelmed for in the four years of school I had only received a dollar or two occasionally. I knew they were scraping the bottom of their financial "barrel" each time they did it. With the package came a letter stating they had found a ride to come out to Wessington Springs for my graduation. For them it was a big event, for no one of my family or close relatives had graduated from college.

On May 29th my folks arrived and I had the joy of introducing them to their future daughter-in-law. They immediately fell in love with her.

The commencement service was on June 1st. I marched immediately behind the faculty with a black robe and a red tassel on my flat academic hat. I received the Bachelor of Arts in Religion degree, the first granted by the college, and also a Second Year Teachers Diploma. Maria received a Stenographic Diploma. For us it was the climax of a struggle to obtain a college education.

My parents left that afternoon for home. A few days later, I followed by hitchhiking, for the car my folks were riding in had no room for another passenger. No problem, I arrived home safely, taking two days to make the trip. Maria also returned to her home and a job for the summer. Many letters passed back and forth during the summer. Early in July we were able to set the date for the wedding. It was to happen August 12, 1937.

The superintendent of the Wisconsin Free Methodist conference, Rev. Aiken, was a member of the Board of Trustees of the college and was present for the commencement. He informed me he had found a job near Platteville, Wisconsin for me so I could earn money to get married and get ready to join the conference and receive a position as pastor of a Free Methodist Church. That spring I had been in correspondence with Rev. Aiken and also with the superintendent of the Iowa conference. I was trying to decide which conference to join. In his correspondence, the Iowa superintendent seemed somewhat non-committal, whereas Rev. Aiken was eager to have me. I felt it was easy to decide in favor of the Wisconsin conference.

June 10th I left home to hitchhike to Platteville. During my travels throughout the summer of 1936 I had visited the Free Methodist churches in Platteville and several nearby towns so the area was not new to me. I quickly made contact with Rev. A.C. Wolcott, pastor at Platteville, and he took me to the farm where I would work during the summer. I found the farm family, Mr. and Mrs. Chester Wright and daughter Marie, pleasant people. I was to work sixty days for a dollar a day and board and room, the standard wage for farmhands at that time.

This would seem to be an appropriate time to look back over my four years of college and evaluate the impact of those years upon my life. In essence, I can say the experiences of those years definitely changed my life and prepared me for a ministry I was committed to follow the rest of my life. I was no longer a shy, troubled farm boy. I was ready for action.

First, let me evaluate the overall situation during the middle 1930's. The decade had started at the beginning of the great depression that was to reduce much of the nation to abject poverty. Jobs and money were very scarce. Then in the early thirties a devastating drought reduced the entire middle section of the nation to a virtual desert, including South Dakota. By the thousands, the population was moving to the West Coast. A few had some extra cash and some of those people were kind enough to support with gifts the goal of Wessington Springs College to train as many penniless students as possible.

During that time, the school was successful in fulfilling their goal of helping as many students as possible gain enough college training for the few jobs that were available. The administration and trustees were especially interested in preparing future ministers. Maria and I were blessed by this vision and the college's success in helping the poverty stricken to gain some advanced education.

We were only vaguely aware of it at the time, but the thirties were afflicted with the turbulent aftermath of World War I. Soon after the war Russia was overwhelmed by the communist revolution. Rumors of this event filtered through to the farm families of northwestern Wisconsin, but few farmers, our family included, had any hard evidence of what was happening in Europe. Few had contact with the outside world. We rarely had a newspaper in our home. Our area did not even see and hear a radio until the late 1920's and telephones began to show up in farm homes about the same time. Electric lines were not yet bringing electricity to farms in that area.

The plunging farm prices did quickly make us aware that the Great Depression had hit the country. In grade school, we had access to a weekly newsletter called "Current Events." The teacher read its contents to us on the first day of the week. We had to take notes and make a report to the teacher toward the end of that week. We called it "Corny Vents." It was some time before I realized the name of the newsletter wasn't spelled the way we pronounced it. We boys were quite excited when we learned several weeks after the event that young Charles Lindbergh had flown across the Atlantic Ocean all by himself. Most of us had never seen an airplane. We were encouraged to hear about the Kellogg-Briand Pact that limited rearmament. Maybe there wouldn't be another terrible world war.

In high school, I took history courses that opened my eyes to a world I knew little about. My memory of the content of my sister Vera's college text on world history, which I had read several years back, was vague in my mind. The high school course helped me to think in broad global terms. The book was quite sketchy about what had happened during the 1920's. The same was true of the United States history book. I was especially interested in the Civil War for my parents had informed me their fathers had served in the Union Army. The details of their service were limited, since their fathers did not talk about their war experiences much. World War I was fairly well covered but little was written about the situation in Europe following the war. Lenin and the Communist Revolution in Russia were briefly discussed, but the names of Stalin, Hitler and Mussolini, as I recall, were not mentioned in the history book.

News reports were telling about the rise of Stalin to power in 1927 and his efforts to abolish family farms and move farm families to collective farms. Many in the cities were forced to work in the new factories being built. The attitude of the reports was basically negative toward communism and the disruption in Russian society that these programs caused. We were concerned somewhat, but the Great Depression was just hitting us and that was what mattered. Mostly people in our area of Wisconsin ignored Europe.

When we enrolled in Wessington Springs College in 1933, the faculty and student body were excited about a student who had immigrated to the United States with her parents and siblings. This young lady had learned English quite well, and soon became popular in the school and community as one who could tell a vivid story about the Russia of the late 20's and the impact of Stalin's programs on her family. Forced by the communists to leave their farm, her family along with other families was able to leave Russia and come to the United States. They followed many others to the Chicago, Illinois and Milwaukee, Wisconsin areas.

Her father was able to get a job in the Monarch Stove factory in Beaver Dam, Wisconsin, so the family settled there. Neighbors introduced them to the local Free Methodist Church where Jenny learned about Wessington Springs College. Since she had just finished high school and had rapidly learned to read and speak English, she was accepted as a student. From her point of view the conditions in Russia were a disaster and had created a sense of terror in the hearts of many Russian farmers, including her own. Her story caused quite a stir in the school and the community. In the summer of 1934, her father died and she could not continue her schooling. Her evaluations of Russia did create a new interest in Europe, an interest that became more acute as radio news reports told of the rise of Hitler to power in Germany and Mussolini's new power in Italy. Nevertheless, Europe was far away and limited money resources, along with South Dakota farmers moving west, seemed much more important concerns of life.

Of interest to us students was the rising popularity of prophecy preachers who were declaring the world would come to an end soon. Jesus Christ would suddenly appear and take all Christians immediately to heaven. One preacher we heard predicted this event would happen in 1935. That year came to an end and no such event happened.

On looking back to that time, I have tended to think these preachers had a keener sense of the seriousness of events that were happening and the ugly character of several newly powerful leaders such as Stalin, Hitler and Mussolini in Europe, than most of the western leaders of France, Britain and the United States. These western leaders tended to regard these men as having significant skills in unifying their countries and bringing a measure of prosperity to their people. These men tended to use some violent methods but the westerners had confidence violence would soon cease and peace maintained by new treaties.

However, in the year 1935 several events took place that bode ill in the future. Hitler announced he had an air force and was conscripting young men into the army, both acts in violation of the Treaty of Versailles. The West responded by trying to isolate Germany. Mussolini became aggressive by attacking Ethiopia in October 1935, from the Italian colony of Somalia and allegedly used poison gas. The League of Nations put some bans on certain products going to Italy but they had little effect.

A series of actions by Stalin, Hitler, and Mussolini in 1936 and 1937 cast a deeper and deeper shadow over Europe. Stalin began his famous Great Purge that continued through 1936 and 1937. The confessions of top leaders of communism about killing many people and sending millions of Russians to forced labor camps stunned the world. Stalin became an absolute ruler by executing all those leaders who might challenge his power. Hitler saw the weaknesses of Britain and France and boldly sent his armies into the Rhine land in March 1936. Mussolini brashly declared himself the Emperor of Ethiopia. In October of 1936, Germany and Italy were united by treaty and in November, Germany and Japan were united by treaty.

A civil war broke out in Spain in 1936 and quickly Hitler and Mussolini sent troops to help the rebels and Russia sent help to the government of Spain. The League of Nations was helpless to correct any of these aggressive actions and in effect became powerless.

In May 1937, Neville Chamberlin became Prime Minister of Britain and chose appeasement as his official policy in dealing with Hitler and Mussolini. He tried to forge some understandings with these men. They would talk freely, but refused to change their ways. In reality, Germany had become a world power again by 1937, with Hitler and his co-horts in full control.

The events in Europe were causing a renewal of dire prophecies by some Christian ministers and we students soon became aware that 1939 was the year selected as the end time for the world. These preachers admitted they had miscalculated Biblical chronology related to the Second Coming of Christ, but that a new study gave them confidence in the new date. We students tended to be skeptical and paid little attention to these prophecies. At the same time, we were increasingly concerned about what was happening in Europe. We did not have a sense of panic, for basically, we accepted the act of the U.S. Congress in 1937 that declared neutrality and thus isolated the United States from the rest of the world. After all, we had pressing money problems to solve and a life to live.

Looking back at my college studies, I must say I have a deep appreciation for some academic contributions available at Wessington Springs College. We had a combination of liberal arts courses and religious courses at a very reasonable price. The liberal arts courses were accredited by the South Dakota Department of Education that meant the Associate of Arts degree was accepted in all state colleges and universities as equivalent to their first two years of college. Since the state regularly examined and approved the A.A. degree program at Wessington Springs College, the credits earned toward this degree were accepted at secular colleges in other states as well. There was no problem having courses in the Bible or theology on the transcript. Regional Accrediting Associations were not yet functioning. The A.A. degree was also accepted as valid by other Free Methodist colleges and colleges of other denominations.

Although I soon realized the college academic curriculum had shortcomings, I appreciated deeply the fact the school had accepted me into its program even though I was literally a penniless farm boy. I worked my way through school with a very small debt when I graduated. However, having to work so much was a handicap for me, for I had limited time for study outside of classes. Nevertheless, I was able to complete the course of study in four years, and every class was like entering an expanding realm of knowledge. The range of courses was too limited, due to small faculty and staff.

My first two years was oriented toward the liberal arts classes. I was fascinated by my science classes, and thought more than once that if I did not have a call to the ministry on my life, I would enjoy being a scientist. My studies in the Bible and about the Christian faith, especially during the last two years, were sources of special joy. To be able to read the New Testament in Greek was an exciting accomplishment.

My love for history was nurtured in the courses dealing with the history of the Christian church, in its various forms, from New Testament times to modern times. The course covered a long time period and thus tended to be sketchy, but it was new to me and I reveled in what I was learning. The same is true of the history of church doctrine in its varieties, sketchy but new to me.

Professor Wilson King was the instructor in the Bible courses I took in my first three years of study and Professor George Turner taught those courses in my final year. Both were graduates of New York Biblical

Seminary and used a method of teaching the Bible which they learned at that seminary. The method was popularly known as English Bible because we studied the King James Version. More accurately, it was also known as the inductive Bible method, for the method could be used while studying the Old Testament in Hebrew and the New Testament in Greek or any translation of those Testaments into any language.

The method brought the student directly to the biblical text. In our first course, we studied the Gospel according to Matthew. The first step was to read the entire Gospel in one sitting, if possible. Ignoring for the time being what other students may have constructed as outlines of the book's content, we attempted to make our own outline or chart. This procedure gave us an overall understanding of the Gospel's content.

The next step was to subdivide the Gospel into major parts. We would compare our opinions in class and if there were several different opinions, the instructor would help us do the task properly. Since the New Testament books, as in the Old Testament, are divided into chapters, the next part of this step is to evaluate the content of each chapter and give an appropriate title to each chapter. Usually there were a variety of titles proposed, so the instructor helped the students, sort through the titles and compare them to each chapter's content. The next phase of this step was to group the verses of each chapter within a subdivision into paragraphs and provide each paragraph with a title. These paragraph titles were compared and fine-tuned in class discussion with the Professor. By this time, we students had a fairly good understanding of the Gospel as a whole.

The next step was to look at the sentences in each paragraph and ask questions about the meaning conveyed by nouns, verbs and other parts of speech. Questions were then raised about the references to the Old Testament, if any, and about the customs and the concepts held by various Jewish groups mentioned in the text.

Since our work schedules prevented us from doing intensive research, each professor would summarize the data, which would help answer these questions and alert us to commentaries and Bible dictionaries, which we should read as we could. This phase of the study went slowly and the professor found it necessary to pick important chapters of the Gospel so we could have an encounter with them before the course came to an end.

Mixed with the previous step was another important aspect of the study, namely the application of the teachings of the Gospel to our daily Christian living and also the best way to explain the gospel to people we would meet in our daily lives and in our ministry.

Other bible courses would center on one or the other of the large books of the Old or New Testament, or a grouping of several smaller books like the Minor Prophets or the epistles of Paul, John or Peter. Both Professor King and Turner, emphasized that the method they were using should become an essential part of bible study the rest of our lives, and especially when preparing devotional messages or sermons. I took their advice seriously.

Maria Saarloos

Wessington Springs College

Herbert Livingston and Maria Saarloos

CHAPTER 4

MARRIAGE AND EARLY MINISTRY

The summer of 1937 seemed to never end yet, it was brightened by many letters from a young lady in Timber Lake, S.D. and many letters addressed to that young lady. We were working out details of how to arrange for the trip from Platteville, Wisconsin to Timber Lake and return, for the Free Methodist Annual Conference was to meet in Platteville the last week in August. Whom would we have perform the ceremony and who of my family would be able to attend? Above all, how would I get out to Timber Lake and back again, for I did not own a car or a small truck to transport people and baggage? We had faith the Lord would help us solve all these problems.

It is time I should introduce you to my beloved Maria. She was born November 19th, 1915 in Mumster, Netherlands; it is a suburb of the national capital called The Hague. Her birth name was Maria Geertriuda, second daughter of Bastiaan Dirk Saarloos and Neeltje Ziel. Bastiaan was born in Hekelingen, Netherlands on September 3rd, 1886, son of Jan Saarloos and Maria Bakker. In his early twenties, he joined the national mounted police force of his motherland and soon was stationed at Vollenhoven, a fishing and farming village on the east shore of the Zuider Zee (sea). While there, Bastiaan Saarloos met a lovely blue-eyed blond, named Neeltje, born May 10th, 1889, daughter of Jannes Zeil and Loutien Prins, who lived on a farm near Vollenhoven.

Bastiaan and Neeltje were married May 23, 1912. Soon after their marriage, Bastiaan was chosen to be a member of Queen Wilhelmina's personal bodyguard. One picture shows eighteen men in the guard.

Their first child, a daughter, was born at Mumster on February 17th, 1914 and was named Lutien Maria Adriaantje Jansje. As noted above, Maria was the second daughter. Bastiaan served the Queen at her several palaces in the Netherlands, throughout World War I. Fortunately, the Netherlands was not invaded by Germany, so Bastiaan never had to serve in combat.

While serving the Queen, Bastiaan was patrolling the English Channel beach when a young girl swimming in the surf cried out for help. Bastiaan quickly discarded his sword and boots. He was a powerful swimmer so he soon had the girl safely on shore. The Queen gave him a special citation, a picture of herself, and a medal in honor of his bravery. The medal was passed on to his son William. We have the picture of the Queen.

After World War I, the economic situation in Europe was a disaster and Bastiaan soon thought of moving elsewhere. Already one of Bastiaan's brothers, Leonard (Leon, pronounced Lane), had moved with his family to a Dutch community in northwestern Iowa. He had been writing to his relatives in the Netherlands about the fertile farmland in that part of Iowa. He urged Bastiaan to come to the United States and take up farming in the area about 30 miles east of the Missouri River and from 30 to 40 miles south of Minnesota.

The family passport shows Bastiaan and Neeltje obtained it on January 22, 1920. They applied for passage to the United States at the Holland-Amerika Lijn's office at Rotterdam on May 12,1920. Vollenhoven is given as the family home. They sailed on the SS. Noordam on June 9th. The total cost for the family of four was five hundred ($508.00) and eight dollars. They entered the United States at Ellis Island. Any visitor can find their record on the computer. The officer who serviced them suggested they Americanize their first names. Bastiaan took the name Burt, Neeltje took the name Nellie, and Lutien took the name Lucy. Maria was given the name Marie and her middle name was changed from Geertruida to Gertrude. The family immediately boarded a train for Boyden in northwestern Iowa.

Burt was soon working on a farm near the town, but the birthplaces of three of Maria's younger sisters indicate that the family moved from farm to farm every several years. Tillie Johanna was born November 29, 1920 in Boyden, Jeannette Gertrude was born June 11, 1922 in Alton and

Fanny Pauline was born January 04, 1924 in Hospers. Maria remembers when the family moved to Newkirk.

Since most of the population of the community was made up of Dutch immigrants, Burt and Nellie were under no great pressure to learn English. However, as soon as Lucy and Maria entered the first grade they had to learn the new language and the parents picked up English words from the girls. About 1926 or 1927, word was circulating that land was becoming available in the northwestern section of South Dakota. American Indians were being settled on reservations in that area.

The Standing Rock Indian Reservation was coextensive with Corson County, a long rectangle of land bordered on the north by North Dakota, then on the east by the Missouri River. The southern border ran west about 80 miles. The Cheyenne River Indian Reservation followed the Missouri River and went straight south to the Cheyenne River. The county line then followed west for eighty miles. Dewey County, where Timber Lake was the county seat, was coextensive with this reservation. A strip of land on both sides of State Road # 20 was set aside for homesteading by white people. Land was cheap and after the sod was broken by plow and seed was planted, excellent crops were harvested.

Burt and Nellie and their family moved to a rented farm in 1927. This farm was located five miles northeast of Timber Lake in Corson County, just north of State Road # 20. A narrow hill called Long Butte arose abruptly several hundred feet above the prairie just to the west of the farm. The nearest grade school was three miles west of the farm and the girls made the trip along the north side and over the butte to its southwest corner every school day by horse and buggy. In the winter the west wind was bitterly cold.

For several years, the move seemed to be a wise decision, but after 1929, the income from farm products fell sharply, followed by the Dust Bowl days of the 1930's. It wasn't long before the family had to move into Timber Lake and Burt had to work for the WPA. However, the move made it possible for the girls to attend Timber Lake High School from which they graduated. Lucy got married but Maria was able to find a job in a local restaurant.

While Burt and Nellie lived in the Netherlands, they were devoted attendees of the Holland Reformed Church and in Iowa faithfully attended the Dutch Reformed Church. In Timber Lake, there were only a few Protestant churches, the most popular being the Methodist Church and the Baptist Church. The family favored the Baptist Church. There were several Dutch families in the area and they arranged with the Baptist Church for services in the afternoon. Mostly the services were in the Dutch language and laymen read the Dutch ritual and prayers, and sometimes gave short messages. Mrs. Leeds Greene, the Baptist minister, also helped as she could. The Saarloos family attended two services each Sunday, with a communal dinner at noon in the Baptist church. In 1933, the Methodist Church, knowing Maria's reputation in the town as an excellent singer, asked Maria to direct their choir, which she did for two years. During this time, her family often attended the morning services at the Methodist Church.

Maria graduated from the Timber Lake High School in 1934 and worked a year in the town. She learned about Wessington Springs College through a high school classmate, Clara Williamson, who attended the College during the1934-35 school year and soon got a teaching job in a rural school near Timber Lake. Clara persuaded Maria to enroll late in August 1935 at the College.

A while back, I paused in my narrative in the summer of 1937. I was working on a farm near Platteville, Wisconsin and Maria was working in Timber Lake. Some of the problems associated with getting out to Timber Lake and back again were slowly being solved. One Sunday morning early in July, a couple, Howard and Dorothy Moeller, who had been our classmates at Wessington Springs College, came to the Free Methodist Church in Platteville to worship. They had heard I would be preaching that morning. They lived in Montford about twenty miles north of Platteville.

After the service, they asked me about our wedding plans and I told them I had no transportation for the trip. They informed me they had a vacation period during the middle of August and had a 1931 Chevrolet. They offered to take me by car to Timber Lake and back, if I would pay for the gas and oil. We quickly made a deal, but what about the baggage?

At the farm, I had noticed that the Wrights had a rather old two-wheeled trailer with wooden spokes in the wheels for a Model T Ford. The tires, known as 33 by 3 tires, that is, 33 inches in diameter from rim to rim and three inches wide. I grew bold and asked them if they would let me take the trailer behind Moeller's car. They thought about the matter for a few days and informed me I could take the trailer. Maria wrote she had arranged for the Methodist pastor to marry us.

Consulting with my family, I learned that mother and my sister, Dorothy, wanted to go. Helen Stuve, who had taken Mother and Dad to my graduation at Wessington Springs, wrote asking whether she could go with us by way of Wessington Springs. She was willing to buy the gas for that part of our trip. She would travel with her fiancé, Bob Short, to Timber Lake so they could attend our wedding. That meant seven people would ride in the car. No problem. My brother Ralph, best man, would hitchhike to Timber Lake from wherever he was located at the time. His summer job was with a harvesting and threshing crew that was following the wheat harvest from Nebraska through South Dakota and North Dakota.

On August 8th, I went to Montford and left early the next morning with the Moellers for Eau Claire, stopping at Humbird to pick up Helen Stuve and staying overnight at my parent's place. Very early on the 10th we headed for Wessington Springs, left Helen with Bob Short, and arrived at Timber Lake at 11 p.m. Very soon Maria informed me the Methodist pastor had been called to conduct a funeral out of town.

The next day, Maria and I asked Rev. Mrs. Leeds Greene, the pastor of the Baptist Church, to marry us, and she kindly gave her consent. Later, Ralph, Bob Short and Helen Stuve arrived. As soon as the Dewey County court house, located in Timber Lake, opened on Thursday, I went with Maria, her sister Tillie the bridesmaid, and my brother Ralph the best man, to obtain our marriage license and in a few moments it was signed and sealed.

I married Maria Gertrude Saarloos on August 12, 1937 in the living/dining room of Maria's home. The ceremony was simple and short but solemn. Only the family and a few close friends were present. For Maria and myself it was a glorious moment. We were now man and wife. Maria's parents served a delicious meal and a number of pictures were taken.

We found out we had a problem. Maria's sisters had picked up information from friends that young people, who knew Maria, planned to serenade us that evening with a party called a shevaree. Sometimes a shevaree could become an unruly party. We had a family consultation and decided Maria's boxes of clothes and gifts should be placed in the trailer and we should leave for Wisconsin late that afternoon. Soon

Maria's sister Lucy and husband George made a request. Could they go with us as far as St. Paul, Minnesota? George's relatives had written that welding jobs were available in the city. George was a blacksmith and a welder and few such jobs existed in Timber Lake. My brother Ralph had asked whether he could ride with us as far as Andover, South Dakota, where he would leave us to hitchhike north into North Dakota, where his harvesting crew was located.

After loading the trailer, we found there was enough room at the rear of the trailer for two people to sit. That seemed to solve the problem. Two of us men would take turns riding on the trailer. With that problem solved, at 4 o'clock that afternoon we said good-bye. There were tears in Maria's eyes, for she would soon be living far away from home. It had been a beautiful, though hot day with no rain in sight. Whereas, the trip out to Timber Lake had been uneventful, we soon learned our return trip would border on the chaotic.

The car and trailer were heavily loaded and the graveled highway was rough. We could scarcely exceed 35 miles per hour. A few miles west of Mobridge, the tire on the trailer toward the ditch side went flat. We quickly discovered that Lucy's husband was an excellent mechanic and the Moeller's had adequate supplies for fixing tires. They were prepared for flat tires. Soon the rubber tube in the tire was removed and a patch cemented over the hole in the tube. We were just entering Mobridge when the tire went flat again. George suggested the wooden spokes on the trailer wheels were too dry and were making the wheel so loose it was causing a pinching action on the rubber tube. We found an auto junkyard and its owner. A much more solid wheel with used tire and tube was purchased for a couple of dollars and installed. During this break, all of us ate a few sandwiches from the supply provided by Maria's family. We decided to travel as much of the night as possible.

We were now on US Highway # 12 and thought the road would be in better shape, but it too was graveled and quite rough. We could not go any faster than on the state road. The men took turns driving the car and riding on the trailer. As much as possible, we all tried to sleep some, but early in the morning, we decided to stop. We men found places in the fairly wide ditch and the ladies cuddled in the car. There was very little traffic, so we did get some sleep. This was our wedding night on our "honeymoon." Exciting!

We were approaching Ipswich, west of Aberdeen, and we heard air escaping from the trailer tire on the other side. We fixed it but it went flat again at the edge of the town. The tire had been damaged so we waited till a store opened and bought a new tire and tube. I was getting worried. My money resources were rapidly shrinking. Things went better the rest of the morning.

At Andover, Ralph left us and we continued east. The road was still graveled and rough, so we worried the tires on the trailer would give out again, and one did. At Milbank, we had turned south to connect with US # 212 for I wanted to stay overnight with my friend, Rev. Bill Dietz, pastor of the Nazarene Church. We had entered Minnesota and a couple miles west of Dawson we heard an explosion and knew the tire we had purchased at Mobridge was ruined. It was after six o'clock in the evening. What should we do? George suggested we remove the tire and very slowly drive to Dawson on the rim of the wheel.

Rev. Dietz was home and quickly made us welcomed and congratulated the newlyweds. He found places for all of us to stay overnight. He also thought he might have a solution to our trailer tire problems. A widow who lived close by could not drive the Model T Ford her husband had cherished, so she had a man place the car on blocks in her garage. Rev. Dietz asked me to go with him to see the lady, who listened to our story. Rev. Dietz suggested that she loan three of the wheels with good tires and tubes to me with the understanding I would ship them back as soon I arrived in Platteville. I offered to pay her for the use of the wheels but she refused to accept anything. She was happy to help us out and insisted on meeting my bride.

Mother, Dorothy, Maria and I were given cots in the basement of the church with minimum privacy. We were all exhausted, so we slept soundly. Such was our second honeymoon night.

The next morning, after a wonderful breakfast, the lady's car wheels were transferred to the trailer. One replaced the damaged wheel and two were secured on top of Maria's boxes. We were off to St. Paul and delivered Lucy and George to his relative's home, then the six of us headed for Eau Claire. We were back on US # 12 and it was paved. No matter, just east of Menomonie we heard a boom and realized the back tire on the passenger side of the car had blown out. The spare tire was installed and we continued, but at the west edge of Eau Claire we heard another boom from the same rear side of the car. There was no spare tire so we repeated what we did at Dawson, Minnesota. We drove slowly through the west side of Eau Claire past a hospital till we arrived at my parent's home at 1 a.m. Sunday morning. The noise of the car wheel rolling on its rim was very loud and we expected the police to pull us over any moment. Happily, it didn't happen. We went to church Sunday forenoon but spent the remainder of the day relaxing and reviewing the past week with the family and friends. Howard Moeller and I were able to find used tires and tubes for his car Monday forenoon. Soon we were on our way and had no more car problems.

Mr. and Mrs. Wright welcomed and joyfully congratulated us. They had a surprise announcement. While we were gone, they had decided to take a week vacation and visit his people in Missouri, leaving us alone on the farm. Our responsibility would be to milk a dozen cows morning and evening, gather the eggs and feed the pigs. They would pay us ten dollars and board and room. We were happy to agree to the deal and had a wonderful honeymoon. At the Sunday worship service, Maria joined the Free Methodist Church.

The Wisconsin Annual Conference convened at Platteville on August 25 and I was "admitted on trial" as the official minutes recorded the action. On Saturday the 28th, I was appointed pastor of the Free Methodist Church at Beaver Dam.

We had another problem. The parsonage had no furniture and we had no furniture. At the conference, Rev. Aiken announced he was transferring to Oregon to become a pastor of a church there. He and his wife had furniture that they could not afford to ship to Oregon right away. They offered to let us use their furniture at the Beaver Dam parsonage for at least one year. We gladly accepted the offer, and early the next week we arrived in Beaver Dam with a truck loaded with furniture.

We were welcomed by a small but friendly group of church members. I think they were surprised we were so young (both of us were 21 years of age) and newlyweds. No matter, we were their new pastor and wife and all helped us move in. The church and parsonage were wooden buildings with clapboard painted white. Actually, both needed new paint. They were side by side in a nice neighborhood. There were stately oak and maple trees lining the street and the houses were close together. The church property had a yard at the rear large enough for a small garden. Best of all, we were in a house we could call home.

I preached my first sermons as a pastor at the Sunday morning eleven o'clock service and at the seven o'clock service. The congregation was about 20 in number made up of a mixture of older people, several families with children and a few young people. In the congregation was a Russian family led by a widowed mother of five children. One of the girls had been a student at Wessington Springs College during the first year I was a student there. She and her older sisters had jobs in the small city. They had a younger sister and brother. They were loyal supporters of the church program and we became close friends. Another middle-aged couple with six younger children also became our close friends.

During visits with older members, Maria usually went with me. We learned that the church had a history of over fifty years and had built the existing church and parsonage. The church had difficulty growing because after World War I there was an influx of immigrants from Europe. Many were from Germany, Sweden, Norway and Poland and were loyal Lutherans and Catholics. Few immigrants from an English background and with Methodist leanings were coming to Beaver Dam. The Free Methodist congregation had become so small they couldn't support a pastor. During the past ten years, the church had started to grow again and there was an optimistic attitude.

Maria and I agreed being a pastor was an exciting way to serve the Lord. We did have to make some adjustments. Both of us had grown up on farms and had limited contact with people in small towns. The past several years we had close contact with young people at the college, so suddenly to be placed in the center of a thriving industrial city of about 15,000 was a new experience for us. Almost all the people in the congregation were older than we. To them we were just youngsters, taking on a job best filled by older people. At least we were tempted to think that way.

I found that preparing two new sermons each week was a real challenge. I worked long hours on each one. We had no telephone in the parsonage so I was not interrupted by having to answer a phone many times a day. We did not have a car; because the salary was so meager, we couldn't afford one, so we did a lot of walking as we called on our members. I was beginning to feel inadequate for the task of being a pastor of even a small church. I doubted whether my call to be a pastor was valid. I didn't tell Maria much about my inner tensions. In fact, I had always been inclined to say little about my inner feelings to anyone.

I should have been much more open with Maria, for she was proving to be a wonderful companion and helper.

One evening at a church service I knelt with Maria and others at the church altar to pray about my inner tensions. The Lord clearly assured me he had called me to serve as a minister. For the second time in my spiritual journey I yielded myself to the Lord's call. Wonderful peace and joy filled me to overflowing. No doubts about my call to ministry have troubled me since that occasion.

As Maria and I thought about the activities of the church, we decided we should concentrate our efforts on the Sunday school that had from 25 to 30 in attendance. We spoke to the teachers and others and found they agreed. They asked us to provide some training, for they felt they knew little about how to teach children. I got out my college class notes and the few books on teaching I had in my very meager library and held a series of classes over a number of weeks for the four or five Sunday school teachers. Efforts to find families with young children paid off and the Sunday school began to grow.

Early in February, Maria began to feel ill in the mornings. A church member recommended a doctor and we went to see him. He soon told us that we should expect a child sometime in August. We were excited but asked about payments for his services. He assured us he did not charge ministers. We thanked him for his generosity.

During the spring, Maria's parents asked us to inquire about owners of dairy farms who might need help. They wanted to move from South Dakota. We learned the factories in that part of Wisconsin were hiring so many laborers the farm owners were indeed looking for farm managers. We suggested Maria's parents should move to Beaver Dam so farm owners could interview them personally. Burt and Nellie decided to take the risk of moving and asked me to come by train to Mobridge where they would meet me. They had a 1929 Pontiac and a four-wheeled trailer to transport their family and their personal items. Since I had traveled through that area so often and knew the roads, they wanted me to drive the car for them. They would pay the train fare.

Fortunately, the train I would take went directly from Columbus, ten miles from Beaver Dam to Mobridge. I boarded the train early June 1st and arrived in Mobridge the next morning. The family was ready to travel. Since Burt had driven to Wessington Springs several times, he decided he would drive that far. A few miles west of Mobridge the engine suddenly stopped and the trailer began to sway. In a blink of an eye, we found ourselves in the low broad ditch and the trailer leaning against the side of the ditch.

We had been going rather slowly on the graveled road, so to our relief, we found only limited damage to the trailer. A car stopped to help us and together we had the trailer on its four wheels. The driver of the car offered to take Burt to Mobridge to hire a wrecker to come pull us into town. While Burt was gone, I used a hammer and some nails and repaired the trailer and with the help of Tillie, Jeanette and Fanny refilled some boxes. We were ready to go when the wrecker arrived. A garage mechanic in Mobridge quickly found the problem. A timing gear chain at the front of the engine had broken. It was late in the afternoon before we continued the trip.

Soon the sun went down and we had to make a decision. Where would we sleep? We decided we would turn off the highway as soon as possible into an open field, laid down some blankets and sleep the best we could. Because the air was dry there was no dew on the ground. For three more days and nights we followed this procedure and finally arrived in Beaver Dam, Wisconsin. Maria's family stayed with us for a few days while Burt looked for a job on a farm. He soon located a farm owner who had just lost the manager of one of his dairy farms. An agreement was reached and Maria's family moved to the farm located about ten miles east of Beaver Dam. We were all happy, for the family could drive to Beaver Dam to attend our Sunday service.

On the morning of June 23rd, Maria had gone out of the house into the back yard but returned soon saying, "Herbert I am afraid our baby wants to be born. How can we get to the doctor?" I took her to the bedroom and asked her to lie down while I went to a neighbor to phone our doctor about the problem. He said he would come to the house immediately. I had scarcely returned to the house when I heard the screech of brakes in front of the parsonage. The doctor rushed in and quickly examined Maria. He asked whether a midwife might be available in our congregation. A lady's name came to mind and I made contact with her. She helped the doctor deliver a baby boy at 10:20 that morning. The doctor left the baby with us but instructed us to call him if the baby's face should start to turn blue. About an hour, later Burton's face did show a blue tinge. I immediately called the doctor and he came quickly and took him to the hospital on the west side of the city and placed him in an oxygen incubator. Burton was born about two months before his due date and his lungs were not developed enough to breathe properly. He weighed a bit more than five pounds at birth but during the first week, his weight dropped to four pounds four and one half ounces.

According to the medical practice at that time, a new mother had to stay in bed for at least a week to recover from the stress of giving birth. Maria's family came to our aid by having her mother and three sisters take turns staying with us. Maria had seen Burton only briefly before he was taken to the hospital and she was reacting to the separation with considerable emotional pain. The doctor had given me permission to be with the child one hour each day, but Maria was not to go the hospital until he was released. The doctor felt the sight of her baby struggling for his life would be too much for her to take.

Every day I spent an hour at the side of the incubator, mostly praying for Burton's survival. The nurses felt I should learn a few skills about caring for a baby, so they taught me how to prepare the formula and how to hold the bottle to his mouth while he sucked on the nipple. He had to be fed every two hours. I arranged to be at his side during his feeding time. They also taught me how to bathe him and how to change his diaper. Day after day, I walked the mile to the hospital and back. I reported each day how the baby was coming along.

The second week Burton gained five ounces and the doctor and nurses were encouraged. The critical time was the transition from the incubator with its oxygen to being outside the incubator. The doctor decided the nurses should begin the process at the beginning of the third week. When I arrived at the hospital Monday forenoon, the nurses told me they had placed Burton in a crib but his face started to turn blue after one half hour so they quickly returned him to the incubator. They said they would continue placing him in a crib several times during the day. The second day they reported Burton still was unable to breathe properly outside the incubator. The third day they had the same result and I could tell they were becoming very concerned. It was difficult telling Maria about the failure of Burton's transition to natural air. The church people were also concerned and assured us they were praying for us.

The fourth day the nurses reported some improvement in Burton's ability to stay outside the incubator for a longer period of time, but they felt his progress was too slow. It was not until the sixth day that Burton successfully stayed outside the incubator for the entire day. During that week, he also gained another five ounces. I must confess that while I rocked him and fed Burton his formula, tears of thanksgiving trickled down my cheeks.

I had good news for Maria when I returned home and we rejoiced together. Maria was ready to bring Burton home right away, but we had to wait another week. On the day of Burton's release from the hospital, Maria and I walked to the hospital and for the first time Maria held her son in her arms and fed him his formula. The nurses insisted that each of them put one garment on the baby. They were as excited as we. We placed Burton on a small pillow we had brought with us. He now weighed five pounds one and one half ounces.

Maria's family had come to the parsonage and we all were happy people as we took turns holding the tiny tike. Added to this joy was the Lutheran Hospital's invoice stating they had a policy of not charging ministers for any services rendered to them or their families. We have always been thankful for the generosity of the Lutheran Church.

Two pressing concerns filled the summer days that followed Burton's return home. One concern was keeping the twenty-four hour schedule of feeding Burton his formula every two hours. The other concern was a pressing need to can the abundant vegetables grown in our garden and the fruit brought to us by friends. By the middle of August dozens of glass quart jars were full. Burton slowly gained weight and by the middle of August, he weighed six and one half pounds.

A second surprise came to us the last week of August. I was aware that the policy of the conference was to move new, young pastors every year for several years in order to broaden their experience. We hoped that because Burton was so young and small that we would not be moved. At that time, neither the congregation nor the pastor had any role in the decision of the conference stationing committee about where a pastor would serve. At the end of the conference session, the assignments of the pastors were announced. There was no appeal to the committee's decisions. Fortunately, that policy was abandoned several decades later, but we were shocked to learn we were to move within a week's time to a church at Birchwood, a summer resort town in northwestern Wisconsin about three hundred miles from Beaver Dam. The conference would provide a limited amount of money for moving costs.

I found it difficult to tell Maria about our move, for she would have to leave her parents and family who had just moved near Beaver Dam. We began packing our belongings and placing the furniture borrowed from the Aikens in a room on the upper floor of the parsonage. The pick-up truck that would transport us to Birchwood did not have room for that furniture. We spent the first night of the trip at my parent's home in Eau Claire and arrived at our new pastorate the next afternoon. Birchwood was a village of four hundred people and located at the juncture of several beautiful lakes and was surrounded by extensive woodland. Chopping down the forest had created small farms. In the town, there was a small factory that hired only a few men.

In the summer, from Memorial Day to Labor Day, people from larger cities to the south would move into small cottages along the lakes to enjoy the cool temperatures. Boating, fishing and swimming were the attractions of the area. Very few of these people took time to attend church but the money they spent helped the local economy.

In October, November and the early part of December, there was an influx of men from the cities whose intent was to hunt deer, which were plentiful in the woods. We often heard gunfire in the woods during those days.

The parsonage was a disappointment to us. It had a cellar with a dirt floor, three rooms but no bathroom. A well in the back yard provided us with water. An open stairway led to an unfinished upper floor. There was no insulation in the building. A wood-burning kitchen stove and a heater heated the house. We had a struggle keeping warm in the cold winter months. No bus or train passenger service connected the village to nearby Rice Lake and we had no car. Several small stores provided the essentials of fuel, food and clothing.

The congregation and Sunday school were small and we were the only pastoral family in the village. Pastors who lived elsewhere served the other small churches in the village. We felt isolated but put our best effort into our ministry and slowly the attendance at the services and Sunday school grew. Finances were very tight and we were glad we had those jars of produce to help our menus. However, we knew we did not have enough canned goods to supply us through another year. Burton grew rapidly during the year and was an active boy. He brought much joy into our lives.

We began thinking about moving elsewhere. We were disappointed with the new leadership of the conference and some of the conference projects. In the matter of assignment, a Free Methodist pastor at that time, had only one choice available, he could seek admittance to another conference. If accepted, he would be assigned to a church.

Our thoughts turned to the Iowa Conference and the response to our letter of inquiry informed us that there were openings for several new pastors at their annual conference in mid-August. The conference would be glad to accept a certificate of transfer from the Wisconsin conference.

We did not attend the annual conference of the Wisconsin Free Methodists, but sent to the conference leaders my written report of my pastorate at Birchwood. My annual salary that year had been about two hundred and thirty dollars. My report was read during the conference business meeting. Immediately after the report, a lady delegate from Birchwood announced to the gathering she and her husband took us to pick blueberries to help our food supply. A friend told us the conference delegates were quite amused.

During our two years of being a pastor, I had met the requirements for being ordained a deacon. I had successfully completed and passed several correspondence courses and had been a pastor for two years. The Iowa conference would ordain me at its annual meeting at Oskaloosa, Iowa. The conference would also pay our train fare to this meeting.

In August 1939, the Wisconsin Conference granted me a certificate of transfer and the Iowa Conference accepted it. We arrived in Iowa on schedule and at the beginning of an evening service, Bishop Fairburn had Maria and me come to the front and together we knelt at the altar during the ordination ceremony. It was a high moment for both of us. I was now a full-fledged minister. At that conference, I was assigned to the Free Methodist Church at Marion, Iowa.

Marion was a small city of about ten thousand situated about ten miles northeast of Cedar Rapids, a much larger city. The church buildings, sanctuary and parsonage, were built when Marion was a small country village and were in the wooden, white clapboard style of a small country church. The Sunday congregation numbered in the 40's and welcomed us warmly. We were the youngest pastoral family they had installed in the parsonage for some time. Burton soon became their favorite person. The parsonage was an adequate building of five rooms.

We were pleased it had a telephone and a furnace. The parishioners soon supplied it with needed furniture.

A week after we moved into the parsonage an event that shook the world occurred. On September 1, 1939, Hitler's armies invaded Poland. Hitler had already signed a non-aggression pact with Russia on August 23rd. The agreement meant Stalin would not oppose the invasion. On September 3rd France and Britain declared war on Germany. World War II had begun. I remember vividly the anxiety and fear that swept through our congregation, community and across the nation. How soon would the United States be swept into the war?

I remember pouring over European maps trying to figure out what could happen next. In my sermons, I tried my best to point my people toward full commitment to God and urge them to pray earnestly for His mercies during those days.

As the Holiday season approached, Maria began to feel ill in the mornings and the doctor gave us good news. We could expect another child in June.

On the morning of April 3, 1940, I stepped outside to work in the yard and heard the voice of an elderly lady next door call my name. She and her husband were immigrants from Norway and she was very agitated. She had just heard on the radio that German armed forces had invaded Norway. She was concerned about her many relatives who still lived in Norway. I tried my best to console her, but inwardly felt unprepared to deal with this kind of crisis in a neighbor's life. We all asked the question, "Who could stop Hitler?"

Maria and I responded by giving our best efforts to encourage those in need. There was an increased interest in spiritual matters but no real movement toward God, though attendance at the worship services and Sunday school did increase.

The situation was scary for beginning on May 10th, German forces swept through the Netherlands, Belgium and northern France. From May 27th till June 4th, British forces were barely able to escape across the English Channel. On June 10th Italy declared war on Britain and France. By June 12th, France was defeated.

As the months slipped by, we began to think about how to get to the hospital in Cedar Rapids. We still did not have a car. A middle-aged man offered to take us to the hospital, if the big event happened at night or on a weekend. A lady offered to take us during the daytime.

About 2:00 a.m. June 16, 1940, Maria awakened me. She was having pains and suggested I should phone Mr. Hansen. He soon came to the parsonage, leaving his wife to care for Burton. Together we sped to St. Luke's Methodist hospital. I mentioned to the nurses I had been at the delivery of our son and requested I might be in the delivery room with Maria.

The nurses were hesitant, for such permission was not commonly given. Nevertheless, they allowed me to sit at the far side of the room. Labor did not last long. At 4:45 a.m., the nurses congratulated me for being the father of a beautiful, healthy girl. Maria and I had already decided that a girl would be named Nellie Maria. Maria and the baby stayed the required week at the hospital and then returned home. Burton adored his little sister.

We were deeply touched to learn from the administration of the hospital that ministers and families belonging to whatever denomination were not charged for services rendered. Our family doctor also would not charge for his services. We thanked God for those who showed us such kindness. On June 21st, France signed the Franco-German Armistice. On August 13th, Germany began bombarding England, hoping to invade the island quickly.

Another event significant for us in the fall of 1940 was the purchase of a used car. An elderly couple in Cedar Rapids informed us they no longer needed their 1932 Chevrolet. We agreed on $75.00 for the car, $15.00 down and $5.00 a month for a year. Iowa required a driver's license, so I took the test and soon had the important document in my pocket. This was our first car and it helped us to be more mobile. We could call on members who lived several miles from Marion.

Maria enjoyed attending the interdenominational monthly meetings of the Women's Christian Temperance Union (often called the WCTU) along with other women of our congregation.

During the winter, at one of these meetings an elderly lady approached Maria and asked if it was true her little daughter Nellie had been born with a small growth on the side of her left cheek. Maria replied the report was true and that hair was growing from the growth. The lady said she knew a doctor in Marion who removed such growths and requested permission to contact him in Nellie's behalf. She was sure his services would be free.

Maria gave her permission to contact the doctor, A few days later; the lady called the parsonage and informed Maria the doctor would be happy to remove the growth at no charge. The lady gave Maria a date to visit the doctor's office. On that date Maria and I took Nellie to the doctor's office and in a few minutes the growth was removed and when the lesion healed no scar remained. Again, we were thankful for kind people who scarcely knew us. We were more and more convinced we made the right decision to move to Iowa.

During the two years at Marion, I successfully completed several correspondence courses required by the conference. I was eligible for ordination as an elder. I was also completing two years tenure at the Marion church. Would the conference appoint us to another church?

We were pleased the superintendent came to our parsonage to talk to us about the next year. He informed us several churches would need a new pastor and one church was planning to build a new parsonage. I grew bold and told the superintendent about my carpenter experience while a student at Wessington Springs College. He gave us no commitment.

Early in August 1941, the annual conference was again held on the campus of Kletzing College at Oskaloosa. Along with several other young pastors, I was elected to elder's orders. Bishop Ormston conducted the ordination ritual, closing by laying hands on each candidate and wife. Maria and I were deeply moved as hands were laid on our heads and a prayer of ordination was uttered. I was now eligible to vote on conference legislative actions. I could serve as chairman of any conference committee, and could be elected to any office in the denomination. Of special importance to me, I could officiate at communion services. On Saturday afternoon, the stationing committee gave its report and we learned I was appointed to the Free Methodist Church in Cedar Falls, Iowa. This was the church that was planning to build a new parsonage.

We felt a sense of sadness as we moved from Marion, for we had bonded with several of the young couples in the congregation. We would have enjoyed serving the church for several more years. On the other hand, we felt some excitement moving to Cedar Falls, a larger church and helping the congregation build a new parsonage.

The old parsonage was in bad condition and sold for only eleven hundred dollars. There was space behind the church to build a small parsonage. So the church committee assigned to direct the construction project decided on a building about 26 feet by thirty feet. Since the ground sloped south away from the street, the committee decided to have a full basement, part of which would be a garage. There would be a floor with two bedrooms, a bathroom, a rather large living room and a small kitchen. The attic would remain unfinished.

New material for construction was becoming scarce, but one of the committee members knew a man who tore down old barns and houses. This man consented to build a cement-block basement wall on which he would put together a wood frame structure made of the recycled lumber. Within a month, the contractor and his sons finished their work, which included shingles on the roof, old boards nailed to the framework, new windows and outside doors. The work and materials cost eight hundred dollars.

Several carpenters belonging to other Free Methodist churches in the area were not working full time so they came as they could to put the clapboard and trim on the house. We were able to find enough boards at the lumberyards in town to meet our needs. A plumber in the congregation installed the water system and I put in the electrical system under the supervision of an electrician in the city.

Finishing the interior walls was a challenge, for house construction was moving from the long used method of nailing narrow wood lath to the joists and studs and covering the lath with plaster. The new method was using plaster-board. Four-foot by eight foot sheets were not yet available. The current size was two foot by four foot nailed to the joists and the studs and then covered with plaster. Groups of parishioners, mostly young people, would gather at the parsonage in the evenings and Saturdays to nail these sheets in place. A man in the congregation did the plastering. At that time insulation bats were not yet invented, nor were plastic sheets available to cover the joist and studs.

Providing a heating system for the house was a major problem. In March 1941, congress had passed the Lend-Lease Act, which allowed the United States to manufacture military equipment and send it to countries fighting against Germany and Italy. The countries receiving this aid, especially Great Britain, were allowed to pay for these goods whenever and however they could. Immediately, factories were humming, but resulted in many materials becoming hard to get at stores.

After much searching, a coal-fired furnace was purchased and installed in the basement. Nowhere could we find hot air and cold ducts made of metal. As the weather cooled down, kerosene heaters kept the house warm, so workers could do their job.

Finally, in early November, I found a shop that had four-foot by eight-foot sheets of galvanized steel. In desperation, I bought as many sheets I thought I would need, tied a rope around them and drug them over the snow to the parsonage. I then used two planks, a large hammer, a drill, screws and screwdriver to form square pipes. I installed some of them in the ceiling of the basement for hot air ducts. Some sheets I cut into sixteen-inch wide strips and nailed them to the bottom floor joists as cold air ducts. By Thanksgiving, the furnace was heating the parsonage and we were ready to move into the parsonage. The construction of the building cost two thousand ($2,800) eight hundred dollars.

We didn't complete moving into the parsonage until December 7th. Tired from a long day's work, Maria, the two children and I were eating a late supper at the kitchen table. We were listening to the seven o'clock evening news when suddenly the newscaster hesitated and stated "President Franklin Roosevelt desires to make an important announcement." The President's voice was unsteady but clear. He said that at six o'clock p.m. Eastern Standard Time Japanese warplanes bombed Pearl Harbor in Hawaii and badly damaged ships and planes, with many men killed or wounded. He went on to say that the United States had just declared war on Japan. No one had expected Japan would attack American armed forces.

On December 11th both Germany and Italy declared war on the United States. We were involved in World War II on two battlefronts, in the West, with a severely crippled navy facing Japan, and in the East, with the British Isles and North Africa as fighting fronts.

The routines of daily life changed drastically. Quickly, a conscription program to draft young men into the armed services was put into operation. Every man between eighteen and forty-five were given numbers through a lottery system. In every county, a committee was formed of local citizens to carry out the draft. Men with low numbers were processed first. Volunteers were accepted immediately. Under a set of rules, some men were not drafted immediately, depending on physical health and family situations. Ordained ministers in active church service, especially pastors, were not required to enter active service. They could volunteer as chaplains, if they qualified.

The stress caused by these events was strong, because Floyd Zimmer, only son of my Aunt Maude, had volunteered to serve as a radio technician in the U.S. Army Air Corps in August 12, 1941. He was sent to England early in 1942 as a member of the crew of the first "Flying Fortress," (B-24 Liberator) bomber to cross the Atlantic.

I was a pastor and did not meet the educational requirements for being a chaplain, so I was never called into service. My job was to minister to families whose sons quickly left to one of the hastily constructed training camps. There was a great deal of shock and sadness in the community, but there were no communal protests or parades. Everyone exhibited a high level of patriotism.

Neither cars nor trucks were available on the market. In their place, tanks and a wide range of military equipment, including airplanes, were being produced on a twenty-four hour schedule.

Gasoline, tires and oil were rationed and replacement auto parts could best be found in junkyards. All the basic foods, such as sugar, flour, corn meal, etc., were rationed, but before the rationing went into effect, people everywhere rushed to the stores and bought as much as they could. Quickly, a black market developed.

A shortage of workers caused many women to take jobs in factories. Grandparents and older relatives became caretakers of children whose mothers were working. This situation caused a lot of stress. Wages were good but prices of food and clothing were steadily rising. People on a fixed income, such as a pastor's salary, felt the loss of buying power keenly.

Schools of higher education lost most of their male students. The state-teacher training college in Cedar Falls soon had a majority of women students. Within the year, women auxiliary organizations for each of the military services were established. A naval unit called the WAVES came to the local teacher training college for special training. Some attended our church services.

The winter months of 1942 were largely given to military preparation and sending military armaments to countries allied against Germany, Italy, and Japan. Little known by the American public at the time, much of this armament was sent to Russia to aid in pushing back the German army that had attacked Russia in the summer of 1941. Much armament was sent to Egypt to equip the British and American resistance to the German thrust across North Africa. Mainly, the armament for the

Allies went to England, though German submarines sank many ships in the Atlantic. Shipyards were rapidly building warships to counter the Japanese goal of controlling the entire western section of the Pacific Ocean. Our government gave few details of these activities to the American public, though we suspected something big was going on.

During 1942, submarine warfare against ships carrying cargo to England was intense. In the air, Allied and German planes fought a desperate battle over Britain and Germany with both sides suffering horrible losses. Russia and Germany renewed their battles on Russian soil. Germany had almost conquered Russia in1941 but American military equipment shipped to Russia slowly gave that country the edge. In the Pacific, Japan's armies were sweeping through the islands of the West Pacific and the Indonesian areas. Newscasters gave us a general picture of these happenings but few details.

Toward the end of 1942, the war news began to provide more encouraging information. With repaired naval vessels and a number of hastily built ships, the United States, on June 1, 1942, challenged the Japanese navy at the Midway Islands in the Pacific Ocean. It was a hard fought battle but the United States navy devastated the Japanese navy. Control of the Pacific Ocean switched to the United States and the Japanese could not stop the United States thereafter.

The crucial battle of El-Alamein at the west border of Egypt began October 20, 1942 and was lost by the Germans. British Empire troops with new equipment from the United States rapidly pushed the Germans far to the west and within a month forced them to leave North Africa.

Late in November 1942, Russia began winning the siege of Stalingrad. Newly equipped Russian soldiers went on the offensive against the German army and pushed it back some distance before severe winter weather stalled both armies.

Within Maria's family, two events were important to us in 1942. In March, Maria's youngest sister, Jeanette, was married to Harvey Schmidt of Hustisford, Wl. On inquiry, we discovered we could get extra gasoline-ration coupons to attend weddings. We obtained enough coupons to make the trip to Wisconsin. The wedding took place in the Wesley Methodist Church in Hartford, Wl. and the couple took up residency on a farm near Hustisford. Harvey had a high draft number so didn't have to worry about going into the armed forces for some time.

The other event came as a shock to the entire family. Maria's dad and family had moved near Oconomowoc, Wl. to manage a farm. One day in mid June we received a phone call informing us that Burt had accidentally fallen from a wagonload of hay. In the process of unloading the hay in the loft of the barn, a rope had broken and Burt fell from the top of the loaded wagon to the plank floor of the loft. He broke several ribs and dislocated the shoulder joint on his left side. A doctor was called to the farm and ordered Burt to cease all work on the farm. Immediately, we requested more gasoline ration coupons from the rationing board and drove to Wisconsin. I helped with the farm chores for a week while the owner arranged for an older man to finish harvesting the hay crop and milk the cows.

During that week, Tillie was able to obtain a few days release from her job at the West Bend Aluminum Factory in nearby West Bend and Jeanette quit her job as a housemaid in a home in Oconomowoc to help with the farm chores. We returned to Cedar Falls, IA believing Dad Saarloos would recover quickly. The doctor discovered a blood clot by the ankle of his left leg. He ordered Burt to walk very little.

As the weeks slipped by, Burt improved steadily so Tillie decided to return to work. She had trouble getting the car out of the garage and Burt went out to help her. He returned to the house and sat on a chair. Suddenly Burt began to groan and then slumped to the floor unconscious. The doctor was called to the farm and informed the family the blood clot had gone to Burt's heart causing his death. The date was August 3,1942. Burt's age was 56 years and eleven months.

Maria's family called and gave us the sad news. We were both stunned. We left within a few hours to return to Wisconsin. Maria's mother and family were grief stricken and we did our best to comfort them. We learned the funeral was set for August 7th. Burt was buried in the La Belle Cemetery, Oconomowoc, Wl. Maria's mother had to move from the farm as soon as possible. Tillie was able to get her mother a custodial job at the West Bend Aluminum factory and permission from her landlord to allow her mother and brother Bill to live in an apartment Tillie rented. We helped Maria's mother and brother to make the move, and returned to our home in Cedar Falls.

A few days later, we had to drive to Oskaloosa, Iowa, to attend the annual conference. I was assigned to Cedar Falls for another year.

The grief we experienced helped us relate better with the parents of the boys who had to join the armed forces. Many were on the way to England and North Africa preparing to invade Europe. Other young men were on their way to Hawaii to fight the Japanese. In our congregation, and in our neighborhood, people were heavily burdened with anxiety and stress. In spite of the encouraging news from the war fronts, there was not enough uplift from this news to ease the pain of uncertainty about the future of their soldier sons and fathers. The same was true for us, for my cousin Floyd Zimmer was sending little information about his activities in England. We suspected he was flying in his bomber quite frequently and therefore was in serious danger.

The daily demands of pastoral work kept us busy. Each week I had to prepare a lesson for a Sunday school class for youth, a sermon for the morning and evening Sunday worship services, and a lesson for a mid-week, evening prayer service. I had to do all the repair work on the church property, all the custodial work and provide activities for the young people. Making pastoral calls on people in the congregation, who were sick or needed counseling, consumed a number of hours each week also. Maria kept busy with the two children but also helped with the young people and children in the Sunday school. She helped lead congregational singing, playing the piano or organ, and often sang a solo. As she could, she went calling with me.

Late in February 1943, we learned from my mother that her sister Maude had received word from the Air Corps her son Floyd, was missing in action. At the time, little was known what had happened. We felt deeply for Aunt Maude.

During the winter, we learned Maria's sister Tillie was dating a young man who faced a draft consignment to the army. On April 8,1943, Tillie married Russell Ritter of West Bend. We were not able to attend the ceremony in the Methodist Church in Hartford, WI. A few weeks later Russell was drafted and left for an army camp. Late that fall he was shipped to England where the Allies were preparing for an invasion of Europe. The stress of worrying about Russell filled our minds. The serious losses which German submarines were inflicting on ships carrying cargo and soldiers to England weighed constantly on our spirits. Information about the loss of many bombers and fighter planes, along with their pilots, was bringing shock and grief to many families in Cedar Falls. None of the young men in our congregation were lost in these raids. Through those weeks, the question constantly plagued us, "Was cousin Floyd a prisoner of war or was he dead?"

In the spring of 1943, Germany opened her third offensive against Russia but everyone was relieved when in July Russia stopped the German army and began pushing the Germans to the west. Italy surrendered on September 8th. The listings of American dead and wounded in that operation gave pain, but some felt relief that at least one of the enemy nations had ceased fighting.

The war in the Pacific Ocean was raging with intensity. American forces were able to reclaim some islands in the Pacific, especially the Philippine Islands in October 1943.

In August, in the middle of these war events, we acquired a new address. The annual conference promoted us to a larger and stronger church in Oskaloosa. In a way, it was like coming home. We had special memories of the place. I was ordained a deacon and then an elder on the nearby campus of Kletzing College. This new assignment also brought us close to my birthplace, Russell, which was about fifty miles to the southwest.

After moving our belongings into the two-storied, square parsonage and enjoying a welcoming party put on by the friendly congregation, we decided to care for two family needs. My sister Dorothy, who had earned her teaching certificate at Wessington Springs College and taught one year in a one-room school, asked if she could live with us while she completed her college degree at Kletzing College. We agreed to her request and she moved into the third bedroom on the second floor of the parsonage and enrolled at the college.

The other family need was a trip to Russell to visit my Aunt Maude and do what we could to comfort her as she endured the uncertainty of what happened to her son Floyd. The army had informed her that Floyd had just returned from a long reconnaissance flight when an accident occurred. His squadron of bombers was approaching the southern coast of England to land at their airfield. There was a dense fog and his plane and another bomber struck each other's wing. Both planes plunged into the sea off shore from Seisey Bill, England. No survivors of the crash had yet been found and no bodies had been recovered. The army promised they would continue their search for survivors. The army had determined the date of the crash as February 16, 1943. This date meant that the search would continue until February 17, 1944 and if there were no results, the army would declare Floyd dead.

We found Aunt Maude devastated emotionally. We had several crying spells together as we tried to lift her spirits. My cousins who lived in and near Russell, Iowa, joined with us in our common sorrow. Maria and the children joined their love with the relatives they had just met. We left Russell burdened for Maude and family.

A burdensome anxiety also reached into Maria's family as Russell was sent to England the fall of 1943 to join others, preparing for an invasion of France. His letters to us had scant information, but the tone of loneliness and concern came through clearly.

This burden also reached into several families in our congregation, for several sons had been drafted and soon sent to England for the same purpose. Thus, the fall of 1943 and the early spring of 1944 was a difficult time for all of us, but it also drew us together in our common needs, and helped us as a pastoral family and congregation to develop bonds of fellowship. We as a family experienced pastoral duties as a challenge and an encouragement, as we tried to point our people to full trust in God.

On March 12th, 1944, we traveled again to Russell, Iowa, to attend a memorial service for Staff Sergeant Floyd Zimmer. The service was held in the Methodist Church with the pastor and several army officers in charge. Maria and I sat with Aunt Maude, with our children close by. After a short sermon by the pastor, an army officer presented Aunt Maude with a folded flag and several medals given in honor of Floyd's military service. He was awarded The Flying Cross, the Silver Star and the Purple Heart. Aunt Maude came through the service very well, though I could feel her body tremble as she received the flag and medals. It was not easy to say good-bye late that afternoon. The horror of war felt oppressively near.

The winter and spring of 1944 was tense, with great loss of ships on the Atlantic due to German submarines. There was also great loss of planes over Europe as British and American bombers tried to wipe out German factories and rail centers. Inevitably, these raids caused huge fires in German cities and German bombers caused the same kind of destruction in England.

The climax came on June 6, 1944, known as D-day, when a huge fleet of ships swept across the English Channel during the night and attacked the northwestern beaches of France. We listened breathlessly to our radios as a limited description of the fighting was released to the American public. We strongly suspected that our brother-in-law, Russell, was part of the invading force, and most likely the same was true of the boys from our congregation.

In fact, within a few weeks word came to one of the families in the church that their son had lost his life on the invasion beach on June 6th. It was my sad duty to arrange a memorial service in our church to honor this fallen soldier.

Later we were informed Russell had not gone to France until late in July. In October we learned our brother-in-law had been wounded near Aachen while his unit, the 109th Infantry was driving through the northeastern part of France into Germany. He was in the hospital briefly, and then was sent back to the front lines.

In the winter of 1944, Maria and I began thinking about my enrolling in Kletzing College in order to earn an authentic Bachelor of Arts degree. I presented my Wessington Springs College transcript to the admissions office for an evaluation. I discovered they would allow three year's credit for my academic work; I could enroll as a senior in the fall semester. This I did and started attending classes with my sister Dorothy who was also a senior. I soon discovered that being a full time pastor and student was no small task.

On the war fronts, the United States and its allies were making progress. On August 15th, the Allies invaded southern France and moved north. Two weeks later, the allied armies moved into Paris with flags waving and many French people giving them a rousing welcome. A few weeks later in September the Germans made a desperate counter attack called the Battle of the Bulge. In December, the Germans were forced to retreat. To the east of Germany, the Russians, early in January, began a powerful offensive that captured Warsaw a month later.

Late in February, the American forces began an offensive that soon crossed the Rhine River. It was in this action that Russell lost his life. He was on patrol at night not far from Cologne and stepped on a land mine. He died instantly. The date was March 3,1945. His shattered body was buried in Belgium. The official news of Russell's death that the army delivered to Tillie, his wife, shocked all of us. Maria and the two children took a train to Watertown, Wl. to be with her sister. A week later, I was able to get gasoline coupons to drive to Wisconsin and join in helping, during Tillie's time of grief. She was devastated. We soon learned a memorial service would not be held until May 6,1945. Reluctantly we returned to Oskaloosa.

Early in the winter of 1945, two other events affected our lives. We don't know the exact date, but Ralph, a brother two years older than me, was drafted into the navy. He was married and had several children. We assumed he was being trained to invade Japan. We knew little of his whereabouts.

The second event was a new opportunity that would affect our future ministry. A series of issues of the FREE METHODIST, a magazine published by the Free Methodist Church of North America, carried an announcement that the Board of Bishops was planning to establish a theological seminary in a few years. They wanted to begin with students qualified to enter the three year program, some as freshmen, some as middlers, and some as seniors. They were planning to pay the tuition for students who had earned a Bachelor of Arts degree and had gained acceptance to an existing theological seminary. After two years, they would enter the new Free Methodist seminary as seniors.

With two regular semesters of classes at Kletzing College and a summer class at William Penn College, also located in Oskaloosa, I would have a Bachelor of Arts degree in July. After discussing the matter with Maria and praying about whether to respond to the advertisement, I made contact by letter with the Board of Bishops, explaining my situation. Shortly, I received a response stating I should contact a seminary seeking admission.

In April, Dr. Harold Kuhn, a professor at Asbury Theological Seminary, came to Kletzing College to lecture for a week. I contacted him, seeking information about the school. I was impressed with him and his description of the curriculum and policies of the seminary. I wrote immediately for an application blank and a catalog. My application was accepted, depending on my completion of college courses and gaining a diploma. The Board of Bishops was pleased and promised me a full year tuition scholarship. At the annual conference early in August, I was officially released from my pastoral duties and assigned to attend Asbury Theological Seminary.

To the profound joy of everyone in America, the war in Europe came to an end on May 6, 1945. While we were in conference session on August 6th, we were stunned to learn that the United States had dropped an atomic bomb on Hiroshima, Japan, utterly destroying the city and killing many people. A couple days later, another atomic bomb was dropped on Nagasaki. On August 15th, Japan surrendered to the United States. A horrible war was over. We all sang "Praise God from whom all Blessings Flow."

As I look back over eight years of pastoral service, half of them when the United States was engaged in war in Europe and in the Pacific area, I feel thankful for the privilege of serving five Free Methodist Churches. One of these churches, Birchwood, Wl., was in a small town/rural area. Four churches: Beaver Dam in Wisconsin, and Marion, Cedar Falls, Oskaloosa in Iowa, were small cities. I tend to be reserved and found it somewhat difficult getting acquainted with new people, but Maria has always been open and friendly. She established fruitful relationships quickly with members of the congregation and with neighbors. I learned a lot as I watched her interact with others. Slowly I acquired some skills in interpersonal relationships.

During the war, I felt deeply the stress and anxiety evident in almost everyone we met, especially when the toll of battle reached into both of our families and caused profound grief in the lives of close relatives. As the years passed, I realized more and more I needed more training in pastoral counseling. I needed to learn how to listen effectively, and advise those who were suffering.

In the 1850's, a group of Methodist Episcopal ministers and lay people in western New York and in north central Illinois took a strong stand in favor of the abolition of slavery and in ministering to poor people. A crisis developed among the Methodists and these dissenters were expelled from the church. In 1860 these expelled people joined together to form the Free Methodist Church. Within decades, the Free Methodist Church spread across the northern states and into the Far West, following the migration routes. The church's abolitionist reputation has made it difficult to penetrate the southern states.

In the communities I served as a pastor, there was almost no African-American population, but occasionally we were able to establish friendly relations with an African-American minister or layperson.

The church's concern for the poor was needed in each church we served. Since Maria and I both grew up in poverty, it was easy to appreciate the economic struggles of many people in our congregations and communities. It was the Depression period and the War period and the challenge of helping people in need was pressing.

Since most of our church members were poor, the financial resources of the church were limited. That meant our salary was meager and we had to watch our pennies carefully. The members had to sacrifice to keep the church property in repair, and in Cedar Falls, they provided a large amount of labor to make the new parsonage livable. There was no money to engage in social service projects, though people did their best to aid friends and neighbors who were in financial difficulty. All of us were poor and knew few people who were upper middle class or higher. The war created more jobs but inflation and shortage of supplies did not really improve the situation.

Another problem connected with having a congregation that was made up of mostly poor people was their level of education. Almost all the elderly people had only an eighth grade education or less. Only a few of the middle-aged people had a high school diploma. Many had only a year or two of high school. I found while visiting with them that two statements often came to the fore: "I don't understand," and "I don't know how to teach a Sunday school class or lead a church committee."

The first statement challenged me to explain the teachings of the Bible and the church in easy to understand terms. The second statement challenged me to form training classes and motivate each person to at least try teaching a class or leading a committee in church work. I discovered that both tasks demanded my best efforts, and fortunately, with some success. I felt fulfilled when a hesitant, poorly motivated member would tackle a task and succeed.

I enjoyed greatly my preaching responsibilities, my Bible classes and leadership training classes. I discovered quickly that few of my listeners enjoyed "heavy sermons." They didn't respond well to messages that had a lot of tightly knit logic or theology with words that were too technical. I was inclined to preach that way. I slowly learned I needed to illustrate the points of my messages and translate strange words into a language of simple sentences and everyday words. Some said I was more of a teacher than a preacher.

World War II had shaken me to the foundations of my intellect and my emotions. My limited knowledge of medieval Europe told me that Christianity had flourished in almost every country of Europe during the seventeenth, through nineteenth centuries. Yet, Germany, where the

Reformation began, embraced Hitler and his Nazism. Italy, the center of Roman Catholic power, had accepted Mussolini and his Fascism. Lenin and Stalin and their communism soon controlled Russia, the center of Orthodox Christianity. What had happened in Western society that these countries could plunge the whole world into a horrible war and cause the destruction of millions of women, children and the Holocaust? I had to have some answers and I hoped that further education would help me.

Nellie and Burt Saarloos during WW I

Nellie Ziel Saarloos's home in the Netherlands

Herbert and Maria Livingston after the Wedding
To the right, Rev. Mrs. Leeds Greene

Nellie (2) and Burton (4) Livingston

CHAPTER 5

BACK TO SCHOOL AGAIN

Asbury Theological Seminary opened its fall quarter the day after Labor Day, so we had about three weeks to sell some furniture, take care of other business transactions, pack our remaining belongings and travel to Kentucky. The Dean of the seminary had informed us he knew of no house or apartment for rent in the small city of Wilmore. We decided to take with us a fairly large tent we had used for camping and in which we could live for a short period of time. We trusted we could find a place in which to live soon after arrival. As days went by, we felt like Abraham and his family obeying the call of God to move to Canaan and start a new life in an unknown land. We knew little about Kentucky and Wilmore. Maria and I encouraged each other, believing we were following God's will for our lives.

Early in the first week of preparation, we noted in the city newspaper two ads offering small trailer houses for sale. Each was priced for three ($300.00) hundred dollars. We decided to look at the trailer houses. One was ready for use but the better one would not be fully remodeled before September 1st. That evening the congregation had a farewell party for us. We explained to everyone the nature of our educational opportunity and the challenges we had in preparing to leave. I mentioned the possibility of getting a trailer house to take with us but would need money to purchase it. After the meeting, a member of the church came to us and offered to loan us the money.

The next day we purchased the trailer house and brought it to the parsonage so we could load our clothing and a washing machine in it.

We also went to the rationing board to apply for extra gas coupons for the trip. We were granted the coupons. We bought some good used tires (for which we did not need coupons) in case of a blowout.

At last the day of departure came. Several of our church members came to say good-by. Tears were shed. We crowded into our heavily loaded 1938 Chevrolet and pulled the trailer house onto the highway leading south to Ottumwa. We averaged about thirty-five miles an hour. Just a few miles north of Ottumwa, we heard a loud sound behind and noticed the trailer house was swaying somewhat. I realized one of the trailer tires had blown out. There was a driveway just ahead of us, leading into the yard of a farm home. We pulled into the yard and parked. Indeed, we did have a blowout and the tire was ruined. The tread was completely worn off the tire.

I put a car jack under the side of the trailer house and lifted it up so I could look underneath. I noted that the springs on the axle bar were almost flat and the bottom of the trailer house was only an inch above the tires. Bumps and slight swaying caused the bottom of the trailer house to touch the top of the tire repeatedly wearing the tread thin and then blowing out. The tire on the driver's side of the trailer house had some damage, but it was not yet critical.

I went to the farmhouse and met the farmer's wife. I told her my problem and asked permission to park in the yard until I could get a new tire. She was very gracious and asked Maria and the children to come to the house while I drove to Ottumwa. She was knowledgeable about tire rationing and gave me directions to the rationing committee in Ottumwa that was about five miles away. I found the rationing committee sympathetic. The chairman of the committee informed me their allotment for granting a tire permit to travelers was exhausted. The chairman said I should go back to Oskaloosa and get a permit from the rationing committee there.

I found the location of the committee and presented to the chairman my predicament. He was a kindly man but said they too were out of tire coupons allotted for travelers. However, he advised me the rule of the rationing commission was that county rationing committees were obligated to provide tire coupons to travelers stranded in their county. He said there are ways county committees can make exceptions for travelers in need.

I felt like I was getting a "run around" but returned to Ottumwa with some hope. While making the trip, I was trying to figure out how to fix the trailer so its bottom would not rub the tires. I decided to get a short piece of 2" x 4", cut it into two pieces and fit each piece between the bottom of the trailer house and the flattened springs. This would negate the cushioning action of the springs but would keep the bottom of the trailer house from rubbing the tire treads.

When I returned to the Ottumwa rationing committee, I discovered the committee had found a way to help me buy a tire. They had contacted a tire wholesale company in Ottumwa and promised to grant them a tire coupon, if the company would sell me a tire that day and wait till September 1st, for a rationing coupon. Why didn't they think of that procedure right away and save me a round trip to Oskaloosa?

I was a bit upset, but nonetheless thankful I could immediately buy a six-ply tire. I got back to the farmhouse where our trailer house was parked, put on the new tire and fastened between the springs the boards I had just bought in Ottumwa. By the time I was finished it was late in the evening. The farm owner and wife kindly gave us a good meal and we retired to sleep in our trailer house.

Early the next morning we drove to Ottumwa and headed east toward Burlington, Iowa. We crossed the Mississippi River and worked our way diagonally southeast through Illinois. We wanted to get to Greenville, IL that night if possible. We had to follow the road map carefully for we had to turn onto a highway with a different number quite often. We averaged only about forty miles an hour, so the trip was taking longer than we expected. We were nearing Petersburg on State Highway # 97 when we heard a boom from the driver's side of the trailer house. The highway had a wide shoulder so we could safely pull off the concrete roadway,

I carefully sized up the situation and decided to move my best car tire, which was on the driver's side, to replace the damaged tire. Both wheels had the same number of bolts, so it was easy to make the switch. I placed on the car a mounted, used tire I had in reserve. I had to be careful doing this task, because I had to work close to the passing traffic.

We made our way into Petersburg and were glad to see a courthouse, which meant the county rationing committee was located in that small city. Our problem was we got there after four o'clock. This meant we would have to stay overnight. We found a small city park and settled in for the night. The next morning I went to the rationing committee office and explained to the secretary my tire problem and why we were moving from Iowa to Kentucky. She said the chairman would not be in the office until one o'clock. I was informed they did have one coupon left but it was reserved for traveling military men. I returned at one o'clock and got the good news the chairman had returned early, and had looked at my application. He noted I was a minister and decided to grant me the remaining tire coupon. I went to a Sears store and bought another six-ply tire.

Within an hour I replaced the tires correctly and we were on our way south. We arrived in Greenville, IL in the middle of the afternoon. A Free Methodist school called Greenville College is located there. On the staff were a professor and a registrar who served at Wessington Springs College when Maria and I were students in that school in the 1930's. We found them and had a wonderful visit and introduced them to our two children, Burton and Nellie. They were happy we were going to Asbury Theological Seminary.

The next morning we headed east toward Kentucky, and with no more tire trouble, we arrived in Wilmore late in the evening. We found a place where we could park the trailer house and the family settled down for a good night's sleep. The next morning we meet Dean Larabee and we were shown where we could park on a lot owned by the seminary. A small house, occupied by a woman and several small children, and a trailer house, occupied by a seminary couple, were located on the lot. Each of us could connect our dwelling to electricity, but water had to be pumped from a well and we shared an outhouse. The Dean said I could start working with the crew preparing the premises for the influx of students over the next weekend. The job would pay fifty cents an hour. I was soon at work.

We had a happy surprise that first week. We learned that Professor George A. Turner, who was at Wessington Springs College the last year Maria and I were studying there, had been hired by Asbury Seminary and would arrive with his family in a few days. He had been studying at Harvard University and would be completing his Ph D. dissertation while teaching at the seminary. When they arrived in town, we helped them settle into a rented house and had a great time getting acquainted with his wife, Lucille, and two children, Allen and Carol. I was determined to take as many courses as possible under his guidance.

Asbury Theological Seminary was begun on the campus of Asbury College, which was across the street from the existing seminary, in 1923 by H. C. Morrison, president of the college.

Later, Asbury Theological Seminary was housed in one building, now known as Larabee-Morris Hall. Dr. Larabee was a Dean and Dr. Morris was a Professor of Theology at the Seminary while I studied there. At the beginning of the three years, we were in Wilmore. Burton was seven and attended second grade and Nellie was five and attended a day-care center. Maria soon had work as a secretary during the week and I worked on the maintenance crew on Saturdays and Mondays. Classes were held Tuesday through Friday, each week. I carried a full load of classes and soon discovered my eyes needed glasses in order to handle the extensive reading required by the professors. I thoroughly enjoyed my studies. My biggest problem was finding time to be with my family on more than Sundays.

Several interesting incidents happened during the school year. Our trailer house was only seven feet wide and sixteen feet long on the inside and had some shortcomings. I could not stand up in it: the ceiling was too low. The only way we had adequate sleeping space for the four of us was to use a table that had two storage boxes for seats. At night, we would detach the table top from hooks in the front wall and lower it to cleats that made it level with the tops of the seats. We placed a thin mattress on this "bed" for Maria and me to sleep on at night. Burton and Nellie slept on a bed at the back of the trailer-house.

In cold weather, a small "pot-bellied" stove that was fueled with coal briquettes, heated the trailer house. By the middle of the night, the coal would be consumed. One night in January, the temperature outside fell to below zero. When Maria and I awakened in the morning, our bedding was frozen to the wall. We then saw that all the interior of the trailer was covered with ice. We checked the sleeping children and found their bedding also was frozen to the wall. There was no fire in the little stove.

Quickly we started a fire in the stove, but as it poured out heat, the ice on the walls and ceiling began to melt. Maria and I grabbed all the towels we had and frantically wiped the water from walls and ceiling From then on we set the clock alarm at three in the morning so

I could put enough fuel in the stove to last until we got up for breakfast. Usually, we found Kentucky weather was moderate, but we discovered the hard way it could get very cold at times.

Another incident concerned the lady and her children who lived in the small house on the lot. She was not very friendly. Her husband was still in the army but we noticed that at night men would visit her house. One day in the spring of 1946, her husband came home unannounced in the middle of an afternoon. Maria and the children were in the trailer at the time. Suddenly there was a terrible racket. Maria looked out the window and saw pots, pans and dishes flying out the door of the house. The husband was cursing terribly. Maria was frightened and ran with the children to the seminary building to report the situation. When Dean Larabee arrived on the scene the man had quieted down some but still was angry. It seems the soldier soon found out about the male visitors who came at night. Fortunately, he did not hurt his wife or children. Dean Larabee requested that the family move to another house, which they did. We felt much more at ease the remainder of the school year.

Other incidents had to do with health crises in the family. During the spring of 1946, Burton had two operations a month apart: one was the removal of tonsils and the other was the removal of his appendix. He came through both operations successfully.

At the beginning of June 1946, I began working as a carpenter on the new administration building the Seminary was constructing. I worked forty hours a week all summer and continued to do so on weekends during my second school year. My new wage was a dollar an hour. What a big boost that was to our budget. There was one disadvantage. The seminary was also going to build an apartment building on the lot where we were living. We had to move several times during the summer while excavation and construction was going on. During the spring, the seminary had purchased about a dozen expandable military surplus trailer houses from Fort Knox near Louisville. In July and August, they were placed in a vacant area on the east side of a small creek that ran through the seminary property. Eventually in August, we settled by the creek at the edge of the new homes for veterans, who were enrolling in the seminary. During that summer, I improved our trailer house on Saturdays and evenings by putting on a new roof high enough for me to stand erect while inside.

The school year, dating from September 1946 to May 1947, continued to challenge us intellectually. Professor George Turner earned his Doctor of Philosophy degree from Harvard University and took over duties as Professor of Inductive Bible Studies. He along with Dr. Kuhn, who already possessed a Doctor of Philosophy degree from Harvard University, gave us in depth lectures and extensive reading assignments in Christian philosophy, theology and biblical studies. I spent long hours in the library, for other new professors with earned doctoral degrees were just as rigorous in their fields. I fear I spent limited time with my family.

In the Free Methodist community, the number was growing. More students, most with families, had come to Asbury Seminary. Dr. Turner took leadership as our pastor. A large room was rented from the seminary where we held Sunday evening services. In the spring of 1947, Dr. Turner organized a small group, which included Maria, as a Free Methodist society. I worked Saturdays and Mondays as a carpenter on the two new buildings being constructed, namely, the H. C. Morrison Administration Building and the Betty Morrison Apartments. Maria worked as a secretary for Doctors Turner and Kuhn. Both Burton and Nellie attended elementary school. It was a year of spiritual and intellectual growth.

In the middle of June 1947, several superintendents of the Ohio Conference of the United Methodist Church came to the campus searching for supply pastors for several churches. I offered my services for one year and was appointed to the Lynchburg, Ohio charge which had one small city and three small country churches. We did not have to change our denominational affiliation and needed to be at the charge only on Sunday mornings. I preached at two churches one Sunday and the other two churches the next Sunday. These churches were 120 miles away, with a crooked U S 68 to travel each Sunday. I was able to work during the week in the summer and attend classes during the school year, working on Saturdays and Mondays. Maria continued to work as a secretary for two professors at the seminary. It was a strenuous schedule for all the family.

An unexpected change happened in the Free Methodist community. In mid winter of 1947, Dr. George Turner had recommended to the Board of Bishops that they should consider negotiating an affiliation with Asbury Theological Seminary. The bishops had failed to raise enough money to begin the proposed John Wesley Theological Seminary and agreed to approach Asbury Seminary. The negotiations were successful and a John Wesley Seminary Foundation was created as an affiliate to the seminary. Free Methodist students would enroll in the seminary, receive tuition scholarships and be guided by a Dean who would be a faculty member of Asbury Theological Seminary and also set up a John Wesley Seminary Foundation office near the campus.

To our surprise and joy, the bishops selected one of our former professors at Wessington Springs College, Dr. W. Curry Mavis. Dr. Mavis had enrolled at the University of Southern California and earned a Doctor of Philosophy degree in pastoral psychology. Dr. Mavis had then joined Greenville College as a faculty member and served several years before coming to Wilmore with his wife Marion and son Donald. A happy reunion awaited them in Wilmore and I enjoyed several of his classes during the school year. I earned a Bachelor of Divinity degree May 30, 1948.

During my senior year I was much concerned about the future. Was it the Lord's will for me to return as a pastor to the Free Methodist churches in Iowa or go to a university to earn a Ph. D degree so I could teach in a Free Methodist college? I made application at several universities and was accepted by Drew University in Madison, NJ. It had a highly rated Ph. D. program and was related to the United Methodist Church. We needed a church to serve in that area while in school. So did three other fellow graduates who had been accepted by Drew University. The first week in June 1948 four of us traveled by car to Madison, NJ as the New York Conference of the United Methodist Church was having its annual session there. There were no Free Methodist churches in the area that needed a pastor so I thought I could serve as a supply pastor as I had in Ohio. Fortunately, the Catskill district of the New York conference needed pastors so three of us received appointments in that mountainous area of southern New York. I was appointed to serve four United Methodist churches in and around Callicoon, NY.

Returning to Wilmore, we sold our trailer house and bought a two wheel utility trailer to haul our meager belongings to NY. Toward the end of our third day of travel, we arrived at the parsonage in Callicoon, NY, which was furnished with basic furniture. The main church of the charge was beside the parsonage in Callicoon, a small church was six miles north at Hankins, a small church was six miles east in North

Branch, and the country church, Fremont Center was northeast another five miles. One Sunday I would preach at Hankins, Fremont Center in the forenoon and Callicoon in the evening, the next Sunday I preached at North Branch and Fremont Center in the morning and Callicoon in the evening. During the school year, I would leave home after dinner Monday, and travel 110 miles to Drew University. I would have a class that evening, two classes on Tuesday, one on Wednesday and return to home that afternoon. We maintained this schedule for two years.

Maria stayed in Callicoon, taking care of Burton and Nellie, worked part-time as a seamstress, repairing sheets and pillowcases and the nurse's uniforms for the local hospital. Burton and Nellie enjoyed their three years at Callicoon and its satellite churches. They had fun attending box dinners with us. Several times Burton played his violin, Nellie would sing a solo and Maria would play the piano. At one church Halloween party, Burton (as a girl) and Nellie (as a boy) dressed in unusual clothing and enjoyed not being recognized by the church people. We came later to the party.

In the spring of the first year, 1949, I passed my qualifying exams and was accepted for the Doctor of Philosophy program, so in my second year my classes were on that level. In the spring of the second year, I decided to do research on the spiritual experiences of the Old Testament prophets, with special emphasis on Jeremiah.

My major professor, Dr. John Paterson, suggested I read and analyze a book, DIE PROPHETIE, (in English, THE PROPHETS), by Rabbi Abraham Joshua Heschel as part of my research. This book was written in German. I was able to locate the book in the library at Princeton Theological Seminary and checked it out through the Drew University library. I was able to locate Dr. Heschel at Jewish Theological Seminary in New York City. I had an interview with him and was encouraged by his interest and warmth. I spent my third year translating and analyzing his book, and had several more interviews with him during the year. My class work at the University was completed, so in the fall of 1950 and the spring of 1951, I did all my studying at home.

Toward the end of 1949 Maria became pregnant and spent seven of the nine months in bed. On May 23, 1950 David Herbert was born at the small Callicoon hospital.

Early in October 1950, an event occurred that left me with a vivid memory. At about two o'clock p.m., the phone at the parsonage rang.

The voice of an agitated woman asked if the Boy Scouts at Callicoon could help her. I informed her that the scouts were out of town at a retreat. Between sobs she said her little daughter was lost in the woods near her home that was on the west side of the Delaware River in Pennsylvania about five miles away. I told her I would try to get the members of the fire department to help her. She gave me her phone number and directions to her home.

I contacted the chief of the fire department, but he declined to send men into Pennsylvania, saying it was illegal to do so. I then contacted the editor of the county newspaper that had a printing press in Callicoon. He said he would talk to the chief, his brother-in-law, about the matter. In a few moments, he phoned and said he had convinced the chief he had to send a truck and men to the home to search for the girl. I phoned the lady that men would soon be at her home. With another man, I drove to the lady's home, and soon a fire truck followed us. Men in cars arrived to discover what was wrong. The tearful lady pointed to the east at trees and much brush. Between sobs, she said, "I think she is out there somewhere." A line of men, spaced about six feet apart, moved into the brush intent on finding the child. A few men checked out the cistern and a "backhouse" with no success. The line of men returned with no girl. They searched several other areas, but still could not find the girl.

A state policeman arrived and organized men as search teams, but their efforts were in vain. The girl's father came home from work and walked through the brush calling the girls name, but had no response. The air was getting chilly. If the girl stayed out there overnight, she might not survive the cold. Farmers were going home to milk their cows, and the policeman had to leave in response to a call for his services. As it began to get dark, a neighbor, the father and I were standing in the yard discussing what to do next. Suddenly a small voice came out of the brush, "Daddy! Daddy!" The father dashed towards the voice at full speed, and soon came back with a very cold child with only a light sweater wrapped around her. The mother came from the house, and with many sobs hugged the girl tightly. The other man and I watched the scene with tears in our eyes. Together we congratulated the parents. I said a prayer of thanks for divine mercy. I was filled with joy as I returned home, and broke the good news to a very concerned wife.

Looking back over my academic studies during the decade of 1945 to 1951, I sensed a feeling of accomplishment. At both Asbury

Theological Seminary and the Theological School of Drew University, I was introduced to the thinking of the great philosophers of Europe and America from the beginnings of Christianity to the decade mentioned above. I also became much more aware of the basic premises of the writers of the Scriptures and how those premises, or doctrines, compared and contrasted with the cultures of the ancient Near East, including Greece and Rome.

The theological professors at Drew University, Edwin Lewis and Carl Michelson, who were liberal in their views, nevertheless led me into deeper encounters with the thinking of Kant, Hegel, Decartes, Hume, Locke and a host of others. I was aware that Hegel's dialectical theory of history had heavily influenced the Old Testament scholar Julian Wellhausen. I was glad the more conservative Dr. Stanley Hopper introduced me and the other students to the criticism of Hegel launched by Soren Kierkegaard, a Danish contemporary of Hegel. The writings of Kierkegaard were just being published in English and Dr. Hopper was quite excited about this scholar's thinking.

Akin to the impact of Kierkegaard's writings was the eruption of a hot dispute between two famous Old Testament scholars, Dr. R. F. Pfeiffer of Harvard University and Dr. W. F. Albright of Johns Hopkins University. Pfeiffer wrote a book, INTRODUCTION TO THE OLD TESTAMENT that quickly became a popular textbook among liberal Old Testament scholars. The book is a detailed presentation of the Wellhausen JEDP theory that assumed four documents lie behind the present books of the Old Testament. Pfeiffer also describes how the religious thinking of the Hebrew people developed. This development was patterned after Hegel's thesis-antithesis-synthesis theory of history.

W. F. Albright soon publicly criticized Pfeiffer for not giving enough attention to the witness of archaeological research in regards to ancient Hebrew religion. Albright was the leading American archaeologist at that time and his views carried great weight. The controversy between the two men waxed hot. Albright set forth his views in a book, ARCHAEOLOGY OF PALESTINE. Later in 1957, he published FROM STONE AGE TO CHRISTIANITY. I found his presentation of the support archaeological research was giving to Hebrew religion, as presented in the Old Testament, exciting and I wanted to learn more about the subject.

In 1948 the news of a remarkable discovery of a number of leather scrolls of portions of Old Testament books in several caves near the ruins of a small village called Qumran was just becoming known in Europe and America. We students were excited but our Old Testament professor, Dr. John Paterson, was skeptical, especially when Dr. W.F. Albright estimated the date of the scrolls to be first century to second century B. C.

I also was uneasy about the way Old Testament scholars were applying the abstract and rigid framework of dialectics to the composition of Old Testament books and the development of religious thought among the Hebrew people. The imposition of a Western system of thought on ancient documents and on religious experience seemed arrogant to me. Why should Western thinking be superior to that of a people of a different, though older, culture? Perhaps the people of that older culture should be studied more carefully. Thus, archaeology became important to me.

My inductive study of the book of Jeremiah, especially the spiritual experiences of the man central to that book, alerted me to another factor important to Old Testament studies. H. Wheeler Robinson, more than Abraham J. Heschel, was unable to understand fully Jeremiah's spiritual experiences, because their rational presuppositions kept them from seeing the interpersonal dynamics central to the Hebrew prophetic consciousness. I was determined to study this fact more extensively.

After a difficult test, I was told I qualified as a candidate for the Ph.D. degree. Three Professors were assigned as my guidance committee and I was told I should decide what area of Old Testament studies I wanted to research for my dissertation. I reported I wanted to do research in the characteristics of the spiritual life of the Old Testament prophets with special emphasis on the prophet Jeremiah. Dr. Paterson informed me I should do this research as an interaction with the views of Dr. H. Wheeler Robinson of England and Dr. Abraham J. Heschel, a refugee from Germany. I have already described my interviews with Dr. Heschel but Dr. Robinson was dead and I had to depend on his writings, especially his article "The Hebrew Conception of Corporate Personality" published in 1935. I described Heschel's theory in Chapter 4 of my dissertation and summarized my detailed study of Jeremiah's spiritual struggles in Chapter 5. I looked at Robinson's theory in Chapter 6 and set over against his viewpoint my inductive evaluation of the dynamics of God's interactions with the Israelites in Chapter 7. I concluded my research by comparing the views of Heschel and Robinson with the data present in the book of Jeremiah. I found that the views of both Heschel and Robinson failed to deal adequately with factors that were vital in Jeremiah's life and ministry.

CHAPTER 6

As Dean and as Professor

During this third year, we were also praying about the future and began to contact several Free Methodist colleges. Our alma mater was interested and so I agreed to become Dean of the college beginning June 1, 1951. In May, we packed and shipped some of our heavier furniture to Wessington Springs, SD. We also bought a better utility trailer and packed it full. It was a long, slow trip to South Dakota and we were able to visit my sister Dorothy and family. Her husband, Fay, was attending Marion College in Marion, IN., right on our way. We drove to Hustisford, WI and visited with Maria's mother and three sisters, who lived just northwest of Milwaukee, Wisconsin. We next stopped at Eau Claire, Wl. to visit with my family and help my parents celebrate their fiftieth wedding anniversary.

Finally, in the middle of May 1951, we arrived in Wessington Springs, and unloaded the trailer. We needed to drive to Oskaloosa, IA where we had stored some furniture in 1945. These items were loaded and soon we were back in Wessington Springs where we settled in a surplus army barracks that had been moved on campus to meet housing needs.

My first task was to supervise the summer school program of the college through June and July. It was my first administrative and teaching experience and challenged the best I had. In January 1952, a retired professor, who served as principal of the high school department of the college, died suddenly of a heart attack. I had to take over his duties, which created a heavy load for me.

Along with caring for baby David, Maria taught two typing classes and worked in a local hospital. She also typed pages of my dissertation, as I was able to write them by hand. It was a manual typewriter and she had to do five carbon copies with no errors. Two-year old David would sit in his high chair at the dining room table near Maria, and do simple math problems provided by his mother. Burton and Nellie attended the city junior high and elementary school. We enjoyed the year and looked forward to another year. A new high school principal was employed and the new school term started out well.

Early in October, a crisis developed in the local United Methodist Church. The pastor was in conflict with leaders in his congregation and without notice one night he packed his belongings in a rented truck and left for another state. I was asked to preach on Sunday mornings until a replacement could be found. No one was available, so I took on the task of being a part-time pastor until the next conference in June 1953. Our family moved into the parsonage, but I continued to carry the full load of the dean of the college. That year the registrar passed away and I had to take on that task. All of these jobs proved to be very taxing.

A very important event in our life happened in the late winter of 1953. A letter arrived from Dr. J.C. McPheeters, President of Asbury Theological Seminary, dated March 7th. I remember vividly the moment I opened the letter and read the contents. I was overwhelmed as I walked to the window of my office and looked out over the small city of Wessington Springs. Could this be happening to me? Dr. McPheeters was asking me to consider seriously coming to Asbury Theological Seminary to be Guest Professor of Old Testament, beginning September of that year. If I did well, I would become full Professor at the end of two years. Maria was overjoyed, for she had happy memories of our three-year stay in Wilmore. Our response was positive and we soon began preparations to make the move back to Kentucky. The agreement was that I would teach a two-thirds load and work on my dissertation. To help supplement my limited salary, l contacted the superintendent of the district where I had served four churches in 1947-48, offering my services as a supply pastor of any United Methodist churches for which they did not have a pastor. In early June word came from the superintendent that he would like to appoint me to serve two churches in and near Aberdeen, Ohio. We should be in Aberdeen by the third Sunday in June. We were able to rent a small house in Wilmore, so a moving van took our furniture to Wilmore while we traveled by car.

We were obliged to conduct two services in Aberdeen and one service at a small country church called Ebenezer each Sunday. Many weekends, we would stay overnight Saturday and come home Sunday evening. During the week, I would work diligently on my dissertation as well as on my lectures for my fall quarter classes that were on the Pentateuch and Hebrew grammar. The children quickly readjusted to life and school in Wilmore and Maria spent full time caring for the family, and doing a great deal of typing for me. At the opening of the first school year, several times I was mistaken for a new student. In fact, I was the youngest member of the faculty and some students were older than I.

On a Thursday afternoon of August 1953, our family faced a serious crisis. Our thirteen-year-old daughter Nellie loved to go bicycling with her friends. Soon after lunch, Nellie and her friends were cruising down Main Street just east of the railroad tracks, when suddenly the front wheel locked. She was thrown from the bike and her head struck the asphalt.

A lady, who was sitting on her front porch, saw the accident, and running to the road, she asked for the girl's name and home address. She stopped a car and asked the lady driver to take her and Nellie to the address (at that time bikers did not have helmets, and there was no 911 service or an ambulance in Wilmore). We responded to the knock on our front door and were shocked to see blood on Nellie's head. She seemed not to know what was going on. A neighbor, who was a nurse, appeared at the door and seeing Nellie's bleeding right ear, asked to use the phone.

The nurse knew that doctors usually closed their offices on Thursday afternoons but tried to find one still in his office anyway. She found a doctor in Nicholasville, seven miles away, who agreed to stay open until we got Nellie there by car. We drove as fast as we dared and both Maria and I silently but fervently prayed for divine mercy and help. The doctor immediately asked permission to call an ambulance. We agreed and said we preferred Good Samaritan hospital in Lexington. While the doctor cleaned the wound and put on a bandage, I phoned the seminary and asked a secretary to cancel my afternoon class.

At the emergency room, a doctor rushed Nellie to the x-ray room. He soon returned to tell us Nellie had a compound fracture on the right side of her head that also affected her right inner ear. Nellie was taken to a hospital room where nurses gave her medications and special attention. I had to return to Wilmore to care for the two boys, but Maria stayed by Nellie's bed full time. A week later on Saturday, Nellie was released with the understanding she was to do nothing active for six weeks, which was very hard for her to do. Nellie improved rapidly, but the doctor informed us the second bone in the right inner ear was dislocated and she would have increasing deafness.

The year went well and along with teaching during the summer school, I made good progress on my dissertation. The pressure was heavy to complete the task, for I had but one year left for researching and completing the document. The main section of the dissertation centered on a detailed literary analysis of the book of Jeremiah and an integrative evaluation of the spiritual life of the prophet as revealed in his writings.

During the fall quarter of 1954, Maria and I decided I should resign from my pastorate at Aberdeen, Ohio and concentrate on the dissertation. By the end of the quarter, my literary analysis of Jeremiah was completed and the focus turned to the prophet's spiritual life. Fortunately, Jeremiah left us a number of statements that related to his spiritual interactions with God, to his relations with his contemporaries, including kings, and to his inner conflicts.

I did considerable research on the theological and the psychological aspects of spiritual life and found limited help, until I read the book entitled OUR INNER CONFLICTS by Karen Horney, a lady psychiatrist. She claimed that a basic dilemma lay at the heart of personal conflicts and an analysis of the dilemma in a client's life brought to light a context of tangled interpersonal relationships. Furthermore, she noted that the client's personal choice was crucial to the positive resolution of the inner conflict. The choices centered on whether the client would face up to the dilemma and resolve to work with it, or to deny the dilemma existed and regress into deeper inner conflict.

I decided to test this insight on the data I had from the book of Jeremiah. I found Horney's insights correlated with the data. I rapidly put together a chapter centered on Jeremiah's interactions with God and a chapter analyzing Jeremiah's interactions with the people

Jeremiah confronted day after day. The dissertation gained the title THE HEBREW PROPHETIC CONSCIOUSNESS.

Maria rapidly completed typing the document and it was sent to Drew University the first week in April 1955. Several weeks later, word came from my dissertation committee that the dissertation was acceptable. I was scheduled to defend the ideas in the dissertation during the week before commencement in June. An account of that occasion is found at the beginning of this life story.

After I received my Ph. D. degree, the seminary informed me I had been promoted to the status of full-time Professor that I retained until my retirement.

The fall of 1955, David started kindergarten so Maria decided to go to work. She was able to get a full time job as the office secretary of the seminary's Alumni Association.

During the 1950's, Asbury Seminary used the quarter system plus summer school and I taught, after I received my Ph.D. degree, three classes each quarter and two in summer school. Each year I taught courses on the Old Testament, on Hebrew Grammar, and on Biblical Archaeology. There was a three-week break at Christmas and the month of August was vacation time.

There were about 250 students enrolled each year in the 50's decade and I had three Old Testament classes that all students had to take before they graduated. The enrollment in the required courses ranged from sixty to one hundred which I regarded as a heavy load. Fortunately, during that decade I had few committee assignments. I had to work hard preparing my lectures, but I thoroughly enjoyed teaching the classes. In the last partial decade of my academic career, there were over 700 students in the seminary. The duties connected with being the chairman of the Division of Biblical Studies, and membership in several faculty committees reduced my teaching load. Those were busy years. I regard my last five years of teaching as the most important of my career. As the years passed by, related but new areas of ministry opened, which I combined with my purely academic activities.

During a portion of the December break, during most of the spring one-week breaks and part of August each year, I would lecture at training seminars for pastors in various conferences of the denomination or preach at special meetings at various churches. A portion of each August and sometimes at Christmas, the family and I visited Maria's mother at Hustisford, WI, and my parents at Eau Claire, WI.

Burton had such fond memories of our years at Wessington, S.D. that he decided to go back there to take his senior year of High School studies. He did so and graduated at the head of his class in May 1956. Maria, Nellie and David went out to Wessington Springs for the graduation exercises. The seminary commencement services happened on the same weekend, so I had to stay to attend them and then drove out to Wessington Springs to bring the family home.

My father died in 1957 from a severe case of diabetes, we attended his funeral and had a family reunion celebrating his life.

During the two school years of 1957-1959, Burton decided to attend Seattle Pacific College in Seattle, WA and had gotten a part time job with Boeing Aircraft Co at the same time. Burton liked the idea of earning money so he applied for full time employment and was accepted. We were unhappy for this meant he had to drop his class work, but he assured us he would return to classes as soon as possible. Nellie graduated with the last senior class of the Wilmore high school in May 1958. The Wilmore high school was moved to the new Jessamine high school that fall. In August 1958, Nellie decided to join her brother at Seattle Pacific College and we took her, along with Maria's mother, by car to Seattle and then returned home.

An important event happened in Maria's life on November 22, 1959. She was naturalized a citizen of the United States of America in a federal court in Lexington, KY. I was thrilled to watch her stand before the judge. He asked her a few questions and officially declared she was henceforth a citizen. She was thrilled that the stability of our long employment at the seminary made it possible for her to become a citizen of the USA. That stability also made it possible for me to complete my doctoral dissertation and earn my Ph. D. degree.

Livingston Family 1957
Front: David
Middle l-r: Nellie, Maria and Nellie Saarloos
Back l-r: Burton and Herbert

CHAPTER 7

Israel/American Institute of Bible Studies

About 1958, the trustees and administration of Asbury Seminary decided on a professional improvement program for the faculty. The decision was to grant a sabbatical of one quarter with pay, after a faculty member had taught for at least nine quarters. I qualified, so I applied for a sabbatical to be taken during the fall quarter of 1959. About that same time, Dr. G. Douglas Young, Dean of Trinity Divinity School, located at Deerfield, Illinois, sent out an announcement to a number of seminaries that he was planning to establish an Institute of Biblical Studies in Jerusalem, Israel in the fall of 1959. He reported he needed professors who had a sabbatical that fall semester to apply for a teaching position in this new Institute. Plane fare plus board and room would be provided. Maria and I discussed and prayed about this opportunity and decided I should apply for a position at the Institute. We were pleased when we learned I was accepted for the faculty position. When Burton heard of my opportunity to go to Israel to teach at the Israel-American Institute of Biblical Studies he informed us, he would like to go with me and take some college work in Israel, hopefully at Hebrew University. Maria and I decided to agree to his proposal.

This incident happened during the spring break of the first semester of 1959. During this time of tenure at ATS, I often received requests that I give a series of lectures on the Old Testament prophets, especially

Jeremiah, at study conferences for Free Methodist ministers. In this case, I was scheduled to speak to pastors in Oil City, PA.

Before leaving for this conference, I learned that a ladies quartette was scheduled to present several concerts at a United Methodist church near Oil City. We agreed that I would meet them at this church Monday forenoon, and we would go together to Wilmore.

When I met them, I discovered that at the last minute they had decided to bring with them a lady student from India to speak to their congregation about Christians in India. It also happened that the pastor of a nearby church had heard them sing and asked them to give a concert that Monday night at his church. They had agreed, but they had a problem. The lady from India needed to return to Wilmore that day, because she had a class on Tuesday forenoon. The members of the quartette asked me to take her with me.

All went well until we approached the entrance of the Blue Licks State Park in Kentucky. It was in the middle of the afternoon and the sun was shining through our windshield. I noticed a State Police Car parked at the gateway of the park and that its driver was talking to a park employee at the gate. A half-mile down the road I suddenly heard a siren sounding off, so I parked by the road and got out of the car. I was surprised when I saw the state policeman standing by the rear of my car with his right hand grasping the handle of his gun.

I asked, "Sir, what traffic law have I broken?"

Without answering my question, he gruffly demanded, "Show me your driver's license."

While I was taking my wallet from my pocket, I noticed he was watching very intently. I removed my license and gave it him. As he looked at it, I noted that a frown was forming on his forehead. He stepped back and looked at the car license on my car's rear bumper.

Somewhat upset he demanded, "What is your occupation?"

I informed him I was a minister and a professor at Asbury Theological Seminary in Wilmore, KY.

His eyebrows went up and he exclaimed. "You have to be kidding. Show me proof of that statement!"

I took an I. D. card from my wallet and handed it to him. He uttered a brief whistle, and pointing a finger to the inside of my car, he demanded, "Who is this woman?"

I explained she was a lady from India who was student at the seminary. Then I explained our weekend meetings and why she was with me.

The policeman replaced his harsh attitude with a softer tone. Briefly, he explained why he stopped me. That morning a white man had robbed a bank in the middle of Indiana and had escaped in a car, taking a black woman as a hostage. The State police department had issued all police departs throughout Indiana and neighboring states to be on the lookout for a white man driving a car with a black woman as a passenger. The man was regarded as dangerous.

"When I saw your car coming toward the parkway, a white man driving and a black woman sitting beside him, I said to myself, "Oh, Oh, here is the bank robber! That is the reason I stopped you. Instead of a bank robber, guess what, I was about to arrest a professor! Please accept my apology."

As we were shaking hands, I said, "No problem, I honor you for doing your duty."

As we continued on our journey, a very nervous lady asked, "What was that all about? I noticed he pointed at me!"

I told the story and she giggled and said, "When I tell this story in India, they will surely laugh."

I murmured, "And so will my wife, I hope!"

In July, I had Bible study engagements at a church conference in Idaho and one in Bellingham, Washington, so Maria, David and I drove out there and I fulfilled those assignments. While in Washington, we kept in close contact with Burt and Nellie. It seemed best to take Burt's belongings to Wilmore in a rental trailer after my obligations to the church conference in Washington were met. All of us, including Nellie who would return to the college, drove almost day and night to Wilmore, for Burt and I were due to meet the Institute faculty and students in New York City. Our group was scheduled to travel by plane to Israel. Burt was with me and Dr. Shultz's teenage daughter was with him. There were eleven students, and more would join us in Jerusalem.

Our first stop was Copenhagen, Denmark. August 1st, we flew in a four motor, DC7 owned by Swedish Airlines and it took eleven hours to fly across the Atlantic. We were exhausted but managed to enjoy a tour of the city. We had fun spending a few hours at Tivoli, the Danish equivalent of Disney Land, and finally had a good night's sleep in a nice hotel room.

The next day our group flew to Gutenberg, Sweden and rode a train to a religious camp close to Ljundskile, where we spent several days. Here we met our leader, Dr. G. Young and Mr. Woehrle, a photographer. I gave a message about the call of the prophet Jeremiah at one of the services. Our next stop on August 6th was at Rome, Italy where we spent several days sight-seeing. Finally, on August 9th, we arrived at the airport in Israel. From there, we rode in limousines to Jerusalem. It was dark when we arrived, but the excitement of being in the Holy City made the long trip seem wonderfully worthwhile.

The next morning we took stock of the situation. We found we were in a stone building owned by the Christian Missionary Alliance Church (aka CMA) and used as a mission in Palestine. It was originally a school with a stone church attached but had been closed since 1948. The CMA had missionaries in another building in the city. The head missionary had agreed to allow the Institute to have the building free of rental costs. He had found some metal cots, some sheets and wool blankets for sleeping and some chairs and tables. The kitchen had an oil-burning stove, an ancient refrigerator and an assortment of mismatched cutlery and dishware. These items were available until a shipment of furniture and supplies arrived from the United States.

Maria and I set up a communication contact by the only reliable means possible at that time, by airmail letters, which we have kept in folders. Their contents provide much of the detail of this narrative. Telephone connections between Israel and the United States cost twelve dollars a minute and were very unreliable.

Dr. Young arranged for our group to assist Dr. Johanan Aharoni, a leading archaeologist in Israel, in an excavation project at Ramat Rachel three miles south of Jerusalem. The site was located on a hill from which we could see Bethlehem three miles south. Dr. Schultz would take half of our students one forenoon and I would take the rest of the students the next day. This schedule lasted for several weeks. It was my first participation in a major dig and I was thrilled. We were working around the remains of stonewalls of an ancient building. We were constantly bringing to light artifacts that dated to about 600 B.C. Wow! (the text of this excavation is found in Appendix A under the heading "Ramat Rahel.")

Burt did some excavation, but the photographer, Mr. Woehrle, needed an assistant and asked Burt to go with him on a series of trips throughout Israel. Mr. Woehrle was taking movie pictures of a number of important places, for promotion of the Institute in the United States.

On the morning of August 15th, Dr. Young said he wanted to talk to me. He immediately asked me to take responsibility for the school's operations for the fall semester. He and the photographer would be returning to the United States in about a month. My new status would be the Field Director, besides teaching a class. I felt honored, but also burdened, for I knew this was a new venture with no model to serve as a guide. Dr. Young introduced me to a number of Israeli government officials, especially Dr. Chaim Wardi, Director of Christian Affairs in the Ministry of Religious Affairs. He would be the liaison man between the Institute and the government.

On Friday, August 21st, six of us decided to make a trip through the coastal area and the northern area of Israel. We rented a battered Jeep cheaply. Our first stop was where David slew Goliath, then on to Lachish. Our next stop was Ashkelon, close to a sand beach on the Mediterranean Sea and we walked over a sizable mound of ancient ruins. Archaeologists had done some digging there, but in recent years, extensive excavation has revealed the remains of a number of city ruins stacked layer upon layer. We drove up the coast, stopping briefly at Joppa and Caesarea. We soon learned the engine consumed a lot of gas and often coughed and jerked. One student had some skills as a mechanic and at repeated stops was able to coach the engine to run smoothly again. Near sun down, we arrived at Haifa and found the Swedish Mission (the Director had visited the Institute) where we stayed overnight.

The next morning a Mission servant took us to a Christian mechanic, who quickly solved the motor problems. The engine worked very well the rest of the trip. We stopped at a number of places in the Jezreel Valley, also at Tiberius and Hazor. By mid-afternoon we were at the north end of the Hulah Valley and found an Israeli kibbutz (a communal farm) close to the southern foot of Mt. Hermon. The leader of the kibbutz graciously invited us to eat a meal and stay overnight. First, we had to see the ruins of the ancient city of Dan that was located at the far end of a large field. A man with a gun went with us, since the mound was close to the border with Syria. As we returned to the kibbutz, we heard unusual noises coming from a neighboring kibbutz. My boyhood farm experience told me such noises should not be heard in Israel. Our guide admitted the kibbutz did raise a number of pigs, but reported them to the government as zebras. All of us had a good chuckle about pigs being in Israel.

The next day we stopped at only a few places for it was Monday and we needed to get back to Jerusalem. It was an exciting trip and the six of us had a lot of fun together. One of our reactions was the smallness of Israel in comparison to our native America, but that did not keep us from being almost overwhelmed. We were in the land of the Old Testament and the New Testament. We had visited the boyhood city of Jesus and walked where our Lord had walked in Galilee and by the Sea of Galilee.

Dr. Young already had done preliminary work on putting together a faculty for the fall semester. Dr. Schultz would teach a course on the New Testament, I would teach a course on the Old Testament. We were able to finalize the employment of five Israeli professors from Hebrew University in Jerusalem: Dr. Raphael Warblowsky would teach a course on "Jewish Religious Beliefs," Dr. Johanan Aharoni would teach a course on "Archaeological Excavation," Dr. Aharon Rosen would teach "Modern Hebrew Language" (with an emphasis on how to speak it), Dr. Ruth Amiran would teach "The Archaeological History of Palestine," and Dr. Chaim Wardi would teach "The History of Christianity in Palestine." All these courses would be taught at the Masters Degree level. A college level curriculum would not be set up until several years later. Burt decided to audit these courses and explore the possibly of taking college level courses at Hebrew University with the daughter of Dr. Schultz. However, the University did not begin its fall semester until the middle of October. Burt was relating well with the other students and was having the time of his life exploring Jerusalem.

The Institute enrolled students on August 31st. Several young people already in Jerusalem enrolled, also a young minister and his wife from Switzerland. They were taking a sabbatical in Israel and we found room for them in our dormitory section. We had fifteen students, four of whom were ladies. Classes began the next day and I decided to sit in on the Hebrew language class and the Jewish Beliefs class. The ladies prepared and served the meals and the men took turns washing the dishes. The men also helped the ladies buy products at the street bazaar. The prices were cheaper than U. S. prices.

On weekends, the students scattered too many parts of Israel to get acquainted with the land and the people. At that time, the West Bank and the old part of Jerusalem were under the control of the Jordanian army, so we had to wait till Christmas time before we could go through the Mandelbaum Gate, in order to visit that part of Palestine as Christian pilgrims.

On September 11th, the Institute sponsored an Inaugural ceremony to which many high ranking Israeli officials came. I felt very important as Dr. Young introduced me to all of them. The next morning Dr. Young and Mr. Woehrle went to the airport and returned to Chicago. I was beginning to feel the weight of being the head of this fledgling school. It was up to me to make that first semester a success.

In the next two weeks, Dr. Ruth Amiran, our Professor of Archaeology, arranged with the Israeli government to provide a bus to take all the students on two trips. One trip was to the ruins of Megiddo that had been excavated quite extensively by the University of Chicago. She explained all aspects of the site in detail. She led us down a precarious stairway to a tunnel carved through solid rock to an underground source of water. She also took us through the impressive museum near the ruins. Her professional skill as a teacher impressed all of us.

Another time, Dr. Amiran took us to an archaeological site north of Tel Aviv called Tel Qasileh and then through a glass museum that had a number of the oldest glass artifacts known. We were beginning to realize how rich our class in archaeology was going to be.

During September, interesting events were happening at our home. A women's dormitory had been under construction on the Asbury Seminary campus, but it was not completed at the time students were enrolled early in September. The business manager, William Savage, knew we had a house with four bedrooms, so he contacted Maria about having several women rent some of the bedrooms for several weeks. Maria decided to rent all four bedrooms. She and David, who was nine, would move into my first floor office. It turned out that six women moved into the four bedrooms. I didn't know till after I got home that Maria had moved two lawn lounging chairs with pads into the study for her and David's beds.

Our two months of having borrowed furniture and kitchen equipment was coming to an end. Early in September, Dr. Young had learned his shipment of equipment and canned food had arrived at Haifa, but he was unable to clear it through customs before he left. The last two weeks of September, I was to work with a lady, a government official, to complete the process of clearing customs. Israeli tariff on canned goods was especially high. The customs lady came up with a clever idea. Each of us would have a portion of the canned goods applied free of tariff to our passports. Finally, on Oct. 5th, a truckload of the shipment arrived at the front door and was quickly unloaded. Two days later, another truckload arrived. We were all excited as we put a new stove and refrigerator in place and a complete set of dishes and cutlery on shelves and in drawers. Cots and mattresses, sheets, blankets and towels were distributed to various rooms. It was a new life!

As the weeks went by, I was able to get acquainted with various Christian leaders. Some were Catholic, some Anglican, some Presbyterian and a few were Orthodox. We were invited to visit a Southern Baptist orphanage and school for boys not far from the national airport. I gave a brief meditation, and then we visited with the teachers and students. Our group was amused that the Palestinian boys used a southern drawl in their speech. As the weeks moved along, I was invited to preach to several independent congregations.

What interested us the most were the small congregations of Israelis who had become Christians. They used Hebrew Bibles (the NT was translated into Hebrew) and their hymns were in Hebrew, as was the preaching. Their hymnbooks have an interesting format, which tried to solve a difficult problem. The musical score goes from left to right but Hebrew script goes from right to left. What was their solution? They divided Hebrew words into syllables and strung them backwards so they would fit the notes.

On some weekends, Dr. Wardi had Israeli guides take us on tours of various kinds of Jewish synagogues. A few synagogues were in separate buildings but there were a number of congregations that met in rooms in stores, apartment buildings and factories. Jews, who had immigrated to Israel from various countries, attended most of these synagogues. Each synagogue had its peculiar way of conducting its worship services.

The synagogue services were on Friday evenings and/or on Saturdays, because the Jewish Sabbath is from sundown Friday to sundown Saturday. All secular activities, all stores and factories and all traveling were shut down during that time: Sunday was like any other day of the week. This practice created a problem for Christians. When would they worship, since many had to work on Sunday. The solution was not difficult. Some Christian congregations met on Friday evenings or on Saturdays and others would meet on Saturday nights and/or on Sundays. We could choose which service to attend.

October 2nd was the Jewish New Year's celebration that occurred on the Sabbath (Friday sundown to Saturday sundown) so the government set aside Sunday as a legal extension of the Holy Day. We attended several synagogue services that were in Hebrew. We also attended a Sunday service in the local YMCA, which is housed in a lovely stone building. However, this service was in three languages, none of them English, so we couldn't participate very well. That evening we attended a communion (in English) at a service held in the church building attached to the one we occupied.

A week later, at Sunday sundown, the most holy of Jewish Holy Days, the Day of Atonement began and continued until Monday at sundown. We were not in Jerusalem to observe the events of that day, which followed quite closely Old Testament instructions. Jews were to fast for at least 24 hours.

One of the Christian leaders in Israel was Rev. Alex Wachtel, a Nazarene minister, who had charge of several Nazarene churches, one of which was in Nazareth. Rev. Wachtel and his family lived in Jerusalem and made contact with us early in August. He gave us good advice about how to work with government officials. Once in August, he had taken us on a brief trip to Nazareth and now he wanted to take us there again. He was building a new stone church in Nazareth and he had to preach to the small congregation.

Early Sunday on October 11th, Rev Wachtel, Burt and I left by car for Nazareth. He also took us to the Spring of Gideon at the base of Mt. Gilboa, to Beth-Shan and to Endor. The worship service was early that afternoon. The congregation was made up of several ethnic families, mostly, Palestinians and were very friendly. Returning to Jerusalem that evening we met only six cars over a distance of 100 miles. The Day of Atonement had shut down everything but emergency activity and tourist travel. Rev. Wachtel soon became a close friend and valued advisor.

Ten days later, five students, three men and two women, asked me to go with them by bus to Beersheba to check out a camel market held there periodically. Burt couldn't go because he had a tooth problem and needed to see a dentist. We left early on the 22nd, a Friday, and enjoyed observing the Bedouin owners of the camels, trade them among themselves and sell some to Jewish settlers in the area. The Bedouin even let us ride a camel briefly. We learned that a bus left Saturday forenoon to stop at several Jewish villages located on the southwestern shore of the Dead Sea. The two women returned to Jerusalem by bus and we found a youth hostel in Beersheba. We stayed overnight there where each of us got a cot, two sheets and two blankets for the equivalent of seventy-five cents. It got chilly that night and the blankets were inadequate. It was difficult to sleep soundly. The next forenoon at ten o'clock, we boarded a bus. We made a serious mistake. We failed to buy groceries.

The bus was old and bounced a lot on the twenty-five miles of crooked, graveled road. The small town of Sodom was interesting but the shore of the Dead Sea was fascinating. The cliff behind the town was solid rock and one upright projection was called "Lot's wife." The sand at the shore also had a lot of salt mixed with minerals and a number of pieces of asphalt that had oozed up from the bottom of the sea, floated ashore and dried. Nearby was a factory that extracted salt from the sea and separated the minerals from it. The Israeli owners sold their products throughout the world.

After eating a lunch at a small cafe and doing some more searching for "treasures," we boarded another bus that was going to Ein Gedi, an Israeli kibbutz over twenty miles north along the western shore of the Dead Sea. The road was only a dirt trail with no bridges across a number of shallow depressions. At sundown, the Jewish Sabbath began and the driver very much wanted to get to Ein Gedi before sundown and he drove much too fast. He barely made it before the sun slipped over the edge of the cliff; within minutes, after we got there we were off the bus.

An Israeli couple had also been on the bus, so they helped us get overnight lodging in the hostel for a dollar each. The kibbutz leader could only speak Hebrew. We had with us one large tin can of hash and some tea. We built a bonfire and had hot tea and hash. The next morning the couple from Haifa helped us get a free loaf of bread from the kibbutz. They couldn't sell anything on the Sabbath but realized we needed something to eat.

A member of the kibbutz led us up a deep ravine beside a rushing stream of water. Soon we came to a large spring that gushed cool water into a pool. We had a wonderful time splashing water at each other. The kibbutz piped water from the stream to a field where its members raised plentiful crops the year around. They specialized in grapes, and dates from stately palm trees. One field yielded ten cuttings of alfalfa each year.

At noon, a truckload of young people stopped briefly at the kibbutz and agreed to take us to a junction with a dirt road to Masada. We had to hike two miles in a blazing hot sun and were glad to find a hostel with a dozen young people. They gave us a lunch and cool water. At three o'clock, we climbed the crooked Snake Trail up the very steep east side of Mt. Masada. Its top was 2,400 ft. above sea level and we started the climb at about 800 ft. below sea level. The climb took us forty-five minutes. We spent a half hour looking at the ruins of a Jewish settlement that was destroyed by the Roman army early in the second century A.D. The view of the Dead Sea and steep cliffs to the East and to the West was fantastic.

The sun was close to setting so we hurried down the Snake Trail. It took thirty minutes and darkness overtook us as we reached the bottom. Some of the kibbutz young men noted we did not have a flashlight, so they came with flashlights to guide us to the hostel. We had several hours of playing several games with the youths whose job during the week was serving as guides to tour groups. A good meal and lodging cost each of us the equivalent of $1.05.

The next morning we were up early and caught the 6:30 a.m. bus and were back at the Institute by noon. The trip was rugged but full of thrills.

Over the weekend, a dentist had fixed Burt's teeth for a reasonable fee and letters from home were waiting to be read. At the seminary, the ladies dormitory was completed and the students who had been living in our home were getting ready to move into the building. Maria had a full time job as alumni secretary so their leaving would take a big load off her shoulders. She sent addresses of several of her relatives in Holland, whom I should visit on the way home. She also sent the address of a Methodist minister in London who would help me buy some china plate ware and silverware when I stopped in that city.

The student body was excited about having a Halloween party for the Israeli faculty and various Israeli friends, who said they knew nothing about how an American Halloween was celebrated. Costumes were made and a "ghost walk" was arranged in the basement and Halloween games were selected. About forty Israeli friends came to the party filled with curiosity. Two or three visitors were taken at a time through the "ghost walk" and now and then screams were heard. Those waiting their turn were entertained with the games. Our Israeli friends said they enjoyed the evening and saw some similarity with their annual Festival of Purim, based on the book of Esther.

After reading several of these narratives, one might gain the impression that our activities were mostly taking weekend trips and having parties. Not so. Classes were being held on schedule and the Israeli professors were greatly appreciated. Dr. Wardi, our liaison with the government, saw to it we had important officials speaking to us once or twice a week in the evenings. Dr. Ruth Amiran took us to several archaeological sites with bus service provided by the government. In the middle of October, she announced that the government was providing free bus service to take the entire student body and staff to Eilat at the southern tip of Israel where it had a short stretch of shoreline on the Gulf of Aqaba. Dr. Ruth Amiran and her husband, a Professor of geology at Hebrew University, would lecture to our group about the countryside and the major archaeological sites along the way. The date was November 8th and 9th.

We arose at 4:30 a.m. November 8th and were on the big new bus at 6:00 a.m. We took our bed sheets and blankets and plenty to eat. The government asked us to allow several government employees to ride with us to Eilat. With a total of twenty-four passengers and our luggage, the bus was full. We stopped at several ancient sites and were in Beersheba by 9:00 a.m. From there on south, the land was barren and soon became rugged. Dr. Amiran, the geologist, explained what had happened to the land. He believed a severe earthquake had caused one section four miles wide and ten miles long to drop 2,000 ft. It looked like portions of Utah. In the book of Exodus, this area is called the Wilderness of Sin and the Valley of Paran. Our bus descended the steep, crooked road and down the Valley of Aqaba toward Eilat. The west side of the valley is in Israel and the east side is in Jordan. A few miles north of Eilat, the bus driver detoured to rugged cliffs from which Israel extracts considerable copper. A few miles further down the road, we inspected artifacts and remains of copper mines that belonged to King Solomon. We hurried to Eilat where we ate a good meal and slept on our army cots.

After breakfast, we loaded the bus and visited the seashore where many of our group joined others in swimming and splashing in the salty water. We then went several miles further south to a place where we hired a boat with a glass bottom. Out from the shore we could see through the glass bottom many fish of various sizes, shapes and colors. Below them was a spectacular reef.

We left Eilat about 9:00 a.m. and took another route home. The two Israeli professors kept us entertained and informed with occasional lectures about the barren countryside. Fortunately, the bus was air-conditioned, for the outside, temperature soon rose above 100. Just before noon, we arrived at the base of an impressive cliff. We could see the walls of ruined buildings along its top. The name of the ancient city was Avdah. For a long time the site was a trading post at the juncture of east-west and north-south trade routes.

In New Testament times, a trading group called Nabateans, created a wealthy settlement here. Potsherds of their treasured, very thin pottery were scattered on the ground. When the Romans conquered these traders, they built a strong fortress and taxed the caravans who passed by. Christians were successful in winning converts and nurturing a congregation, when the Romans had to leave in the Third Century A.D. Christians became wealthy and built several beautiful churches, which are now in ruins, but significant portions of the walls and floors remain. On the face of the cliff were man-made caves in which people lived during the summer. We entered those caves and noted how cool they were. About four o'clock, we got into the bus and arrived at the Institute at seven p.m. The trip had been very informative and we thanked the Amirans for their kindness. We read our mail, washed our clothes and were soon sound asleep.

Up until the middle of November, we had no need for heat in the building, but the weather was becoming cooler so we had to purchase kerosene heaters for our study rooms and a large heater for the main room. Light rain would fall at times but the days were mostly sunny. Everyone was beginning to think seriously about the fact classes would end December 18th and about the planned trip into the Old Jerusalem and the West bank area controlled by Jordanian soldiers. We were beginning the process of gaining special permits to enter that part of the Holy Land as pilgrims during the Christmas season.

Besides the daily pressure of teaching a class, monitoring several others and filling several speaking engagements, I was also working on several writing projects, which I will describe in a later chapter. At the same time, Maria and I had decided by mail to attempt a telephone call on November 19th, Maria's birthday. I began the process by contacting the Israeli telephone office so arrangements could be made to coordinate the time of the call both in Israeli and in Lexington. KY. The Israeli telephone operator cautioned me to expect possible difficulty making a connection since weather conditions could disturb the radio transmission of our voices between Israel and the United States.

The time for the call arrived but atmospheric conditions were bad and, after trying for an hour and a half, the effort stopped, for the office closed at 9:00 p. m. and would not open until 2:00 p. m. the next day. Burt and I were disappointed and wondered about Maria's stress as she waited for the call that did not come. It so happened that the American operator kept Maria informed about the problem and about the schedule to try the next day, which would be early morning in Wilmore. To our joy, the connection was made but the voices were transmitted poorly. Burt and I had just time to say Happy Birthday and Maria and David had just time to say they were doing fine. It was a costly phone call but we were glad we could talk, though so briefly.

Another extra-curricular event was a Thanksgiving dinner at the Jerusalem YMCA for all Americans who were living in Israel at that time. A Baptist minister and his wife visited the Institute and asked whether someone could show them about the Israeli part of Jerusalem and guide them on a tour of northern Israel. Burt volunteered for the job so he missed being at the Thanksgiving dinner. We even had turkey and pumpkin pie! Eighty Americans were present for the dinner and we were able to make acquaintance with a number of them.

After dinner, four of the Institute students and I left by train for Haifa. We rented a car and made a three-day trip through the Galilee area, checking out some places we had missed on previous trips. We stayed at a youth hostel one night and at a kibbutz at the base of Mt. Hermon the next night. The third day we stopped at several archaeological sites. At Haifa, we boarded a train, and arrived at Jerusalem just before dark. The next forenoon I went to a mission by the airport and spoke to a group about the Old Testament covenant.

Excitement was increasing in the student body for our pilgrim permits had come through from the Jordanian authorities in Old Jerusalem. We studied maps together to decide what trips to take while visiting the West Bank. I had been in good health all fall but in the first week of December, I caught a bad cold and had severe stomach cramps. A typical Middle Eastern flu was making me miserable. Rev. Wachtel obtained some special pills and within two days, I was feeling great. Burt had escaped this flu.

We were pleased the reservations for our group had been confirmed for staying at the tourist hospice at the Anglican, Christ Church building in Old Jerusalem. The rates for board and room were reasonable.

Christmas time is not observed in Israel so we missed sparkling lights and decorated trees, although, to our amazement, a representative of the Israeli Jewish Agency brought a lovely evergreen tree to our front door. He said the government wanted to express appreciation for our presence in Israel. We were free to decorate it and observe the season according to our customs. We thanked him for the government's kindness and in short order had the tree placed and decorated. We all joined in making chains of colored paper and ornaments of images cut from tin cans. One student was an electrician and invented a string of lights.

The second full week of December was filled with completing last minute class assignments and tests. News reporters from an Israeli newspaper interviewed us for an article about the goals and activities of the Institute. It was good publicity for us. Some of the students decided to go caroling to several Christian centers and Christian friends in the city. We would have to walk from place to place. Late on the afternoon of the 18th we arrived at the Anglican private school, just as the students were released from their classes. The students and the staff joined us in a series of well-known hymns. Walking from one site to another, we had to go past the major synagogue of the city. Several of the students suggested we stop and sing a carol but I talked them out of it.

We did agree to end our caroling at the home of Dr. Wardi and his family. He had often questioned us about Christian practices in America, so we thought he might like to hear an example of our caroling practice. As we sang a carol at the entrance to his home, he opened the door and welcomed us to his home. We met his wife and two young children. After a good chat, he asked us to sing "Silent Night" before we left. The children watched with wide-open eyes and rapt attention as we sang.

During the morning of Sunday, December 20th, we passed through the Mandelbaum Gate into Old Jerusalem. One of our Christian friends had arranged for a Palestinian tour agent to meet us and take us by bus to the Anglican Christ Church Hospice. We set up a schedule of tours to various parts of the Kingdom of Jordan and were assigned rooms in the hospice. We spent the day walking about Old Jerusalem that is entirely enclosed by a thick stonewall. The streets were narrow and the buildings rarely had space between them. A map of the city served as our guide. But the next day our tour guide took us around the city again and gave a detailed explanation of many of the important churches and how the bazaar provided for the needs of the people. Many lived above the stores. He even took us into the Muslim sacred area where the Old and New Testament temples were located.

At five o'clock, Burt and I met Dr. George Turner and his tour group at the National Hotel and chatted for several hours. He delivered several packages Maria had given him to pass on to us. The streets were empty except for Jordanian soldiers, who were gracious to us. We were soon at the hospice. We had much to talk about at our evening meal.

The next morning we took a bus to Jericho and crossed the Jordan River. We were surprised how narrow and muddy it was. We went east up a steep incline and entered Amman, the capital of the Kingdom. The city was not very large but had a nice museum. We next went north to Jerash where stone paved plazas and towering stone pillars reminded us of the luxuries of the Roman Army in New Testament times and the next several centuries. We returned to the Dead Sea and explored the remains of crude buildings and potsherds of a small village that existed there for several hundred years before 3,000 BC. The guide allowed us to pick up some pieces of the pottery. We went down to the seashore and dipped our hands into the extremely salty water of the Dead Sea.

We crossed the Jordan River again and followed a bumpy, dirt road to the ancient site of Qumran where a community of Jewish scholars lived from about 200 BC to 68 AD. Only twelve years before our visit, leather scrolls, on which these men had copied most of the books of the Old Testament, had been found. They were in caves in the cliffs that rose steeply back of the village. Archaeologists had uncovered most of the remaining walls and floors of the site. We listened intently as our guide showed us around the place. Two of the members of this tour group were important people: a justice of the Supreme Court of Canada and his wife. Both were devout Christians.

The next day, Wednesday, we traveled north to visit Samaria, Shechem (modern Nablus) and back to Bethel before returning to Jerusalem. The road was paved with asphalt and curved back and forth, and up and down, over mountainous terrain. Now and then, the sides of a mountain were terraced for grapes, fig trees and olive trees, but otherwise were barren. The narrow valleys seemed fertile, producing vegetable crops. The villages had one story, sometimes two story stone buildings. There was little evidence of farm machinery. Some farmers were plowing behind oxen or mules. The people were friendly. Our guide knew local history well and spoke English clearly.

I ate supper with Dr. Turner whose guests were Dr. Marvin Pope and his wife who was the Director of the American School of Oriental Research in Amman. Burt and another student came at 8:00 p.m. to hear Dr. Pope give a lecture.

On Thursday, our bus headed south of Jerusalem. Our first stop was Bethlehem, the small city we had seen from Ramat Rahel while we were doing archaeological work there. We explored the huge Catholic and Orthodox churches in the center of Bethlehem. In the basement of the Orthodox Church, we spent a few moments at the spot that tradition claims was where Jesus was born. The spot has a marble star implanted in a marble floor. Across the small room was a wooden manger full of hay. We then went east of the city through a field in which tradition asserts Ruth of Old Testament fame gleaned heads of grain and also met her future husband, Boaz. At the north edge of the field was a reputed shepherd's cave. We would return to this spot again. We journeyed toward Hebron, stopping here and there to examine grape vineyards in which the vines lay on the ground.

Hebron is a city with many stone buildings, the most striking of which was a large one dating from New Testament times, but used as a mosque. Through windows in the floor, we could see stone boxes reputed to contain the bodies of Abraham and some of his family. The streets were crowded with Palestinian Muslims. We returned to Jerusalem and at 4:00 p.m. went back to Bethlehem and out to the shepherd's cave where Protestants meet for a special YMCA service. There were more than a hundred present. As the sun went down and it began to get dark, we could look east at an open pasture and imagine the shepherds listening to the angels announce the birth of Jesus in the nearby village. One of the songs the congregation sang was, "O Little Town of Bethlehem." Our sense of awe was overwhelming. After the service, a lunch of Arabic bread and cooked lamb was served to those present.

We went back to Bethlehem and visited briefly a Christmas Eve service in the Catholic Church. The Orthodox Church had no service because they do not observe Christmas until January 6th. Another Protestant Christmas Eve service, led by Anglican priests, was held in the courtyard of the Church of the Nativity at 9:00 p.m. There was a large crowd and the singing of carols was enthusiastic. We returned to the hospice thrilled with what we had experienced that day.

On Christmas day, our group joined with Dr. Turner's group at the Rockefellow Museum just outside the north wall of Old Jerusalem. They then went through the Mandelbaum Gate into Israel where I was scheduled to meet the tour group in Tel Aviv on the twenty-ninth. We did some more walking about Jerusalem and decided to take it easy that evening.

The evening turned out to be anything but calm. Most of the students went to visit some nearby shops, whereas I settled down to read a book. Suddenly, a student came rushing into the hospice with the news one of our students had been placed under arrest and was at the headquarters of the soldiers who policed the city. This headquarters was in the complex of stone buildings called the Tower of David and was just across the street from the hospice. I rushed over to the Tower of David and found the young man in handcuffs and being questioned by an army officer. Soon the Jordanian colonel in charge of the soldiers arrived. The colonel was gracious but concerned. We were American tourists and our passports and permits were in order. What had our student done?

Though I had instructed the students never to go into the city alone, this young man decided to go by himself to Gethsemane which was in the valley east of the city. He made the mistake of wearing a cap, called a beanie, which he had purchased in Israel. Several Palestinian young men recognized the Israeli cap and demanded an explanation. Rex, the student, said he was American and had gotten the cap in Israel, but he was not a Jew. He refused to show his passport to the men, for he had been told not to show his passport to anyone except an official or a soldier. A scuffle ensued and soldiers came running to the scene. Rex showed his passport to them and they brought him to the Tower of David. We were able to work out an agreement with the colonel that no Israeli caps would be worn in the Old City and that none of our students would go about the city alone again. Rex pledged himself to this agreement too. He was a shaken young man.

Christian leaders in Israel had alerted us that prices of groceries and meat were much cheaper in the Old City, and that we should take Institute money with us to buy up to the quota allowed for each tourist to take into Israel. The next day several of us bought our quota and crossed over to Israel and arrived at our Institute building with a nice supply of food. Several students stayed another day and did the same thing. Our friends who had freezers stored the fresh meat.

I spent two days getting the financial matters of the Institute taken care of and my bags packed. Burt was staying at the Institute for five months in 1960 and attending classes at Hebrew University. On the morning of Dec. 30th, Rev. Wachtel took a student and me to Israel's Lod Airport to board a plane.

While waiting in the milling crowd, we noticed two middle-aged men going from person to person. Finally, they came to us. They were government officials who needed to get on a plane to Europe. They asked if we would give our seats on the plane to them. The government would put us up for the night in a nice seaside Hotel, provide us with meals and rearrange our plane ticket to take a plane the next morning. They promised to contact people, at places we were scheduled to stop, of our changed schedule. We decided to release our seats to them and, after getting new tickets, we went by taxi to our seaside hotel. Both of us were bone tired so we took it easy and ate some wonderful meals. A taxi took us back to the airport the next morning and we boarded a Belgium plane.

At Athens, no one was present to meet us. We contacted our missionary friends by phone and they came to the airport and then took us on a tour of Athens. They had not received the telegram the Israeli officials had promised to send. The next day Rev. Pappas took me by car to Corinth and then sightseeing through Athens. I boarded the plane to Paris as originally scheduled but when I arrived, I found the plane had arrived late and so I missed the plane to Amsterdam. I was upset, for I knew Maria's relatives in Holland had promised to meet me at the airport that evening. The airlines took me to a hotel for the night.

The next forenoon I boarded a plane to Amsterdam. I then took a train to Utrecht where I phoned Maria's relatives, who lived in the nearby town of De Bilt. One of Maria's cousins, who spoke good English, answered the phone and promised to come immediately to meet me. I was soon at the home of Maria's uncle and aunt, neither of whom could speak English. Soon more cousins arrived who could talk with me and we had a great time together. They took me on a tour of Utrecht and around the countryside.

Arriving in Amsterdam, a day late interfered with my plane schedule to London, so I sent a telegram to our friend there and informed him that I would be a day late, and also the time of my arrival. Our friend had gone to the airport but didn't find me, but later that day my telegram arrived and he was on hand when I entered the airport terminal. I stayed at his apartment for two days. His wife was a kind person and provided a nice room and wonderful meals. On the second day, my host took me shopping. We found our Wedgwood plate ware at Harrods Department store at a reasonable price and I arranged to have the set shipped to Wilmore. They didn't have the silverware I wanted, so my host took me to another store where I bought a set for twelve to be shipped to Wilmore.

With great anticipation, I boarded a Boeing 707 jet plane and headed for New York City. The ride was remarkably quiet and fast, arriving at the airport on Long Island early in the afternoon. I immediately phoned Maria and we rejoiced all had gone well. Two hours later, I stepped off the plane at the Cincinnati airport and soon Maria and David were in my arms. As we drove home, we talked excitedly about Israel, Burt, Nellie and events in Wilmore.

Fifty years later, looking back on the five months spent in Israel, I find it rewarding to see what has happened to the Institute I helped establish. In January 1960, the future of the school seemed precarious. It had a small student body and almost no financial resources, because of the generous gifts of a few friends the Institute still exists. Slowly the enrollment increased, some students coming from several different countries. Year after year, the Institute seldom went into debt.

In 1967, the Institute moved to a fairly large stone building belonging to the Anglican Church. The building was located on the southwest slope of Mt. Zion. The move enabled the school to enroll more students and enlarge its curriculum with several Master of Arts degrees. It also became known as the Israel-American Institute of Holy Land Studies. I was asked to join the Board of Directors that met every year in the school's American headquarters in Deerfield, IL. In 1970, Dr. Young asked me to organize a group of evangelical colleges and seminaries into a Consortium of Associated Schools that would send students to the Institute and give academic advice to the Board of Directors. Starting with a dozen schools, I built the number to about a hundred schools located in the U. S. and abroad. In 1985, I retired from twenty-five years as a Director and fifteen years as chairman of the Associated Schools.

In 1996, the school chose a non-American style of name and has since been known as the Jerusalem University College. A recent alumni publication of the school provides the following statistics from its present day office in Rockford, IL. Records show that former students total about 18,000. These alumni are serving on every inhabited continent. Students have enrolled from forty countries, including students from 48 of the states in the US and four provinces of Canada. Several hundred Masters Degrees have been granted and many class credits have been transferred to transcripts of students of both the college and seminary levels. I count it an honor to have been associated with the school.

I count being the first Director of this institute one of the top projects of my career. Many others have contributed to its long-term contributions to evangelical scholarship in many nations as well as the United States. Many of its graduates have become significant pastors, missionaries and professors. Being in the Holy Lands for nearly five months blessed me with many new insights into biblical places and times. I was a more effective professor because of this experience.

This trip also gave me an opportunity to stop over in the Netherlands to meet relatives of Maria. Later, she was able to go to the Netherlands and meet these same people. Burton gained an abiding interest in the Palestinian people, including the Arabs. After returning home, he enrolled at the University of Kentucky where he majored in Near Eastern history and languages. He won a federal grant for graduate studies at the University of Michigan centered on Arabic, and the tense relationship between the British Empire and the Ottoman Empire.

Israel/American Institute of Biblical Studies.
This group was starting a flight to Jerusalem to begin this
school. Herbert is on the left at the end, Burton is the tallest
person in the center, and G Douglas Young is on the right
end of the line.

CHAPTER 8

WILMORE AND A TRIP TO MISSION FIELDS

Several events were happening at Asbury Theological Seminary. An American Theological Seminary commission had given accreditation status to our seminary and right away, its enrollment began to increase. Asbury Seminary was required to build a new library, the quarter system was changed to a semester format, the degree "Bachelor of Divinity" was changed to a "Master of Divinity" degree and plans for a "Master of Theology" degree were begun.

I was appointed chairman of the faculty library committee and immediately became a member of a library building planning committee set up by the Trustees. When this planning committee met, I was chosen chairman. This position made me a bit uncomfortable. As I chaired the committee's first meeting, I could not help thinking, "What am I, with a poverty stricken, dairy farm boyhood, doing leading a committee made up of the seminary president, the executive vice president, the Dean, the vice president of business and the librarian?" Within a year, a beautiful new library was completed.

During the winter and early spring of 1960, another project, besides a heavy academic load, was claiming the attention of Maria and me. Burt sent word that several of the students of the Institute were planning to spend the summer traveling throughout the western part of the Middle East and throughout Europe. The students would use buses, trains or boats, whichever cost the least.

At the same time, church leaders and pastors were contacting me, asking me to speak to their congregations about my visit to Israel. We quickly put together a schedule that would take us through the lower Southwest to Los Angeles and San Diego, north to Seattle and home. We decided to buy a seventeen-foot trailer house to attach to our Ford sedan. Maria, David and I would sleep and eat in it on the long trip. We left in the middle of June and spoke at several churches on the way to southern California. After fulfilling all those engagements, we headed north and enjoyed seeing the redwood forests.

Through letter contact with Nellie in Seattle, we learned she and her boyfriend, Ralph Kester, wished we would visit his parents who lived in Portland, OR, and sent the necessary address. We found the house easily and quickly made friends with Ralph's parents who were devoted Christians belonging to the Evangelical Church of North America. Arriving in Seattle, we soon were hugging our daughter who in turn introduced us to Ralph. The young man, who would be a senior at Seattle Pacific College during the upcoming school year, impressed us.

We were informed we would need to start preparing for a wedding ceremony in Wilmore the next summer. We spent several wonderful days getting acquainted with Ralph and bringing Nellie up to date about Burt's travels in Europe. On Sunday, I spoke at several Free Methodist churches in the city. Aside from marveling at the fantastic scenery of the Cascade and Rocky mountains, we had an uneventful but enjoyable trip back to Wilmore. Burt arrived home from his summer travels with many pictures and interesting stories about what happened in the various countries he had visited. He enrolled at the University of Kentucky, Lexington, KY, majoring in history and the Arabic language.

I carried a heavy teaching load during the 1960-1961 school year, including two basic Old Testament courses, Hebrew language, a course on biblical archaeology and a course on Jeremiah.

As a family, our extra-curricular projects centered about committee work related to a new church building for the local Free Methodist Church, and preparations for Nellie and Ralph's wedding that was scheduled for June 23, 1961. Being a very good seamstress, Maria spent many busy hours cutting out the pattern and sewing a lovely wedding dress.

The church building was not quite completed when the wedding date arrived, but with only the organ installed in the sanctuary, we teamed together to construct a temporary wooden trellis on the platform. We decorated the trellis with ivy vines and wild roses. The bare wood of the floor in the pulpit area was visible, so we rented green funeral grass from a funeral home to cover the platform. Folding chairs were borrowed from the seminary and set in rows in the sanctuary area. Ralph's sister-in-law played the organ, the new pastor of the church; Rev. Clyde Van Valin sang. Ralph's brother, Rev. Eugene Kester, and I conducted the wedding ceremony. The reception was held in the church fellowship hall. Our pastor was able to sneak Nellie and Ralph away from the house and deliver them to a hotel in Lexington where the newlyweds spent their honeymoon night.

A few days later, we received a telephone call informing us that my brother Ralph's wife, Opal, had been killed in an automobile accident near Mason City, Iowa. I immediately boarded a train and arriving in Mason City, I found Ralph and his four children shattered by the tragedy of losing a wife and a mother. I did my best to comfort them and returned to Wilmore with a heavy heart. Fortunately, the family came through the ordeal as a unit and two years later Ralph married a widow named Polly, a devout Christian.

A week later Nellie and Ralph left in a new car to set up their home in McMinnville, Oregon, where Ralph had a job as a sixth grade teacher in a public school.

Within a two-week period, our family experienced the joys of a wedding celebration and the deep sorrow of a tragedy. The Lord helped us through the events.

During the school years of 1961-1962 and 1962-1963, Asbury Seminary had an increase in enrollment, and more faculty, was needed. I needed a colleague who could share the regular teaching load and also make possible a Master of Theology curriculum in the Old Testament.

I was impressed with the academic work of a former classmate, Dennis Kinlaw, who graduated from Asbury Seminary in 1947. He had a rich background as an evangelist and as a pastor, but also had continued his graduate studies at Brandeis University in Boston under the tutelage of Dr. Cyrus Gordon. Dennis quickly agreed to join the faculty.

From March 10-14, 1963, I lectured at the Gunter Air Force Base near Montgomery, AL. The chaplain was Rev. Harry B. Ansted, the son of the president of Wessington Springs College while Maria and I were students there. He was also a classmate at Asbury Theological Seminary for two years.

At the convocation that opened the fall semester of 1963, Dennis and five other men were welcomed as new faculty members. The student body now numbered 363 and the faculty numbered thirty. Most of them possessed, or would soon possess, academic doctoral degrees from major universities in the United States and Europe.

My next sabbatical leave from my teaching duties was scheduled for the second semester and summer of 1964. Maria and I were captivated by the possibility of teaching for short periods of time at a series of mission schools around the world. The more we prayed about the trip, the more we were sure the trip was in God's will for us. I asked the seminary administration to make this trip an approved sabbatical project. The seminary's policy was that a professor on sabbatical would receive full salary and receive a limited allotment for travel.

I received approval and made contact with the Free Methodist Missionary Board about teaching at several mission colleges and seminaries in various countries. We also contacted the World Gospel Mission Society and the Oriental Missionary Society. By early fall of 1963, a full schedule of teaching had been organized and necessary funds were available.

One of our pressing problems was what to do about providing a place for our thirteen-year-old David to stay while we were gone. Burt and Nellie agreed that Maria should go with me on this trip. Burt would no longer be home, for he had earned his college degree and had won a government scholarship to study Arabic at the University of Michigan. In August, we moved him to an apartment near that school's campus in Ann Arbor, Michigan.

Our prayers were answered when Nellie and Ralph offered to move to Wilmore. Ralph found a teaching job in Midway, KY. Ralph signed a contract, and Nellie and Ralph moved in with us in July. They would take care of David and the house while we were on the trip.

Having never been on an ocean liner, we decided to book passage on the Leonardo da Vinci, a luxury liner owned by Italy. Fare for two of us from New York to Naples, Italy was cheaper than plane tickets to Rome. We were able to get two tickets on the ship that would leave New York City on Christmas Eve, 1963. Using KLM, the Royal Dutch Airlines, as our basic airplane ticket agent, we obtained a book of tickets that would take us from Rome, Italy to Athens, Greece, to Cairo, Egypt, to Beirut, Lebanon, to Nagpur, India, to Madras, India, to Calcutta, India, to Hong Kong, to Taipei, Taiwan, to Tokyo, Japan, to Osaka, Japan. Our return trip would begin at Osaka to Tokyo, then on to Hong Kong, to Cairo, Egypt, to Beirut, to Amman, Jordan, from Lod, Israel, to Amsterdam, the Netherlands, to Lexington, KY, where we would arrive on the evening of August 15,1964.

How would we travel from Wilmore to New York City? We decided to go the cheap way. We would take a bus to Cincinnati, Ohio and a train to New York City. We did not anticipate a snowstorm that left eight inches of snow on the ground. Ralph, Nellie and David were able to take us to the bus station in Lexington on the morning of December 23rd, but the Greyhound bus scheduled to take us to Cincinnati was snow bound in Bowling Green, KY. The company found another bus that would get us to Cincinnati only a short time before the train left for New York City. A taxi hurried us from the bus depot to the train station and we were able to board the train five minutes before it left the station.

We arrived in New York City in the forenoon of the next day. We telephoned our family in Wilmore, telling that we had arrived safely. After the call, Maria began to cry. I asked why and she said she was homesick and wished David was with us. She didn't know whether she wanted to continue the trip or not. I comforted her and she soon consented to board the luxury liner at four o'clock. We were assigned to a small room, called a cabin, on the tourist deck. Imagine our surprise when we found on a small table a lovely bouquet of white mums and red carnations with a card stating it was from the congregation of the Wilmore Free Methodist Church. A card assured us of the thoughts and prayers of everyone in the church, while we ministered on several mission fields. Beside the vase was a pile of ten cards from seminary administrators and faculty. We were thrilled our friends would be praying for us.

We had time before the seven o'clock dinner to make a limited tour of the huge ship. Crowds of passengers were everywhere, though we found later the snowstorm had kept many travelers from getting to New York City and to the ship. At six o'clock, the ship was pulled from the dock and pointed south. With sirens blaring and Christmas decorations fluttering, we moved through the harbor to the Atlantic Ocean.

The dining room for tourist class occupants was huge. Waiters were dressed in formal uniforms, the menu folders were fancy and the food offered was appealing. The food we chose was delicious and we could ask for second servings. Several other passengers sat at our round table and we enjoyed getting acquainted. We found the single beds in our cabin were comfortable, so sleep came soon.

We awoke and went to breakfast, but the liner swayed in a rough sea. Both of us soon became seasick and went back to bed. We awoke just before noon lunch and carefully holding to ropes attached to the corridor walls we were able to get to the dining room. We told our waiter we didn't feel well and he suggested we eat a steak to settle our stomachs. It worked! The waiter advised us to order steak for breakfast if we felt seasick. We did this more than once. Among our new friends were Rev. and Mrs. Krist of Dearborn, MI. We spent a good deal of time together on the voyage. A porter told us there was a larger, empty cabin near us. We could move into it at no extra charge. We quickly had our belongings moved.

As we sailed further south into the Atlantic, the wind subsided and the sea became smoother. We spent more time on the deck and at excellent concerts each night. Rev. Krist and I decided to ask the captain of the ship whether we could have a Protestant service on Sunday. He agreed and suggested we have it in the lounge on the Cabin class deck. Thirty attended an informal service that I led and Rev. Krist preached. After the service, several who had rooms on the Cabin deck invited us to an afternoon tea.

At four o'clock on December 30th, the liner docked at the port of Las Palmos on one of the Canary Islands. The Krists and we ate at a restaurant and did some shopping. The prices were very reasonable. We headed north on a smooth sea and were due at Lisbon, Portugal the next forenoon, which was New Year's Day. Maria found excellent linen cloths at very cheap prices at tables on the dock. The Krists and we had a full day roaming the city of Lisbon by taxi. A multitude of Christmas lights were strung all over the business section. The beauty of the city impressed us. All too soon, the day ended. We decided to watch our cash balance carefully.

By noon the next day, we were docked at Gibraltar. It was a duty-free port and we yielded to temptation and bought things for next Christmas. We sailed overnight in the Mediterranean Sea headed for Sicily. All the next day we saw the north shore of Algeria. A Canadian lady we met at the Sunday service invited us to the Cabin deck for tea. We had a delightful visit. The sea was rough, so a breakfast of beefsteak helped settle our stomachs.

We docked at Palermo about noon and with the Krists, we walked through the business section. We stopped at a restaurant and asked for American coffee with our meal. To our surprise, the coffee cups were large and filled with very strong coffee. The waiter thought we wanted a lot of coffee. Overnight we sailed to Naples and passed through customs early in the forenoon.

One of our fellow professors at Asbury had suggested we book a room at a Methodist orphanage, called Casa Materna, in Naples, which we did. We walked about a mile to an archaeological site where the remains of a city called Hercalanium was totally covered by ash from an eruption of Mt. Vesuvius in 79 A.D. After several hours, we returned to the orphanage, ate a good supper and retired. Our room was in a stone building and had no source for heat. The night was chilly and the blankets were inadequate. We did not sleep well.

The next forenoon we boarded a train for Rome and spent the forenoon marveling at the beauty of the country. The farms were small and there was little evidence of modern equipment on them. The many villages looked in poor repair and dirty. We arrived in Rome at noon and checked in at the Columbus Hotel located within a block from the Vatican. We spent several hours visiting remains of ancient Rome and when we returned to the hotel, we found that Rev. and Mrs. Krist had arrived. We also learned Pope Paul would arrive from a trip to the Holy Land and his procession would go past our hotel. The Pope was late but we enjoyed watching the excitement and colorfulness of the procession as he returned to the Vatican. We enjoyed taking Rev. and Mrs. Krist on a tour of the ruins of ancient Rome and also a tour of the huge St. Peters Cathedral, the Library and the Sistine Chapel. We took our friends to the train on which they would travel to Genoa later that afternoon.

The next afternoon, January 8th, we boarded an Air France plane headed for Athens, Greece. It was Maria's first ride in a jet and she was thrilled how quiet and smooth it was. The plane was behind schedule so we landed in Athens too late to fulfill a seven p.m. preaching appointment at the OMS mission headed by Rev. Pappas. We took a taxi to a hotel and the next morning notified Rev. Pappas of our problem getting to Athens too late for the meeting. Nevertheless, He and his wife were gracious. Previous speakers had the same problem. They picked us up and took us by car to tour the ancient sites in Athens. That evening I preached at the mission as scheduled, with Rev. Pappas translating my English into Modern Greek.

The next forenoon, January 10th, we took a bus downtown to find a post office so we could ship some small boxes to Nellie and Ralph. A Greek who knew English led us to the post office and we found it was not easy to go through all the paper work necessary to ship packages. We found a nearby restaurant and had a Greek meal then returned to the mission to pack our bags. We went to the airport late in the afternoon and boarded another Air France jet for Cairo, Egypt. Rev. Norman Cooke, a Canadian missionary, met us and took us to the Windsor Hotel.

During the forenoon, we had to register with the Egyptian government. All our documents came back to us except our health certificate, which the authorities admitted they received but could not find. Before we left Egypt, we had to get a replacement from our doctor in Wilmore. Our car ride south to Assuit was comfortable, for the bright sun produced a temperature that rose to the upper 70's. We followed the impressive Nile River along which were many small villages filled with people. Fertile soil and extensive irrigation produced plentiful crops. At the end of the day, we enjoyed a beautiful sunset framed by palm trees and a camel caravan. It was a long ride and by the end of the trip, I was beginning to feel a bit ill. I ate a bountiful supper anyway, but my stomach revolted and I had to run to the bathroom to get rid of it. I had a miserable night.

The missionary residence in Assuit was scheduled to be our home for the next three weeks. Rev. and Mrs. Cooke were the leaders of the mission team, which included two single ladies, Miss Naomi Lindsay and Miss Irma Ergezinger, also Canadians. Besides teaching duties at the Wesley Theological College located in Assuit, this team worked with local churches and their pastors, all of whom were Egyptians. The residence was a concrete building with a propane gas heater that was turned on very seldom. The sleeping rooms were on the second floor. Though warm outside in the afternoons, the interior was chilly so we borrowed sweaters and slept under heavy blankets at night. Maria soon learned that washed clothes were taken to the flat rooftop where the hot sun dried them quickly.

I was scheduled to speak the next day, Sunday, at a nearby Free Methodist church, but the illness had made me too weak to do so, however, I was able to bring greetings that afternoon to the congregation of about fifty people. That evening I was able to preach at a Presbyterian chapel. I preached many times, with the aid of an interpreter, while in Egypt where the spoken language is Arabic.

Maria and I immediately noticed that the Egyptians worshipped differently than Americans or Canadians. The Egyptians often entered their plain concrete sanctuary a half hour before the announced time and began to sing and pray until the ministers arrived. They sat in roughly made pews but the women and men were separated. Facing them from the platform, the men and boys could be seen seated on one side (usually the right side) and the women and girls on the left side, Often a wooden partition went down the center of the aisle. The men would take the lead and the women followed along. I found it easy to preach to them and they responded well. After the service, the entire congregation would stay another half hour to an hour, singing and praying. Everyone was dressed in long robes, usually three or four robes thick. The people were friendly and emotionally uninhibited.

On Tuesdays, Wednesdays and Thursdays, my task was to teach two Old Testament classes and give a devotional message at each chapel service. The Presbyterians had a Bible School in the city also and the faculty brought their students to the classes I taught. There were between forty and fifty students and all my lectures were translated into Arabic. This schedule lasted three weeks and I thoroughly enjoyed my contacts with the Egyptian students and faculty. The two missionary ladies kept Maria busy helping them prepare Bible school materials and speaking to groups of women and young ladies. She enjoyed being an assistant.

Several nights a week Rev. Cooke and I would visit nearby Free Methodist churches and I would preach to fifty to two hundred people. On weekends, we would go farther distances to preach at a Free Methodist church and also visit important archaeological sites.

The first weekend we left early Friday morning to go by car to Luxor. For half the way the road was a narrow asphalt strip on top of the dike that followed the Nile River and kept it from flooding the country-side during the summer. People, leading donkeys and camels loaded with produce, also used the road, so travel was quite slow. The scenery was fascinating. We stopped at Abydos to visit the remains of ancient temples and tombs of Pharaohs Seti I and Rameses II. Artwork on walls and ceilings were still in good condition and amazingly well done. These remains date from the Thirteenth to Fourteenth centuries B.C. South of Abydos the road became little more than a dirt path but the animal traffic was much less. We arrived in Luxor about five o'clock. I preached at the Free Methodist church that evening and we lodged at the Presbyterian American Mission. The two denominations worked very well together in Egypt.

The next morning, January 18th, we all took a horse and buggy ride to the Nile River and crossed it by boat. On the west side, two old Chevys served as taxis to take us to the Valley of the Kings where a number of Egyptian Pharaohs were buried over a period of many centuries. All the tombs had been dug deep into the cliffs of the valley. The first tomb we visited belonged to King Tut (Pharaoh Tutankhamen) and we entered three or four others. All the tombs were empty, but all the walls and ceilings were richly decorated with chiseled figures and images, which have retained their rich coloring. We visited the restored temple of Egypt's famous woman Pharaoh, Hatshepsut. The temple had been cut into the stone cliff and an elaborate facade of decorated pillars gave the building a measure of elegance. An image of the Queen, dressed like a man, can be seen carved on the side of a large pillar deep inside the temple.

We returned to Luxor and Rev. Cooke took all of us by car to nearby Karnack to view the remains of several large temples that were being restored. They were amazing. We next went to the remains of a large temple at Thebes mostly built by Rameses II. For everyone in the party, the day had been eventful.

The next day was Sunday and I preached at the Free Methodist church at eight thirty a.m. and also at three thirty p.m. to a congregation of about sixty-seventy people at each service. The Egyptians were not as emotional in this church. Afterwards, we visited the Chicago House staffed by specialists in preserving and translating the inscriptions on surfaces of both the tombs and the temples. They gave us a tour of their library and explained their work. The next day we returned to Assuit. It was a great trip, but we felt quite tired.

After classes on Thursday, Rev. Cooke and I went to a city called Timah, about twenty miles away, to attend a regional ministers conference. I spoke in the afternoon and evening. About fifty Egyptian pastors were present in the afternoon but about five hundred people attended the evening service. On Friday, we went back to Timah to speak in the forenoon, afternoon and evening services, with about the same attendance. At the end of the evening service, the singing and praying continued for an hour. During this week Maria enjoyed working with the lady missionaries and visiting at several Egyptian homes.

Saturday was sightseeing day again; this time to Tel el-Amarna, the capital city of Pharaoh Akhenaton who reigned in the Fourteenth century B.C. The road we took was on the west side of the Nile River so we had to board a sailboat called a falluca. On the eastside was a small village of mud brick houses. The people were obviously very poor. There was very little left of the ancient city, for it too had been built mostly of mud brick. The site is famous because in recent years hardened clay tablets have been found in the ruins on which were inscribed in several languages, the diplomatic letters that were sent and received by the Pharaoh. A little over two miles east, burial tombs had been dug into the soft stone of a cliff. We all mounted mules, which were led by teenage boys who continually begged for money. We were glad to get back to the riverbank and sail across the Nile.

Sunday we returned to the Ministers conference at Timah, so I could preach at a morning service, which lasted about three hours, and an afternoon service that was also lengthy. Maria and Mrs. Cooke spent the afternoon at a school operated by a Plymouth Brethren lady missionary whose home country was Holland. Maria had a great time visiting with her.

Monday was another sightseeing day. This time only Rev. Cooke and I went to a place called Malawi, which is noted for sizable underground cemeteries for mummified monkeys and birds called Ibis. These creatures had been worshiped as gods and goddesses and had been carefully preserved. The mummies were not a pretty sight and I could understand why the lady missionaries suggested Maria stay with them in Assuit. On the way home, we stopped to visit a Coptic monastery called Deir el-Maharra. It was an impressive building. The place is special to the Coptic Christians, because they claim Joseph, Mary and

Jesus stopped there when they fled from King Herod in Palestine (Matt. 2:13-15).

Wednesday, January 29th, was my last day lecturing in classes at Wesley Theological School. I also preached two nights in nearby Free Methodist churches and then a second Ministers conference, this time in Assuit, on Thursday, with about 40 pastors present. I preached at two services that day and Friday forenoon and afternoon. That evening I preached at another nearby Free Methodist church to nearly 200 people. On the way home a most unusual thing happened. Two Egyptian pastors in the back seat of Rev. Cooke's car began to talk excitedly in Arabic. I asked what was going on. Rev. Cooke replied, "Do you see these rain drops on the windshield and the flashes of lightning in the northwest. Rain is a rare event in Egypt, and I don't have windshield wipers. I had to take them off, because boys would steal them. This is the first time I've needed them since coming to Egypt." We had to stop so he could wipe the dust, which had turned to mud, from the windshield. The sprinkles stopped but began briefly again after we got to Assuit. On Saturday, we drove to Port Said in northeastern Egypt. This beautiful city was located at the spot where the Suez Canal joins the Mediterranean Sea.

We were housed in the Peniel American Mission, associated with the World Gospel Mission. Early forenoon the next morning, Sunday, I preached to over 100 at the mission chapel. Two-thirds of them were women and girls. The men and women were separated, but we noticed the lack of a partition between them. Another difference with the southern churches was the presence of piano accompaniment to the singing. The congregation was very attentive but there was very little expression of emotion during the service, and there was no singing or praying before and after the service. The people were, nonetheless, very attentive. In the afternoon, we crossed the Suez Canal by ferry to Port Fuad to preach in a Free Methodist church. There were 125 present and again no partition. We enjoyed a warm worship service.

On Monday we returned through a stiff wind and drifting sand as we crossed the desert areas between Port Said and Cairo. We were scheduled to stay in the Windsor Hotel during this last week in Egypt. In the afternoon, Maria went shopping with Mrs. Cooke, and Rev. Cooke and I visited some huge Islamic mosques and an ancient fortress in the city. All of us ate a delicious meal at the Nile Hilton Hotel, our favorite restaurant in Cairo.

Tuesday was a day of sightseeing at the giant pyramids, dating from the Third millennium B.C. The three major pyramids are on a sandy hill west of Cairo. They are truly amazing. Burt had been here in the summer of 1960 and had climbed to the top of one of them. We did something different. We climbed up a passageway inside the largest pyramid to a fairly large, but empty, burial room. It was eerie. We got to ride some camels and we visited the large Cairo museum. That evening I preached to an attentive congregation at one of the several Free Methodist churches in the city. Maria was informed she was scheduled to speak to a group of women the next day.

A third ministers conference began Wednesday forenoon at one of the Free Methodist churches in Cairo with about seventy present from seven Protestant denominations. I spoke on Old Testament topics three times that day and the next day. Maria spoke at several women's meetings. One of her assignments was at a Free Methodist church in a poor section of the city, but the fifty women present were very appreciative of Maria's message. We had to rush back to the evening service of the conference by taxi. It was a wild ride through narrow streets, dashing between people, camels and donkeys, with the horn almost constantly blowing. We made it on time. In each of the three evening services, between 500 and 600 people were present. Maria spoke to another group of 65 women on Friday afternoon. We were exhausted by the time the conference was over, but it had been an exciting three days.

Saturday, the Cooke's took us by car to Alexandra on the Mediterranean Sea. The irrigated farmland was a rich green with abundant crops. This was the western edge of the land of Goshen of Moses' time. We also caught a glimpse of some of the pain and joy of missionary life. Cooke's two children, a boy and a girl of pre-teen age, went to a Presbyterian school in Alexandria and this visit was one of the few times the parents and children had seen each other since September. Tears and joy mixed easily as they met. The children stayed close to their parents all weekend. That afternoon we drove to ancient sites, and then to the opulent palace of King Farrouk, when he ruled Egypt a few decades ago.

On Sunday, I preached at several thriving Free Methodist churches, one of which had a congregation of over 300. At one church, the pastor gave me a copy of a beautiful bust of Queen Nefertiti, the famous wife of Pharaoh Akhenaton. It has had a prominent place on my study desk through the years.

Monday, February 10th, was our last day in Egypt. After returning to Cairo, Maria and I packed our bags and the Cooke's took us to the airport. We have many pleasant memories of our visit to Egypt. We visited only a few of the nearly 100 Free Methodist churches. I spoke sixty-two times, eighteen at three minister's conferences. Maria spoke at least twenty times. We remembered often in prayer our Christian brothers and sisters in Egypt.

When we arrived at Beirut, Lebanon, Rev. Reilley, of the World Gospel Mission, met us and took us to his residence. In the evening, Mr. Babikian, principal of the Mission school in the suburbs of the city, came to discuss our speaking schedule for the several days we would be in Beirut. They planned to keep us busy. The next forenoon I spoke at his school. In the afternoon, the Reilleys took us north to the ancient ruins of Byblos, located on a bluff above an excellent port serving the Mediterranean Sea. Extensive excavations have revealed the walls and floors of impressive buildings.

In the Old Testament, Byblos' inhabitants are mentioned once as Gebelites (Joshua 13:5), which means the city was known in ancient times as Gebal. Many centuries later, the Greeks called the city Byblos. Local Arabs now call the place Jebeil. The site has been occupied since about 5,000 B.C. It was destroyed and rebuilt many times, leaving layer upon layer of ruins.

That evening, I preached at the Armenian Brotherhood church. The next forenoon Rev. Reilley took several of us by van over the snow-capped Lebanon mountain range, famous for its majestic cedars, to the remains of ancient Baalbek in the Beqa Valley.

The remains of Greek and Roman temples cover the site completely, so archaeologists have found only a limited number of walls of older temples to bring to light. Primary attention has been focused on restoring Greek and Roman temples. A mammoth temple, 290 feet long and 60 feet wide, overwhelms one with its columns, 62 feet high and seven and one-half feet in diameter. Originally, there were nineteen columns on each side and ten on each end. Many are still standing. Other smaller temples are also impressive.

The next forenoon, February 13th, the Reilleys took us south to the seaports of Tyre and Sidon. During Old Testament times, Phoenician kings ruled these cities. The most famous of these kings was Hiram who provided cedar logs and expert architects, masons and carpenters to help Kings David and Solomon of Israel build a temple and palace in Jerusalem.

That afternoon, we boarded a British Airlines plane for New Delhi, India where we arrived at 5:30 a.m. India time. We were taken to the Swiss Hotel where we slept until noon. We caught up on correspondence and walked to the city post office, doing some sightseeing along the way. At 9:00 p.m. a taxi took us to the Air India office and a bus took us to the airport where we boarded a plane to Nagpur, arriving at 3:00 a.m.

Professor Gaekwad of the faculty of Union Biblical Seminary, Yeotmal, India, and a former student of mine at Asbury Seminary, was waiting to greet us at Nagpur. We shared a cup of hot tea before joining the driver of a seminary car to make the ninety-mile trip to Yeotmal. The road was a narrow asphalt strip with wide dirt shoulders. Already the road was crowded with oxen drawn carts loaded with bales of cotton. The drivers of these oxen reluctantly moved off the asphalt to let us pass.

Professor Gaekwad had a rifle with him and when traffic was light on the road, he would position himself on the roof of the car. He would use a powerful spotlight to survey each side of the road, searching for reflections from animal eyes. He informed us he often shot deer. On this trip, he did not have success.

We arrived at Union Biblical Seminary at about 6:00 a.m. and Mrs. Betty Kline welcomed us warmly. Her husband, Dr. Frank Kline, was away on a trip. He had been President of the seminary for many years and was due to retire, and with Betty, return to the United States. After sleeping most of the day, we met the faculty and spouses at a reception that evening. We were honored with garlands of flowers draped around our necks. The next afternoon we went with some faculty and the members of the student council to a nearby park in the jungle for a picnic. Monkeys were everywhere.

Mrs. Kline had a class that studied the book of Jeremiah and requested that I lecture to the students at each class session for the next two weeks. That evening I showed the student body my slides with maps illustrating Old Testament times in the ancient Near East. I did this several evenings during our three-week stay. I quickly learned I did not need an interpreter, due to a long period of British dominance in India. Almost every educated Indian could understand and speak English. Maria enjoyed the gorgeous dresses of the ladies and girls of India. That evening we ate an Indian dinner at the hostel for women students of the seminary. The food was highly spiced but delicious.

On Friday February 21st, we were taken by car to a rural hospital in the village of Umri. Dr. and Mrs. Yardy of the United States were in charge. Patients from the surrounding area formed waiting lines each day, seeking help for physical illnesses. A busy elementary school was on the crowded compound. Several native Indian physicians, nurses and teachers assisted Dr. Yardy. The hospital and school were founded and funded by the Free Methodist Church. I showed my map slides to the staff on Saturday evening. On Sunday forenoon, I spoke to a Sunday school class, to a group of young people and I preached at the regular morning service in the local Free Methodist church. That evening I showed my slides about Israel.

On Monday forenoon we returned to Union Biblical Seminary where I spoke to the faculty in the afternoon. The next morning I resumed my teaching schedule on the book of Jeremiah and spoke in chapel service. Dr. Kline had returned home and immediately asked Maria to help him with his secretarial work. I also gave several lectures on Old Testament theology to another class. During that week, I lectured or preached twice, sometimes three, times a day. We noticed that in the middle of each day the temperature was quite warm. On Friday, we joined other faculty and spouses in attending a rather elaborate Indian "pot-luck" picnic sponsored by officials and leading citizens of the city of Yeotmal. Everyone was friendly and chatted easily with us. The house mother of the ladies hostel, Mrs. Kamaleson, had been dressing Maria in Indian dresses called saris, and provided an especially beautiful sari for the night.

On Saturday, February 29th, Maria and I spent the forenoon tending to personal needs and the mail, at noon the temperature was 105 degrees so we stayed in the Mission house that was quite cool. In the late afternoon, the seminary ladies of the hostel entertained us at a tea. Mrs. Kamaleson again dressed Maria in a stunning sari. She kept this garment on for a student celebration of the end of the Jeremiah classes for the winter semester. I closed the joyous occasion with a fitting devotional.

At an 8:00 a.m. worship service which all students, faculty and staff attended with their spouses, I preached on "The Wonder that Surrounds the Cross." Late in the afternoon, sixteen students of Mrs. Kline's Jeremiah class came to the Kline's residence to pay honor to her as the regular teacher and to me as guest professor. They conducted a short worship service, served tea and then placed beautiful floral garlands on each of us. They thanked us for coming to Union Theological Seminary.

During the third week, the students took their tests. Dr. Kline had requested that I spend the week in their library to assess the needs in the biblical section for new books and compile a list of books the library staff should obtain. I spent every afternoon in the library and by the end of the week had a lengthy list of needed books. Maria continued to do secretarial work for Dr. Kline. I preached at two student chapel services and one evening devotional hour. Most evenings we were invited to meals at various faculty homes. One meal was at the home of Professor Samudre. He had spent a year at Asbury Seminary and had been in several of my Old Testament classes. He had a lovely family.

Toward the end of the week, good news came to the seminary administration. A letter arrived announcing the seminary had been granted accreditation status in India. Only one other Christian seminary at Seramapore enjoyed this status. Union Biblical Seminary was a top rated school in India. This institution had been established by Dr. Frank Kline as a Bible School in 1939, but as years passed by several evangelical missions felt they needed a school on the seminary level, so the Free Methodist Church agreed to join with the other missions and thus created the Union Biblical Seminary at Yeotmal under the leadership of Dr. Frank Kline. Other mission boards would provide Professors. Over one hundred students, men and women, from all across India and several other countries made up the student body. About a decade ago, the seminary moved its campus to a suburb of Bombay.

On Sunday, March 8th, I assisted in serving communion at the Free Methodist church in Yeotmal in the forenoon and preached to a congregation of over two hundred that evening. Maria and I were honored with floral garlands and the love and prayers of the people. The next afternoon we packed and at ten o'clock p. m. were taken by car to Nagpur to board a plane to Madras. It was the end of a most pleasant and inspiring visit to central India.

We had enjoyed receiving a number of letters from home, from Burt in Michigan, from our mothers in Wisconsin and from Nellie and Ralph. Word from Burt indicated he was enjoying his studies at the university and that he was excited about a relationship with a young lady he met in his Arabic class. Our mothers were doing well and we tried to keep them informed about our activities. The most interesting letters were from Nellie and Ralph, for they reported David was doing well in school. The big news was that Nellie was coming to the end of her pregnancy and was expecting their baby during the second week in March. We had sent her instructions to send a telegram announcing the arrival and provided her with a series of addresses, because we would be only a short time at four locations before we would arrive in Japan. We were praying that all would go well.

We arrived by plane in Madras, India at 5:30 a.m. without sleep during the night. We were able to catch a train to Bangarapet at ten a.m., and soon discovered that traveling by train up the long ascent to that city was not pleasant. The coal-burning locomotive had been purchased from Canada and managed to produce a cloud of black smoke that swirled along the side of the passenger car in which we were riding. The big problem was the temperature that registered about 100 degrees inside the crowded car and there was no air-conditioning. People were opening windows to get some breeze but the smoke came inside too. The ride was miserable.

Bangarapet is located on a high plateau at about 3,000 ft elevation so the temperature did drop some as the train climbed to our destination. South India Bible Institute, operated by World Gospel Mission, was closing its school year with a Spiritual Emphasis Week and I was one of the speakers. A Rev. Dewey met us at the station at 7:00 p.m. and took us to the beautiful campus. We were assigned to stay in the cottage occupied by Rev. and Mrs. Lester Hamilton whom we had known for many years. They had graduated with me at Kleltzing College and were students at Asbury Theological Seminary. I was to team with Dr. Samuel Kamaleson, who had been one of my students at Asbury. He was a native of India and a powerful speaker, as well as a fine bass soloist. He, Maria and I were welcomed with beautiful garlands of flowers.

Dr. Kamaleson began the conference by speaking in the morning chapel to about sixty students. The housemother of the ladies was Miss Zechariah a graduate of Asbury. I spoke that afternoon on Jeremiah and Dr. Kamaleson in the evening. This sequence continued through Saturday noon. Dr. Kamaleson had to return to Madras to preach at his church on Sunday, which was the same day, the Baccalaureate and Commencement services were held. I spoke at both of these occasions. There were twelve graduates. The response of the students to the sermons was attentive and wholehearted.

One of the points of my commencement message was an emphasis on the fact that often a pastor will not know the outcome of sessions with come and go people seeking advice. We must commit them to the Lord's mercies. I illustrated the point with an episode from my early ministry.

In the spring of my first year (1937-38) at Beaver Dam Wisconsin, a young man knocked on the front door of the parsonage. He said he wanted to show me some interesting materials on religion. Quickly I realized his articles for sale were not based on orthodox Christian doctrines or experience. Taken back by my objections, he demanded what were correct doctrines and valid religious experiences.

Picking up a nearby Bible I explained its authority in telling us about God the Creator. I told the birth, life, death, resurrection and ascension of Jesus Christ, our Redeemer from sin, and the transforming power of the Holy Spirit. I mixed into the discussion aspects of my own personal experience and why I was a minister. He questioned me closely, but suddenly grabbed his materials and said he must go. He was soon out the door.

I was dismayed. I turned to Maria and said; 'You know, during all that discussion, I failed to ask him to accept Jesus as his savior. I fear I failed to be an effective minister." Being a good wife, she assured me I had done a good job. Her observation helped, but disappointment was still felt keenly. I supposed I would never see him again.

Five years passed by. A part of my pastoral training was moving from church to church in Wisconsin and Iowa. In the spring of 1943, we were at Cedar Falls. IA. One afternoon I responded to a knock on the front door of the parsonage. A fine looking young man was standing on the porch. He said; "I have come to visit you again. Do you remember me?" His face was a bit familiar, but I could not connect him with any episode. I invited him into the house.

As we sat down, he asked: "Do you recall a youngster who came to your parsonage in Beaver Dam, hoping to sell you some religious literature?"

"Oh yes. I now remember! We had quite a discussion and suddenly you got up and left. What has happened to you since then and how did you find me here?"

"I left so quickly because I feared you would soon convert me! I could not shake your testimony so I bought a cheap New Testament and began reading the gospels before going to bed. One evening I became so burdened I knelt by my bed and accepted Jesus Christ as my Savior. Then I sensed a strong urging to attend a Christian college. I remembered you mentioned attending a Christian college in South Dakota. I decided to return to Beaver Dam and obtain from you information about the college. When I knocked on the door an elderly man appeared and told me you had been transferred to a church in northwestern Wisconsin more than three hundred miles away.

Disappointed, I returned to my selling Bibles and biblical literature. I prayed about my desire to attend college. In a few weeks, I learned that some of my clients were Wesleyan Methodists who had the same beliefs as the Free Methodists. When they learned about my interest in college, they soon had me on my way to a Wesleyan Methodist college. Completing four years of training for ministry, I was ready to be pastor. I learned that a Wesleyan Methodist church northeast of Waterloo, Iowa needed a pastor and I was soon installed. A week ago, I was reading the church page of the Waterloo newspaper and I noticed that a Herbert Livingston was the pastor of the Free Methodist church in Cedar Falls. Immediately I thought, that is much like the name of the pastor in Beaver Dam I met five years ago. I have to find for sure. So here I am."

We had wonderful visit, a time of prayer together and a prospect of future meetings. A few months later, we were appointed to a church several hundred miles to the southeastern part of Iowa. Two years later, I started a ministry in higher education that took me to other parts of the USA. I never met the young pastor again. I completed my sermon and began greeting people in the congregation.

I was shocked when I shook hands with an elderly man to my right, He said;

"That was Rev. Bray you were talking about, was it not?"

I reacted; "I don't think I mentioned his name when I told the story. How would you know who he was?"

With a chuckle, he said: "For many years I have been an evangelist in the Wesleyan Methodist denomination and have held many special meetings in churches in Illinois. Rev Bray is the leader of those churches and I have heard him tell that story several times."

I responded; "This is astounding!" Almost two decades after last seeing Rev. Bray I am receiving an update on his ministry from a man I am meeting for the first time in southeast India!

It was an inspiring week. The next morning I spoke at an alumni meeting of the school and then we took the train back to Madras where we were housed in the St. Christopher Training College for Women.

Two concerns weighted heavily on us as we retired for the night. When we had presented our travel documents to the Ticket Master at the train station at Bangarapet, he informed us our visitor visas to India had just expired and we should have them renewed immediately after we arrived in Madras. We had informed Dr. Kamaleson of our problem and he promised to help us obtain a renewal the next morning, after giving a lecture on Jeremiah at 7:00 a.m. to fifty men. This early morning lecture time continued through Friday. I also preached at the church each evening. During the forenoon, we obtained new visas.

The other concern was lack of a telegram informing us of the birth of Ralph and Nellie's first child, who was due to be born soon. We anxiously opened our mail each day but the week ended without the desired news.

That Tuesday forenoon, Dr. Rigby, principal of the Oriental Missionary Bible School in Madras, came to take both of us to his school. I gave a lecture each forenoon that week to the small student body. Dr. Rigby had been a classmate of mine at Asbury. After lecture sessions each forenoon, he took us sightseeing, especially to historic places connected with Thomas, one of Jesus' disciples, who had come to India and introduced Christianity to Madras, India. We visited Mt. Thomas where he was martyred and the Catholic Church where he was buried. The Christian community he started continued to grow and is now known as the Mar Thoma church.

On several afternoons, we went shopping and sent boxes of items home. The first such afternoon, we learned a valuable lesson about how to shop. We failed to take an umbrella with us. Maria was wearing a new, brightly colored dress. The temperature was at least 100 degrees and we tried to walk from small store to small store as quickly as possible. That first evening, Maria washed her dress and to her dismay, much of the color washed out. The hot sun had destabilized the dye. We were careful to use an umbrella after that.

We had an eventful week nevertheless, and Saturday forenoon we packed our luggage to fly by plane to Calcutta. A member of the Methodist church was the radio operator on the plane and he invited us to come to the cabin where he explained the function of all the instruments. At Calcutta, representatives of the Japan Air Lines took us to a beautiful, modern hotel where they provided our lodging until we boarded their plane the next day. The hotel had wonderful meals and our room was air-conditioned. We thoroughly enjoyed that cool air. In a few days, we discovered we enjoyed it too much. We caught a severe cold.

We arrived at Hong Kong the next day and were met by five missionaries; all of them were my former students. That evening I preached at a Free Methodist church that met on the flat rooftop of a high-rise apartment building. We stayed with Harry and Ruth Winslow. Hong Kong proved to be an overcrowded but exotic city.

The next morning, Monday, March 22nd, we spoke at an Oriental Missionary chapel, and then we were taken to visit a tailor. We were told the tailor could make a dress for Maria and a suit for me, in 24 hours at a very reasonable cost. We selected the cloth and were measured for a proper fit. We visited some rooftop schools and saw the tailor again. He had the suit and dress pieces cut and, using safety pins, adjusted the pieces to fit our bodies. The suit and dress were delivered the next morning. They fit us perfectly. We boarded a plane for Taipei, Taiwan soon after nine o'clock and arrived there about noon.

Rev. James Taylor, Jr., and family were at the airport to meet us. Rev. Taylor is a descendent of the James Hudson Taylor who established the China Inland Missions. James, Jr. had come to Asbury and had taken several of my classes. We all took a China Air Lines plane to Kaohsiung, Taiwan where James Jr. was Principal of the Free Methodist School called at that time Holy Light Seminary. We ate supper at the home of James Jr.'s parents, Rev. and Mrs. James Taylor, Sr. who also had fled to Taiwan due to Japan's conquest of China.

I was scheduled to speak a number of times that week, which was Holy Week, but a bad cold almost robbed me of speech. Fortunately, translators were a big help. I spoke loud enough for them to hear me and they translated my words into Chinese. I told the congregations, the translators were my loudspeakers. I spoke to about forty students that first evening and early the next forenoon, afternoon and evening. I also showed slides of the Holy Land that evening. The next forenoon and early afternoon, I lectured at the school. Not bad for a person who was almost speechless!

Mrs. Taylor, Sr. had a special assignment for me that Thursday evening. A short distance south of Kaohsiung there was a growing church that served a small group of Christians who were natives of Taiwan. The bus included us, the Taylors, a student who was a member of the mountain church and Miss Dorothy Raber, another former student of mine. The last mile of the trip we had to walk up a narrow dirt road to the church. Almost 200 mountain people met us at the church. The spirited singing of the congregation was supported by several drums and Chinese type guitars. The speaking arrangement was interesting. I still had a bad cold so I spoke just loud enough for my interpreters to hear me. The student who was a member of the church translated each sentence into the local dialect and Mrs. Taylor, Sr. translated the same sentence into Mandarin, for in the congregation there were immigrants from main land China. That meant the sermon went slowly. A local choir of young people sang a hymn in the local dialect. By this time, it was getting dark and the church had no electricity so they lit a dozen or more candles. The service concluded with a most impressive communion service. With the aid of a lantern, we walked down the mountain to the bus and we were soon in Kaohsiung.

Good Friday, March 27th, was travel day. After breakfast we went to the railway station and found faculty and students of Holy Light Seminary gathered to say good-bye and sing in Chinese, "God be with you till we meet again." The views of workers in rice paddies and of the picturesque villages caused the trip to Taichung seem much too short. Faculty of the Oriental Missionary Society School met us and took us to its campus. I lectured to about twenty students in the afternoon and preached a Good Friday sermon in the evening. A communion service conducted by a Chinese pastor was impressive. Four of the faculty members were graduates of Asbury and two of them were my former students. The next forenoon I lectured on the Dead Sea Scrolls and in the afternoon some of the faculty took us sightseeing. At six p.m. they bade us God speed as we boarded a train to Taipei where Rev. James Taylor Jr. met us at the station and took us to the lovely Omea hotel.

Because Rev. Taylor Jr. was well known in Taipei, he had been able to secure in advance special tickets to attend an Easter service at a Methodist church. The President of Taiwan, Chiang Kai Shek, and his wife worshiped at this church and the President was scheduled to preach that morning. The occasion was very special. About 120 were present at the service. Most were high-level Chinese officials and foreign dignitaries. We saw a number of American military people there. President Chiang Kai Shek spoke fluently in Chinese as we read an English translation of the message. Rev. Taylor, Jr. then took us to the opulent home of C.Y. Chang, Chairman of the Board of the Aluminum Corporation of Taiwan. We had a wonderful meal and an earnest conversation about Christian matters.

After we returned to the hotel we were met by the Principal of the Nazarene Seminary and I preached at a Nazarene church to about 70 people. We stayed overnight at the Nazarene Seminary. I preached at the seminary chapel the next forenoon. We were taken on a sightseeing trip around Taipei and to the airport where we expected to board a plane at 2:45 p.m. for Tokyo, Japan. I was scheduled to speak at a commencement service at an Oriental Missionary school near Tokyo the next forenoon.

We were disappointed when we heard the audio system announce that the plane we were to board had engine trouble at Okinawa and would be delayed until the next day. All the passengers were taken to a hotel to stay overnight. We were taken back to the airport at four o'clock the next afternoon. We arrived at the Tokyo airport at 10:45 p.m. and were met by five American missionaries and a Japanese pastor and wife. Most of them had been my former students. We were taken to an Oriental Missionary Society school about twenty miles from Tokyo. We were exhausted. The next forenoon we took the train back to Tokyo where a missionary couple met us and took us on a sightseeing tour of Tokyo. It is an amazing city, especially the Imperial Palace. We returned to the O.M.S. school for a late supper and were most happy to have a good night's sleep. We had one keen disappointment. No word from Wilmore announcing a new grandchild.

Early the next morning, April 2nd, I returned to Tokyo by train to give two lectures at a Wesleyan Methodist Bible School. A lady missionary took me to the train station and promised to telephone the O.M.S. school when my train would arrive at its last station on the route. The principal of the school was supposed to be there to meet me. When I arrived at the station the Principal was not there. I waited for over an hour and became worried for it would soon be dark. It was getting quite cool, and the train station had closed for the day. I thought I had received a small card that morning with the name of the school and its telephone number but I could not find it. What was I to do?

Just as it got dark, a station wagon came roaring into the parking lot. It was the principal who was very happy I had not wandered off and become lost. It seems the lady missionary in Tokyo had forgotten to call the principal. When no word came to the school about me, the Principal called the missionary I had been with during the day and found out I had been on the last train to go out to this station. We joined in thanking God for His watchful care. We sped out to the school. I ate a quick supper and preached at the evening service. What a day!

I was to give one lecture at the school on Friday, but I knew I had a heavy schedule on the weekend. I was taken sightseeing on Saturday and closed the day by attending a special dinner put on by the Japan Holiness Conference that was meeting at the school. It was my privilege to preach that evening to the assembled ministers of this conference. The Principal of the school took Maria and me by car to stay overnight at the Wesleyan Methodist Bible School where the annual conference of the ministers of the Immanuel Gospel Mission was meeting in Tokyo. On Sunday afternoon, I preached a mission sermon to over one thousand people. Several missionaries took Maria and me to the Tokyo Hilton Hotel for a delicious sukiyaki chicken dinner in an exotic setting.

The next morning, April 6th, we boarded an early morning train, called the Kadoma, for Osaka. The train was clean, electric and very fast. At times, we could see Mt. Fuji, the highest mountain in Japan. There were many pine trees and the plum and cherry trees were in full bloom. The delicious lunch cost one dollar for each of us. We arrived in Osaka at 1:30 p.m. and were met by three Japanese pastors and an American missionary. Osaka was the location of the Osaka Christian College and Theological Seminary supported by the Japanese Free Methodist Church. As we were unpacking our luggage for the first time in a month, we received our mail and were overjoyed to find a letter announcing the birth of Karen Kae on March 21st, at Central Baptist Hospital in Lexington, KY. All was well with mother and child. Thank God the wait was over. We found out later our son-in-law, Ralph, had sent a telegram to us in India. It was another week before it caught up with us.

We had agreed to teach at the college and seminary during their spring quarter that would end the last week of June. The resident missionaries, Dr. and Mrs. Snider, were Canadians and had spent seven years teaching at the school without a furlough. Their replacement, Dr. and Mrs. Parsons from the USA, could not come until August. We had agreed to fill in the gap. The Snider's were scheduled to fly home on April 15th, so, for several days they took us to the registration office and showed us where to buy groceries, where to do our banking, and introduced us to the resident Japanese leaders of the school and the church. We would live in the missionary residence on the college campus. The next day we wrote letters and rested.

On April 11th we attended the first college chapel service of the spring quarter. The Snider's were given a farewell gift and we were introduced and welcomed. There were about 450 students present. Most were girls preparing to be teachers. That evening a dozen seminary students gave farewell testimonies in honor of Dr. and Mrs. Snider and a cordial welcome to us. Maria had been assigned to teach English as a second language to twelve girls and two boys. They would meet one hour each day, five days each week. I had been assigned to teach three different Old Testament classes (Old Testament Theology, Biblical Archaeology and the Book of Jeremiah) three times, a total of nine hours, each week to about twenty seminary students. Japanese pastors in the area took turns translating my lectures into Japanese to the students. I had brought overhead transparencies and 2 x 2 slides to illustrate my lectures. Both of us thoroughly enjoyed our classes. The students were courteous, eager and appreciative.

In addition to my teaching responsibilities, I spoke in chapel several times each month, gave prayer meeting devotionals and preached on Sundays in Free Methodist churches. Maria spoke about aspects of Christian living to student groups and women groups in these churches. Everyone loved her.

After the Sniders left for home on April 15th, we settled down for our almost three month stay in Japan. The residence floors were covered with typical Japanese tatami mats made of tightly packed straw. We decided to follow Japanese custom and sleep on these mats and found them comfortable. Frequently students, some from other nearby Christian schools would stop by to visit. They insisted we talk with them in English. Some students would take us sightseeing on Saturdays. Everyday provided new and exciting experiences. The days flew by quickly, and we enjoyed the letters from home that kept us posted about the growth of our new granddaughter.

Several memorable events happened outside of Osaka. On May 6th, we went by train to Nagoya to attend the dedication service of a new Free Methodist church. This church was started and nurtured by Rev. Jacob De Shazer who in World War II had served as an airman on the first US plane to bomb Tokyo. His plane had run out of fuel over China and the crew had been captured and imprisoned by Japanese forces that occupied China at that time. While in prison he yielded his life to Jesus and after his release, he visited Japan as a missionary. This church was one of the fruits of his labors.

Another event was a weeklong visit to Sapporo. The Methodist missionaries at this city were Rev. and Mrs. Evan Adams. Evan had graduated from the seminary with me in 1948.

Osaka Christian College and Theological Seminary had a spring break May 16th-25th so we traveled by plane, train and ferry to Sapporo on May 16th. The weather and scenery of Hokkaido Island is like Minnesota and Wisconsin and snow even remained in patches on the higher mountains. Yet, the island also reminded us very much of Kentucky, for thoroughbred horses, purchased in Kentucky, were on many of the farms. Evan, Joy and children quickly made us feel at home and put us to work distributing pamphlets about the services at which I would be preaching and showing slides of Israel. The important event of the week was a gathering of missionaries of a number of denominations at Evan's church. I spoke several times to a group of about forty people. We had good fellowship together. I also preached at the church in both services on Sunday. On Monday, we flew back to Osaka, ready to continue our teaching responsibilities. The trip was an enjoyable vacation.

A ministers conference of Japanese Free Methodist pastors and families met at a beautiful resort at the foot of a low mountain range about twenty miles west of Osaka. My assignment was to serve as the main lecturer and preacher. The conference was scheduled for June 8th, 9th and 10th and about fifty people were present. My lectures centered on a brief study of the prophet Jeremiah and showing slides of the Holy Land. It was an inspiration to speak to such an appreciative audience.

One night two of the Japanese leaders, the American missionary, Rev. Overland, and we were taken to the luxurious home of a Christian family who lived in the resort. The second night the Buddhist mother of a pastor's wife took us under her care. She first took us by taxi to a beautiful park nearby and then announced she was providing rooms in a richly appointed hotel for us and the same leaders and missionary. She told us she owned a factory in Osaka that made doors for several large automobile factories in the USA. On several visits to these factories, she had been royally treated by the corporation officers and now she wanted to show her appreciation by giving us a special treat. She placed us in a luxury room with lovely appointments and a large Japanese bathtub with very hot water. Maria and I had a wonderful time enjoying this lady's hospitality. We left that conference feeling special.

We were keenly aware that our time in Osaka was rapidly coming to an end. We would be boarding a plane the 23rd. The Free Methodists in Osaka and at the school were also aware of this fact, so during this final week Maria's students and my students honored us with carefully planned farewell parties. Pastors and wives also held special green tea ceremonies for us and gave us gifts that we have always cherished. All month we had been in frequent correspondence with Ralph and Nellie and Dr. George Turner about the possibility of our fourteen year old son, David, meeting us in Cairo, Egypt and continue with us for six weeks visiting the Middle East and the Netherlands. David would travel with Dr. Turner's tour group to Cairo to join us.

The day before we left Osaka, Maria's English class came to our residence for a farewell party. The class wanted to make a recording of Maria reading stories and poems they had selected from their meager supply of English literature. They wanted to listen to her voice and repeat words as they listened later to tapes. This she did gladly. They did not want me to read for the recording! The students joined in singing English songs with Maria.

Late in the afternoon several of the young men and women left, saying they would be back shortly. They returned with food and a small stove with several burners that were fired with bottled gas. They placed the stove on the dining table, following Japanese practice, and lit the burners. What great food! The students had Maria sit in a chair at a side of the room. I was amazed and thrilled as I saw the students, one by one, kneel at Maria's knees, kiss her hands and tearfully say goodbye. The students asked me to pray for them, which I did gladly. The occasion was a touching example of how the reserved Japanese could express their emotions beautifully.

We had a wonderful time visiting the mission fields for five months. At Asbury, we became acquainted with a number of students from foreign lands. As we ministered in several countries, we found many of them in positions of leadership and serving their people. We also worked with a number of missionaries who also were serving the Lord effectively. We are thankful we had a small part in training them for such service in the Lord's work.

Finally, our bags were packed and we were ready to leave Japan. Bishop Oda and two Japanese pastors took us to the airport on Saturday, June 27th. When we checked in at the desk, we were jolted by a surprise. We were told the first cholera shot had expired its six month period of effectiveness. We could not board the plane until we received a new shot. The doctor and nurse normally on duty at the airport had gone home at noon, because it was Saturday. One of the pastors phoned several nearby hospitals and was told the same thing.

Finally, a Christian hospital five miles away said the doctor would wait until we got there. One of the pastors took us in a car across two four-lane highways and two railway lines. It took twenty minutes to go the five miles. The doctor gave us a shot and a certificate to validate it and we hurried back to the airport. The scheduled time of departure for our plane that came from Tokyo was only a half hour away. We were relieved to see the plane on the tarmac, and were informed it would be leaving an hour late. The Cathay Pacific Airlines got to Hong Kong at two o'clock in the morning.

As we were passing through customs, we were told our new cholera shot had a problem. Technically, the vaccine would not be effective until six days after the injection. The clerk would allow us to go to our reserved hotel room to get some sleep but we could not visit or shop while we waited for our departure on the Japan Airlines at 6:20 p.m. that evening. We now were aware that further problems could develop as we continued our travels.

As feared, we had problems at the Cairo airport where we arrived early the next morning. The immigration clerk refused to let us go to our hotel in Cairo. Instead, we were taken to a quarantine camp close to the airport. A high chain-link fence surrounded the camp and the gate was locked. A nurse was in charge of the camp in which were six other detainees. We were very tired but found the military cots poorly designed for sound slumber.

Besides that, we were concerned about how we could contact Dr. Turner and our son David, who were scheduled to be at a hotel in Cairo. After we awoke, we found the telephone system in Cairo difficult to use, but finally talked with Dr. Turner and David and explained our situation. Dr. Turner promised to take David with his tour group to visit the pyramid area west of Cairo.

We discovered the camp management did not serve meals. Food had to be purchased with Egyptian money from a young man who took orders and brought the food from another location in metal containers to his customers in the camp. The nurse permitted me, under guard, to go to the air terminal to change a traveler's check into Egyptian currency and buy two meals at the terminal. I also informed the KLM office of our predicament and that we would be on hand for our flight to Lebanon the next day.

When I returned to the camp, Maria had a big smile and told me privately she had persuaded the nurse, with some difficulty, to allow David to come to the camp, stay overnight and go with us to the terminal. She made one request. We were not to go out to the gate to get David. As soon as possible, I contacted Dr. Turner by phone and arranged for him to bring David to the camp by taxi that afternoon.

David arrived at the camp as planned. We were sitting on the porch waiting, and when we saw the taxi arrive, we ran to the gate to greet David and thank Dr. Turner. The nurse was not happy we had disregarded her restriction but did nothing about it. David enjoyed showing the things he had bought on his trip so far. When two guards arrived by car to take us to the airport, they were surprised there were three of us. Their papers showed there should be only two people. When they saw David's plane tickets agreed with ours, they shrugged their shoulders and muttered. "Someone at the office had made a mistake", and took us to the terminal.

We flew out of Cairo on Air Lebanon to arrive at Beirut about eight o'clock p. m. We enjoyed the hotel and had a great time hearing David excitedly tell about his visit to Spain, Rome and Athens. He brought us up to date on affairs at home. He stressed especially the wonders of having a baby niece to play with. We were amazed at how much he had grown. We spent a day exploring Beirut and giving David an opportunity to swim in the Mediterranean Sea. On July 1st we flew to the Jordanian airport near Jerusalem.

We stayed at the same Christ Church Hostel in which Burt and I had stayed during Christmas time in 1959. Prices were still very reasonable. We went on a series of trips to all the important places associated with Biblical times on the West Bank and up and down the Jordanian area east of the Jordan River and the Dead Sea valley. David really enjoyed floating in the very salty water of the Dead Sea but did not enjoy the tough job of washing all the salt off his body and from his hair. We met Dr. Turner and his tour group one day and went with them for a memorable visit to Bethlehem and Hebron.

After two weeks in Jordan, we passed through the Mandelbaum Gate into Israel. We were relieved that in Lebanon, Jordan nor Israel had our health documents examined. A big load of concern slipped off our shoulders. We stayed at the stone building on Prophet's Street that was still the location of the Israel/American Institute of Holy Land Studies where Burt and I stayed in the fall of 1959 and Burt during the winter and spring of 1960.

The school was steadily growing but only tour groups visited the school during the summer months. One evening, Dr. and Mrs. Douglas Young, the founders of the school and its President, were our hosts at a gathering of more than one hundred government officials and important people in Israel. I met again a number of men and women I had become acquainted with in 1959. I was thrilled to introduce Maria and David to them.

During the first week of our stay, Dr. Turner and his group came into Israel and we arranged to travel with the group throughout the northern part of Israel. I had a great time explaining to Maria and David how Burt and I had visited the same places. I had an opportunity to discuss with the tour group the significance of the important excavations we visited. On other days, Maria, David and I traveled by bus and train to a number of places in Israel mentioned in the Bible.

At eleven o'clock a.m., July 25th, the three of us boarded a KLM plane headed for Amsterdam. Maria's relatives were at the airport to welcome us to Maria's native country, which she had left with her parents in 1920. Maria was thrilled to listen to her relatives speak in Dutch, which she could understand. She struggled for several days before she could form the Dutch words on her lips easily. Soon she was conversing fluently in her native tongue.

Fortunately, several cousins could speak English quite well so David and I could enter the conversation with some ease. David quickly got acquainted with a girl cousin, Miriam, about his age and soon the two of them were bicycling on the asphalt streets. David thought it was great to wear Dutch, wooden shoes while riding the bike.

We spent three weeks traveling throughout the central part of the Netherlands, visiting its major cities. Our relatives took us by train and bus to the homes of other relatives of Maria's mother and father. It was a great reunion for Maria and her people. The events of those two weeks will long be remembered.

We boarded a KLM plane the forenoon of August 15th and arrived in New York City about three o'clock p.m. Eastern Time. We transferred to an Eastern Airline's plane and at last, at 9:45 p.m. the plane touched down at Lexington, KY. Nellie, Ralph, baby Karen, Burt and several of David's friends welcomed us. It was a joyous occasion. Three exhausted people thanked God for a safe journey.

CHAPTER 9

FAMILY DATA

I spent the next several weeks hurriedly arranging my teaching materials for a busy fall semester. The church and the community kept Maria and me busy showing our slides and telling about our trip. David had some good "show and tell" materials for his class also. Ralph decided to continue teaching in a Junior High School in Versailles, so he, Nellie and Karen rented a trailer for the coming year. Two excited grandparents had a great time getting acquainted with their beautiful granddaughter.

Soon after we returned home, Burt let us in on a personal secret. He and Jeanie had started dating and now were planning to get married on April 25, 1965. We congratulated him and started planning with him the details of the wedding, which I participated in, along with Mary Jean's Presbyterian pastor in Ann Arbor, Michigan. Both soon got teaching jobs in a community college at Somerset, KY. The school was related to the University of KY.

Since the Free Methodist Board of Missions had helped finance our trip, they requested I speak about missions at churches in several states. I was able to do so on weekends and breaks in the school schedule. I found these occasions challenging and inspiring. I was also able to use our colored slides effectively in my classes.

By Christmas time 1964, a new idea began to stir in our minds. The seminary had been given a small tract of land on the northwestern side of Wilmore. The officials announced to the faculty and staff that the tract would be subdivided into lots and offered for sale at reasonable prices and limited loans at a low interest rate. Wasn't it time for us to think about building a new house? Maria and I presented the idea to our children and they concurred, offering their labor in constructing the house. We obtained booklets of house plans and decided we liked a particular ranch house plan. I decided I could draw the house plans myself and discovered several seminary students had carpentry experience and would oversee the construction process.

By April 1965, we had purchased a lot from the seminary, had contracted with a local contractor to excavate and build the concrete block basement walls, which was done early in May. Streets, electric lines or water service had not been put in place yet, but the day after commencement, our carpenter crew began work. Even our fifteen-year-old son, David, and son-in-law, Ralph joined the project.

David did us a special service early in July. We had placed a for sale sign in front of our house on Lexington Avenue, hoping to sell it quickly. One morning David said he wanted to sleep in, so the rest of us left to work on the house. Just before noon he came running across the field to tell us a family from Lexington had stopped and asked about the price of the house. David told them the price and showed them through the house. He promised to tell his parents to be home during the noon hour to talk business with the couple. They appeared on schedule and in a short time the house sold. We gave David a special gift for doing a good job.

The couple wanted to move into the house August 1st and we promised we would move our possessions into our new house by that date. We enlarged our work crew and worked ten hours a day, six days a week. Though the rooms were not painted nor the carpets put in yet, we placed our furniture in the middle of each room and continued painting, putting up curtains and installing the carpets. By the time the new school year began, we were quite well settled and the city had laid a water line, brought electric lines to the house and constructed streets. We were now the happy owners of a brand new, Bedford stone faced house!

It was a challenge to do a number of small jobs on the house and put full time into my classes that fall, but we were thankful everything went well. No one had been injured and we were all excited as we celebrated our first Christmas in front of the white Georgia marble fireplace decorated with Dutch landscape pictures on white tiles.

Our second granddaughter, Sharma Maria Kester was born on October 14, 1965 to our daughter Nellie and Ralph, at Central Baptist Hospital in Lexington, KY.

Early in the semester, Dr. Howard Shipps and I were talking about the entrance of Methodism into Kentucky after the Revolutionary War. He informed me the ruins of the first Methodist school built west of the Appalachian Mountains, Bethel Academy, was located in a field on a farm several miles southeast of Wilmore. He said no one seemed to know the exact size of the original building. We decided to go with shovels to the site and do some digging. We found a stone monument erected on the site that had trees and brush covering it. A few stones of a foundation could be seen here and there. We wanted to find exactly where the foundation walls lay.

I told Dr. Shipps about a technique I learned in Israel. One should seek a section where the ground sloped sharply. We dug at the lowest point of a slope and worked toward the high point. This way we could find the side of a wall.

In about twenty minutes, we had dug a ditch that revealed the face of a wall, and cleared soil from the top of it. We went to the far side of the site and began digging at another slope. Soon the face of another wall appeared and the top was cleared. Our tape measure revealed the foundation was thirty-five feet wide. We thus had located the south wall and the north wall and turned our attention to another slope that might bring to light the east wall. We were successful in finding the face and top of that wall and a short time later had located the west wall. Our measuring tape showed the length of the foundation was eighty-nine feet. The thing that amazed me was that no one had thought to do this bit of digging to determine the size of the building. The outcome of this project was my decision to use my students in the spring semester to do more digging at this site, thus putting into practice what archaeologists do in Jordan and Israel. A description of this project is found in the appendix A.

Early in the spring semester, an unexpected opportunity presented itself. Dr. Joseph Calloway, Professor of Old Testament at Southern Baptist Theological Seminary at Louisville, Ky. sent out an announcement about his archaeological project at et-Tell (also known as Ai) located on the West Bank of Jordan. He needed professors with field experience in archaeology to serve on his staff, during the summer of 1966. I mentioned to my fellow professors I was interested in the project.

Maria was hesitant about me taking another big trip so close to our world trip but after considerable discussion and prayer consented to my going, if finances could be provided from sources other than our meager funds. For a more complete description of that summer of excavation, and a similar one in 1968, (see Appendix A under "Ai'66" and "Ai'68").

After a busy, enjoyable year teaching in the school year 1966-67, I continued to work on the new house and its yard. Several new houses were built near us. We began to feel we had a neighborhood. Our granddaughters, Karen and Sharma, lived with their parents on Asbury Ave. in Wilmore. The two of them gave us a great deal of joy. In 1966 Ralph, Nellie and the two girls moved to Bloomington, IN. Ralph enrolled at Indiana University to do graduate work in education. Burton and Jeanie were teaching at a community college in Covington, Ky. and David was in high school.

One event brought sorrow into our lives. My 83-year-old mother was failing fast at a nursing home in Eau Claire, WI. Early in October, I made a trip to Eau Claire to visit with her a few days. Plane connections to the city were very poor, so I made the trip by bus that took thirty-six hours. My brother Ray met me at the bus station and took me to the Lutheran Hospital. Obviously, my mother was very ill, but she was overjoyed when she realized I had come to see her. The next day was World Communion Day so Ray, who was a deacon in the local Baptist Church, and I decided to have communion with Mother. He borrowed a small communion set and together we served Mother her last communion. She couldn't thank us enough. A man lay ill in a bed in the same room, with his wife standing beside him. They consented to take communion also, for they identified themselves as Methodists. After a farewell kiss, I voiced a prayer. That was the last time I saw my mother alive.

Two months later, we received a call from Ray informing us of Mother's death. This time Maria and I drove to Wisconsin and stopped at Bloomington, IN. to pick up Nellie and the two girls. All of our family except Harold, who lived near San Diego, CA. was at the solemn funeral. In our grief, we felt a calming assurance Mother was with her Lord, who she so deeply loved and knew so well. Mother's body was laid to rest beside her husband.

On our way home, I felt an increasing pain in my left leg. By the end of the trip, the pain was severe. A doctor examined me and said I had a broken tailbone and asked how that could have happened. Thinking back, I realized that I had played volleyball in a match between seminary faculty and college faculty. In one incident of the game, I was in the back line and had jumped high to hit back the ball. I remembered I had fallen backward and hit the floor hard. For over a year I had to wear a steel-framed brace around my hips. On Christmas Eve, I had to be carried from my bed to the living room where I laid on a mat during the opening of presents. When school opened, I was able to meet my classes, though with discomfort. Very slowly, the break healed enough for me to join the excavation at Ai (et-Tell) in 1968. This time the site was in Israel, which had gained control of the West Bank in the Six Day War of 1967.

While engaged in that excavation, I received news from Maria of two shocking events. Every weekend our excavation crew went to stay at the YMCA in Jerusalem at which time I received her airmail letters. One letter informed me that my second oldest brother, Floyd, had been killed by a lightning strike on his farm in Wisconsin. I noted from the postmark on the letter that it was already a week old. I realized his funeral had already taken place. I wrote Maria that when I returned home we should drive to Chetek, WI to visit his widow to express our sorrow.

The next letter had a different kind of news. Maria wrote that the Board of Trustees of Asbury College in Wilmore had voted to hire my fellow Old Testament Professor, Dr. Dennis Kinlaw, as the new president of the college. A mixture of emotions flooded through me. I rejoiced that Dr. Kinlaw was being so wonderfully honored, but I was disturbed by the realization my next sabbatical semester was that coming fall and Dr. Kinlaw was to carry the full load of Old Testament courses. I would have to give up my sabbatical and teach those classes.

I had a research project planned for my sabbatical, that I would do while staying in Wilmore. Now I had to postpone the project until a later date. This turn of events also meant, I would have to look for a replacement for Dr. Kinlaw. We located a Ph. D. candidate who could both teach a couple classes and work on his dissertation, but he didn't stay with us more than two years. Finally, we found the person we wanted,

John Oswalt, who was completing his doctoral dissertation at Brandeis University in Boston. I was happy to have him as my colleague.

In the spring of 1970, another change entered my academic career. The chairman of our Biblical division, Dr. Wilbur Dayton, had resigned his position as Professor of New Testament to become the President of Houghton College. Dr. Frank Stanger, President of the seminary, asked me to take the chairmanship of the division for the coming school year. I agreed to accept the new position. I would still teach several classes, but I would have several new, time-consuming duties. I would be in charge of monthly meetings of the Biblical faculty, but also be with the other divisional chairmen, a member of the President's Educational Consultant Committee and the Dean's Curriculum and Instruction Committee. I would also be responsible for overseeing the search for and recommending to the head officials all new professors and instructors in the division. I held this position for fourteen years.

The school year 1970-71 was a challenge breaking into my new duties as divisional chairman, teaching a full load of classes and engaging in several writing projects, including preliminary work on a textbook on the Pentateuch, and limited translation work with the New International Version committee. The latter project I will describe in the appendix C.

Early in 1972, I began promoting a tour group of seminary students in the USA to spend four weeks during late June and early July at the Israel/American Institute of Holy Land Studies in Jerusalem. The Institute officials helped me arrange with a travel agency in Jerusalem a low priced airfare for students only. If I signed up 24 students, my airfare would not cost anything. By the end of April, I had signed up enough students, so in due course we arrived in Israel. The Institute had arranged for a two-phase curriculum for the group. The first phase would be a two-week excavation of a portion of a site just north of Tel Aviv called Tel Qasileh. The project would be under the leadership of an Israeli archaeologist Ami Mazar. See Appendix A under "Tel Qasileh" for a description of this dig.

The purely academic phase of this trip consisted of four days of intensive classes at the Institute's new headquarters on Mt. Zion in Jerusalem and six days of travel to archaeological sites throughout Israel. A professor at the Institute would travel with us and lecture on the significance of each site in regards to ancient history and to Biblical studies. It was an exciting and inspirational time in the Holy Land.

Our third granddaughter, Deborah Faith Livingston was born on May 16, 1972, daughter of Burt and Jeanie, was born in Ann Arbor, MI.

Maria's mother was finding it more and more difficult to live by herself in her house in Hustisford, WI. Maria conferred with her mother and sisters and together they decided she should spend her winters at our home in Wilmore. In late September, she came to live with us until April of the next year when she returned to West Bend, WI to stay with another daughter Fanny Sommerfeldt. This pattern was repeated for several years.

The spring of 1973 was a time of crisis for our family. On the afternoon of February 28th, I stopped by the seminary registrar office where Maria worked as the assistant to the Registrar, Miss Juanita Spencer. Maria was sitting at her desk crying. Miss Spencer informed me Maria had just received a call from the doctor in Lexington, KY who a few days before had examined her. The report was that Maria had cancer and must report at St. Josephs Hospital for further tests. The result was that Maria was given radiation treatments for a week at the hospital. She was then to rest for at least a month at home. She entered the hospital April 10, 1973 for surgery for a complete hysterectomy. We were all shattered by this turn of events, but the seminary community and the church community joined in earnest prayer for her full recovery. We felt their supporting love.

After a week in the hospital, Maria came home for a complete rest. It was deeply touching how the community, seminary and church assisted us with meals, phone calls, get-well cards and visits. Our two sons came home to help as often as they could. Our daughter and her two girls came down and spent a week to take care of Maria and help around the house.

Two months after the surgery, Maria went through extensive tests. All of us rejoiced when the doctor reported no evidence of cancer remained in her body. Together, Maria and I believed God had joined in the healing of her body. That cancer never did occur again. Maria returned to work but her body was still too weak. She decided to retire on August 1, 1973.

One day that fall, we received an ordinary looking, brown envelope. We opened it and discovered that on the recommendation of the faculty of Asbury Theological Seminary, I had been nominated for special recognition. A certificate read, "This is to certify that George Herbert Livingston has been selected as an OUTSTANDING EDUCATOR OF AMERICA for 1973 in recognition of contributions to the advancement of higher education and service to community." signed by V. Gilbert Beers, Director of Outstanding Educators of America, Washington, D.C. I felt highly honored.

Other members of the extended family had received honors that year. Our oldest son and wife were now professors at Wayne County Community College, Detroit, MI. Nellie's husband, Ralph, was awarded the Doctor of Education degree by Indiana University. At that time, he was doing research work for Ohio State University at Columbus, OH. In celebration of his achievement, they invited us to join them on a one-week vacation trip to Florida.

Our youngest son, David, was awarded the Bachelor of Arts degree in mechanical engineering in December. He took a factory job in Georgetown, KY. For several years he had been racing cars on weekends, a hobby he continued for many years. In December, the New York Bible Society invited me to serve, in my spare time, on the General Editorial Committee as one of the translators of the Old Testament for the New International Version (aka NIV). More on this project is available in Appendix C.

By the beginning of 1974, Maria had regained her strength quite well and spent many hours crocheting many beautiful items. In February my textbook, THE PENTATEUCH IN ITS CULTURAL ENVIRONMENT was published by Baker Book House, Grand Rapids, MI.

In April, Maria went to Columbus, OH and spent a week with her granddaughters and Nellie as Ralph was out of town. On Wednesday, April 24th our fourth grandchild, Kenneth David Shawn Kester was born at Ohio State University Hospital in Columbus, OH. On Saturday I took Maria back up to help take care of Ken.

Besides my seminary responsibility, I spent January and the spring break doing translation work for the New International Version. An announcement came from the New York Bible Society saying the Society was paying the way of translators and spouses for summer work in St. Andrews, Scotland. We would travel by plane both ways and would spend two months of the summer working on the NIV. A narrative of that summer event is also found in the Appendix C. We concluded the summer with a trip to Western Europe for three weeks before returning home.

The seminary granted me another Sabbatical leave that fall semester so I spent September through December at home in Wilmore, doing intensive research on the lives and actions of the Old Testament prophets. I hoped to publish another book, or at least articles, as a result of that research.

The biggest event in our family life during 1974 occurred in December. Soon after we arrived back from Scotland our son David told us, he was dating a young lady from Lebanon, KY. He met her while instructing several people in the fine points of driving a Porsche. He owned an older model that he used in local car races. This young lady needed guidance in handling and caring for her newer Porsche model. She also did some racing with it, and later raced a Formula Ford. The two were soon dating and fell in love. She was a high school counselor and a widow of a soldier who lost his life in the Vietnam conflict. Her name was Mary Raley O'Neill. That fall they decided to get married on December 21st. For several years David worked for Johnson Controls Corp. in Georgetown, KY where he was an engineer. Mary soon became a member of the Livingston extended family circle. The wedding took place in Lebanon and I assisted the Catholic priest in the wedding ceremony.

The newlyweds purchased a house two miles west of Perryville, Ky. on state highway # 150. Years later we discovered their home was about one-half mile south of where David's great-grandfather, Thomas M. Livingston, was camped with the 86th Illinois Infantry Regiment during the battle of Perryville in October, 1862. Fortunately, his great-grandfather was not hurt in that battle.

The second biggest event of the month was a climatic one. December was the coldest on record. The temperature was—20 degrees. To our dismay, when we got home after the rehearsal dinner we discovered that a water pipe that went to the outside broke and a lot of water poured into the basement. The break was in my office and a number of my books got wet, and many of them were ruined. The carpets in the basement had to be replaced.

In comparison to 1974, the next year seemed unexciting. Classes occupied most of my time and several short articles were written. I continued with the New International Version committee doing translation and editorial work on several Old Testament books. Maria's health returned to normal, though she no longer held a job. The three children were happily married and busy in their tasks.

During the fall, a new interest began to capture our imagination. The idea of having a motor home to travel during the summer months seemed attractive so we began searching the classified ads, hoping to locate a good model. In the spring of 1976, we decided to buy a 26 ft. Titan motor home with about 25,000 miles on its odometer. We tried it out on several short weekend trips and liked it. Soon we had a full travel schedule set up for the summer months.

Our first trip was to Washington, D.C. and surrounding historical places of interest. We next headed north to see the Niagara Falls. We wanted to go across the river to view the falls from the Canadian side, but we had overlooked bringing Maria's naturalization papers so we stayed on the U.S. side. About a week after returning to Kentucky, we left for Wisconsin to visit Maria's mother and several sisters just west of Milwaukee. We motored on to visit some of my brothers and sisters in northwestern Wisconsin. We returned by way of Iowa and Missouri. My oldest brother and family lived at Rolla, MO so we visited several days with them. We were really enjoying our motor home.

Early in the spring of 1976, Rev. Robert Short, our classmate in Wessington Springs College in the 1930's, had asked me to come to Wessington Springs in August to give several lectures during the national Bicentennial Celebration. I gladly accepted the invitation, so a week before the celebration Maria and I set out in our motor home for Wessington Springs, SD. The weather was hot during the trip, but late in the second day, we safely arrived.

We had not visited Wessington Springs since 1956, so we were excited to see the remains of the college. Due to inadequate finances, the school had closed in the late 60's and all but one building, a barn had been taken down. A retirement village had been constructed on the campus, which we were happy to see, but the grip of sadness filled our hearts. This was where Maria and I had gained our college education, had met and had become engaged. My brother, Ralph had earned his high school diploma here. My youngest sister, Dorothy, had earned two years of teacher training after which she taught in a country school. Our oldest son, Burton had returned to the high school on the campus and earned his diploma. What an educational and spiritual debt we owed this humble school located in a typical western town on the prairies of South Dakota.

We met many old friends during the celebration. There was a parade dominated by horses and wagons, with plenty of stars and stripes fluttering in the breeze. During the day, horse shows and races kept the crowd excited. During the evening hours, skits and songs dear to the hearts of ranch owners and cowboys filled the schedule. Since my evening lectures would be illustrated by colored slides, I was last on the program. Just as dusk was turning to darkness, I would begin to speak about my adventures as an archaeologist digging five thousand year old ruins and artifacts in Palestine. One evening I centered my address on the Dead Sea scrolls, in which the people were intensely interested.

The trip had a second objective. Nellie and Ralph, who lived in Columbus, OH at the time, had gone to Oregon to spend a few weeks of vacation with Ralph's family in Portland, OR. We had agreed to meet them in the Black Hills, S.D. during their trip back to Ohio. After the celebration in Wessington Springs, we drove over three hundred miles to an agreed upon campgrounds, from which we would make sightseeing trips through the hills. We wanted to acquaint the three children, Karen, Sharma and Ken with the marvels of the Black Hills. We enjoyed viewing Mt. Rushmore, natural rock formations, and the evergreens on the sides of mountains.

After several days, we traveled east on I-90 to Mitchell, SD. At Mitchell, the children were enthralled with the corncob decoration of the Corn Palace. We camped overnight by a small lake near a town where Ralph's mother was born. The next day our travel route separated at Indianapolis. Ralph and Nellie were returning to Columbus as Ralph had accepted the position of Chairman of the Education Department and Director of Student Teachers at Greenville College. Nellie worked in the Development Office. Maria helped Nellie, Sharma and Ken move Ralph and Karen on August 26th. After returning to Columbus, Maria stayed for a week to help Nellie pack their belongings. Late in September, a moving van delivered their goods at Greenville. We were glad they would have this opportunity to serve in a Free Methodist school.

The Christmas season in 1976 was a joyous one for the family, but it ended with an event that brought shock and grief. Maria's mother was spending the winter with us and she seemed to be doing well. One evening she greatly enjoyed the visit of a caroling group made up of the President of Asbury Seminary and his wife, Dr. and Mrs. Frank Stanger, the Vice President of Academic Affairs and his wife, and the Vice President of Finances and his wife. They had come especially to sing for her and she was thrilled beyond words.

Two days later, the shock came. Mother Saarloos had gone to her bedroom after the noon meal for a nap. Maria and I were in the kitchen and heard a noise in the bedroom. We found mother Saarloos partially lying on the bed vomiting severely. We got her fully on the bed, but she could not talk nor move her right arm. She had suffered a severe stroke. Before she became ill, mother Saarloos had requested that she not be sent to the hospital, if she had a severe stroke. She wished to die in the presence of her family. Dr. Dunkelburger responded to our telephone call and was at our home within minutes. He agreed that her stroke was terminal and she should not be taken to the hospital. He gave instructions for her care and promised to visit every day and more often if needed.

Maria's sisters and brother were notified of their mother's impending death, but Tillie was the only one who could come. Our oldest son, Burt, and daughter, Nellie, came toward the end of the week. Since Dave and Mary lived close by, they would come after work and Mary stayed all night several times. Mother Saarloos could not eat solid foods and had difficulty swallowing liquids. She was in almost a constant coma. She recognized us the brief times she was awake but could not talk. By Saturday, she was losing strength and by Sunday noon it was evident she would not live long. Dr. Dunkelburger visited her that morning and in the afternoon stayed by her side for over two hours until at 5:45 p.m. January 2, 1977 she breathed her last breath. Tears were streaming down the cheeks of the family members.

Her body was taken to the Betts and West Funeral Home in Nicholasville, KY. Two days later, a memorial service was conducted in the forenoon, led by Dr. Frank Stanger and Dr. George Turner. Immediately afterward, the casket was taken to the Lexington, KY airport and shipped to a funeral home in Hartford, WI. Maria, Tillie, Nellie, David and I traveled to Wisconsin in our motor home and stayed at Tillie's home. Burton, Jeanie and Debby came from Ann Arbor, MI. and Maria's sister Lucy and most of her family came from Hastings, MN.

On January 7th a funeral service was held at the funeral home at which I gave a tribute to mother Saarloos, and burial was beside her husband, Burt, in the La Belle cemetery in Oconomowoc, WI. It was a sunny but chilly day. Our hearts were sad.

We stayed overnight and in the morning, it looked dark in the sky toward the southwest. We feared a snowstorm. In Chicago, we dropped Nellie off to fly to St. Louis. Everything was fine until we came to Indianapolis and headed toward Louisville. Soon there was ice on the road and snow was falling at Columbus, IN. The storm was coming from the south and got worse as we headed east on I-64. It took David and me five hours to travel 150 miles from Columbus to Wilmore. We were glad to get home without an accident. We immediately noticed that our house seemed empty without mother Saarloos present. We missed her greatly, but were comforted by a statement she had made several times during the fall of 1976. She testified with calmness that she was ready to go. She was a sincere, devoted Christian.

The second semester (winter and spring) went smoothly. The classes were challenging as usual and committee meetings sometimes burdensome, sometimes exciting. A development in lecture presentation was capturing my attention. The overhead projector was gaining acceptance by teachers, so I convinced the business office one should be purchased for the professors to use in the classroom. At first, I was the only one to experiment with the projector and soon found I needed to improve my visual material that should be printed or drawn on transparent sheets. The students liked the visual presentations and gave me suggestions about how I could improve the text size, the quality of the charts and pictures projected, and how to tie the visual projections with my lectures. Soon other professors took an interest in the new equipment and more projectors were purchased.

An updating of the curriculum was in progress and various professors had varying views about what improvements should be made. A consensus was reached and the new curriculum was scheduled to begin the coming fall. The duties of the division chairmen were just as demanding as before, and classes seemed to continue as usual.

Two highlights of 1977, that were not academic, one was the arrival of another granddaughter, Cynthia Jeanette Marie Livingston on May 11th, to Burton and Jeanie in Ann Arbor, MI. She soon acquired the nickname, Cyndy.

The other highlight was a summer trip in our motor home. We visited several of the lovely state parks in Kentucky and visited our families in Michigan, Illinois and Wisconsin.

I did not have to teach in the fall semester, because I had been granted a sabbatical leave to do academic research and to lecture in churches. I spent the month of September lecturing on archaeology and the Bible in various churches in the upper Midwest. My schedule was: Free Methodist churches in Platteville, WI and in Mason City, IA. I also spoke at several United Methodist churches in Lafarge, WI, where my brother-in-law, Fay Johnson and his wife, my sister Dorothy, were pastors. I also spoke at Free Methodist churches in Bloomington, MN, Rapid City, SD and Grand Forks, ND. We were able to spend a night with my brother, Ray, and family in Eau Claire, WI. I gave my last lecture in the United Methodist Church in Manitowoc, WI where David Passett was pastor.

In the fall of 1978, the urge to travel to Israel came to the forefront. Dr. Joseph Wang, Professor of New Testament and a native of Taiwan, and I, with our wives, began to think seriously of organizing a tour in the summer of 1979. We would advertise the tour as covering a three-week trip to the Middle East, visiting Italy, Greece, Egypt, Lebanon, Jordan, Israel, and Turkey. We would provide opportunity for students of the seminary to keep a diary and make notes about the places visited. Students would write a summary of academic quality for credit towards their degree. We urged friends to go along and also help advertise, seeking adults who would enjoy such a trip. By late fall, we had letters sent to friends and ads were placed in religious magazines. Meanwhile, classes and writing several articles for publication claimed our time.

By February 1979, almost two-dozen friends had signed up and paid a deposit. Among these tourists were my brother and wife, Ray and Ellen, Ron and Judy Highhouse and their son, Jeanie's mother, Mrs. Seward, and her friend, Mrs. Broom. Dr. Wang, his wife, Esther and my wife, Maria, helped in the task of sending instructions to the prospective friends. Each tourist obtained passports, health certificates, and plane tickets. We had contracted with Rama Vacations of Chicago,

IL to provide us with promotional materials, to secure reservations in hotels and guides during the trip.

The Bible Lands Seminar Tour members, twenty-seven in number, came from various states and were scheduled to meet at the Kennedy Airport, near New York City, on July 9th. We boarded at 7:00 p.m. a KLM plane to Athens, Greece, with a two-hour stopover in Amsterdam, the Netherlands. We hired a bus to take us on a tour of Amsterdam, an extra we had not counted on. We also had a good guide and bus driver in Greece and we saw the important places in Athens. The tour of the Parthenon impressed us.

On the morning of July 11th, we took a plane to Cairo and after checking in at the Indiana Hotel, we enjoyed seeing the pyramids and several other ancient ruins. The next day, several of our group, under the leadership of Dr. Wang, flew to Luxor and spent the day visiting the remarkable tombs and ruins in that ancient capital of Egypt. The rest of us toured Cairo and enjoyed a boat ride on the Nile River. After supper, we gathered for sharing our impressions of Egypt.

On the morning of July 14th, we flew to Amman, Jordan and toured the significant historical sites of that ancient city. The next day we took a bus south to the ruins of Petra. Archaeologists have spent several decades bringing to light this remarkable crossroads of Nabatean merchants. On one of the cliffs of the gorge leading down to Petra, the Romans had carved the facade of an important building. The doorway led to a large cave that served a storage area for cargo. We arrived back in Amman, after an exciting but exhausting trip.

On July 16th we traveled north to the ruins of ancient Jerash. Still towering high above us was an almost complete circle of pillars of a ruined Roman temple. We returned to Amman and turned west toward the Jordan River, where we stopped to visit the spot where John the Baptist baptized Jesus. We next visited the mound that contained the remains of ancient Jericho. The mound has excavated layers of ruins that go back to about 7,000 BC. At Jericho, the Jordanian guide and bus driver bid us good-bye and an Israeli guide and bus driver took charge of the tour.

Turning north the bus driver took us along the west side of the Jordan Valley and stopped to examine the ruins of ancient Bethshan and on to the Crusader Castle of Belvoir. What a view of the upper Jordan Valley and the southern part of the Sea of Galilee. We continued on to the Hula Valley north of the Sea of Galilee and prepared to spend the night at a Jewish settlement called Kibbutz Hagoshrim. Mount Hermon rose to its snow covered heights north of us.

As we were preparing to depart the next morning, Dr. Wang, who was in charge of keeping track of all members of the tour and their baggage, discovered the suitcases of one of the student couples were missing. Thinking they were probably put on the wrong bus, he noted that several buses had already left. Only one bus owned by a Palestinian company remained.

Receiving permission to search through the baggage of this bus, Dr. Wang found the missing suitcases. About ten minutes after the bags were found, the Palestinian bus left to continue its journey.

We spent July 17th touring the Galilee area, stopping at Hazor that Joshua conquered and places where Jesus ministered, such as the Mount of Beatitudes, Magdela and Tiberius. We boarded a boat to cross the Sea of Galilee to spend a few moments at Capernaum and continued by boat to the east side of the sea where the Golan Heights came down almost to the shore. We had a delightful meal of St. Peters fish, which were about the size of a good-sized bluegill. We returned by boat to Tiberius, had supper and retired for the night.

The next day we motored south to ascend the Mount of Transfiguration, and on to Nazareth where we saw the Chamber of Annunciation and Mary's well. After lunch, we continued on to the second largest city in Israel, Haifa. We went to the top of Mt. Carmel for a terrific view of the Mediterranean Sea and the harbor that serves Haifa. We stayed overnight at the Liv Hacarmel Hotel.

On July 19th we rode the bus to Megiddo and examined the ruins of the two-dozen layers of ancient cities that make up the mound of that important military fortress in northern Israel. We went on to Caesarea that was built by King Herod in 22 B.C. Here are the remains of an old aqueduct, a Roman hippodrome, a large amphitheater and ruins of a Crusader fortress. We followed the shoreline of the sea to Joppa, to Ashkelon and finally to Beersheva, the southern limit of Old Testament Canaan.

The next day we journeyed south through the barren desert, called the Negev, and stopped at the ruins of a fortress city, called Avdat, atop a cliff. Then motored on toward Eilat where we stayed overnight at the Moon Valley hotel. The next morning we went south along the shore of the Gulf of Aquaba. The group was divided and taken in glass-bottomed boats out a short distance to view the marvelous coral reefs and the many varied colored fish. A brief time was given to the young people to swim in the warm gulf water.

Mid-morning our bus took us north to the Dead Sea and a short stop at Masada, a high cliff on which King Herod had built a fortified palace area. Seventy-five years later, Jews found refuge in the fortress from the Roman army, but took their own lives rather than surrender to the Romans. A cable car took us to the top of the cliff and we spent an hour examining the ruins. We next stopped at the ruins of Qumran, on the northwest corner of the Dead Sea. In the cliffs towering above this village, a number of torn scrolls of all but one Old Testament book were found in several caves, in the mid 1940's. Jewish scholars, who refused to live with the high priests appointed by the Greeks to govern the religious life of the Jews in Jerusalem, had built the small village and spent much time copying Old Testament books and authoring other religious literature.

A month or so before we began this tour, Maria and I had copied some hymns and religious songs on tapes so we could play them at special places in Israel. As we motored up the mountain toward Jerusalem we played, "Holy City" and several other songs about Jerusalem to prepare the tour members for the first sight of Jerusalem. Even the guide and the bus driver seemed to enjoy the songs. Late in the afternoon of July 21st we reached the ridge of the Mt. of Olives and everyone gasped as they saw Jerusalem for the first time. The Western sun shone on the local limestone buildings causing the stones to reflect a golden color. We settled down in the Strand Hotel on the north side of Jerusalem.

We spent four days getting acquainted with Jerusalem and its surrounding towns. On the first day, July 22nd, we began with a lecture given by Dr. G. Douglas Young, the President of the Institute of Holy Land Studies, the school I helped him establish in 1959. We then went to the Mount of Olives, with its outstanding view of Jerusalem, and its important churches, including the one that commemorates the spot where Jesus stood just before his ascension. We descended the Mt. of Olives by walking the path followed by Jesus on Palm Sunday, visited the Garden of Gethsemane, with its Church of All Nations.

We then ascended Mt. Zion to stop at the Room of the Last Supper and David's Tomb. The buildings containing these shrines were constructed much later than New Testament times, but a sense of peace was felt. We went on to visit the Shrine of the Book where the Dead Sea scrolls are kept and walked through the Israel Museum with its impressive displays.

We concluded the afternoon by having a special communion service at the Garden Tomb located in a lovely garden. This is a tomb used in New Testament times, but not the actual one in which Jesus' body was placed after his death. However, it serves as a good symbol of that event. A natural stone platform rose about six feet higher than the tomb and had wooden benches for worshipers. Our group sang several well-known Easter songs. Maria and a tour member, who had sung with her during college days in SD, sang a duet and I gave a short devotional. Dr. Wang and I then conducted a communion service. It was a solemn moment.

The next day was spent walking through the walled part of Jerusalem starting at Stephen's Gate, the Pool of Bethesda, the Chapel of Flagellation, and the modern, narrow street now called Via Delorosa, or the Way of the Cross. We also visited the Church of the Holy Sepulcher and Joppa Gate. We next went to the site where the ancient Jewish temple stood, but now is under the control of the Muslims, who built the Dome of the Rock where the ancient altar was located. The Muslims declare their prophet Mohammed went to heaven from that rock. They also have a beautiful mosque called El Aqsa within the walled enclosure. We then found our way to the Wailing Wall where Jews come to pray. After dinner, we had our usual brief gathering at which time I answered questions the tour members may have about the day's events. I closed by giving a brief survey of what to expect the next day.

The morning of July 24th, we motored north; stopping briefly at Gibeon, Bethel, Shechem and Samaria. Returning to Shechem, we visited Jacob's well and drank water drawn from the well. While the tour members sipped their cups of water, I played a recording of the song "Fill my Cup, Lord." The group and the monks, who drew the water, deeply appreciated the song. It was time for dinner when we got to our hotel and all the tourists were tired.

The next forenoon we traveled south. We visited Ein Karem where John the Baptist was born, then on to the ruins of the Israelite fortress of Lachish destroyed by the Babylonians in Jeremiah's day. Our next stop was Hebron where there is a large cave called Machpela in the basement of a mosque. The cave can be viewed through glass windows in the main floor of the mosque. Within this cave are the alleged tombs of Abraham, Sarah and several of their family. Returning to Jerusalem, we stopped at Bethlehem at the shepherd's field, where angels appeared to announce Jesus' birth. We ended the day by worshipping briefly in the room of the Church of the Nativity, marking the spot where some say Jesus was born.

On July 26th, our tour group boarded a plane at the Israeli Lod Airport to fly to Istanbul, Turkey, then on another plane to Izmir, the modern name for Smyrna of New Testament times. The hotel was one of the best we had stayed in and the evening dinner was delicious. We spent two days visiting the sites of the seven churches (Rev. 1:4-3:22) and had an excellent guide.

On the 27th we first visited Pergamus, now called Bergama, and saw the remains of an impressive city of New Testament times. It is on a high hill at the junction of two rivers. Pergamus had a large theater, many temples and public buildings plus an impressive stone sculpture called the altar of Zeus. One of the outstanding health centers of Roman times was located here. We went on to the not-so-impressive ruins of Thyatira, Sardis and Philadelphia. The best preserved of the three is the partially restored pagan temple, the church of St. John and a Jewish synagogue. We ate dinner and stayed overnight at a hotel in Pamukkale.

The second day of this trip, we visited Laodicea, which had few ruins of St. Paul's time to see. The situation at Ephesus was just the opposite. Paul ministered here three years to establish a congregation. Most of the outdoor theater, where Paul was almost mobbed, has survived. A church and a tomb of St. John, who wrote several short epistles and the Book of Revelation, are in ruins here, as well as the temple of Artemis. The last stop of the day was at Miletus where Paul boarded a ship to Jerusalem (Acts 20:17-38). We returned to Izmir. We had been scheduled to stay there overnight, but a Sunday registration of citizens for a national election promised to be turbulent, and caused the Turkish Airlines to abolish all flights that day. Instead, we were placed on an evening flight to Istanbul.

July 29th turned out to be quieter than expected. Soldiers were everywhere and few buses and cars were on the streets. We took advantage of the calm and rested all forenoon. In the afternoon, a guide took us on a short tour of Istanbul but all of the important places were closed. We had to be satisfied with just seeing the outside of the famous Blue Mosque and the St. Sophia Church that is at present a museum. In mid-afternoon we were taken by bus to the airport where we had to wait three hours before taking off for Rome. The Delta Hotel in Rome was a disappointment. It was not clean and was over crowded. The air-conditioning system was out of order and it was a warm night. Guess what. It was miserable.

The next morning we had a three and one-half hour tour of Rome led by a very good lady guide. She left us at the airport where we boarded a KLM plane to Amsterdam, the Netherlands. In that airport, we had to walk quite a distance but were soon settled in a nice KLM jet airliner destined for New York City, where we arrived later than scheduled. Maria and I were able to connect with our flight to Cincinnati and Lexington, KY. Some of the others missed their flights and KLM put them up in hotels and gave them meals until the next day. Nellie, Ralph and children, David, Mary and a few friends met us at the Lexington airport at 9:20 p.m. They gave us a warm welcome and we were happy to be home.

While I was preparing for my fall semester classes, a letter with a surprise invitation came to our house. Thomas Nelson Publishers in Nashville, TN. had sent a letter. The president of the company informed me they were in the midst of revising the King James Version into an updated New King James Version. They had finished the New Testament and now were busy updating the Old Testament. A member of their Executive Review Committee had become seriously ill. The president would appreciate my coming to Nashville for an interview. I made the trip to Nashville and soon received a request to join the committee. I responded that I would be honored to join the committee. An account of the two years I spent on this project is given in appendix C. During 1980 and 1981, many hours and much travel made up my workload. I continued to teach my regular classes and carry on my duties as chairman of the Biblical division of the seminary.

In June, 1980 our granddaughter Karen Kester, and 6 other teens from their hand bell choir and 6 adults from their Free Methodist Church in Greenville, IL went on a 3 week trip to England and Scotland. They played at a number of churches and camp meetings around the area. The group also visited the factory that made their hand bells and did a lot of sight seeing. They had a great time together.

Our sixth grandchild, David Herbert Livingston, Jr. was born on September 6th, to our son of David, Sr. and Mary Livingston in Lebanon, KY.

Our seventh grandchild, Laura Jean was born on April 24, 1981 to our son Burton and Jeanie Livingston in Ann Arbor, MI.

The summer of 1981 found Maria and me at St. Andrews, Scotland working with the committees of the New King James Revision project during June and July. Early in August, we spent several weeks in the Netherlands visiting with Maria's relatives. During that time, Maria's sister, Tillie, came to the Netherlands with a tour group and spent a day exploring Amsterdam with us. We visited with several cousins who lived there.

The beginning of our trip home was hectic. We noticed in the news that air controllers would stop international flights between the United States and Europe. The strike would begin the day we were to fly home; we had to go to Prestwick, Scotland to meet our plane. We took a train to the coast and crossed to England by ferry, and took a train to Glasgow. At the airport, we found a plane with empty seats and flew to Boston, where we phoned our family that we could fly to Cincinnati, but not to Lexington, KY, David and his family met us there. Later, our other two children and their families came to Wilmore to celebrate our summer trip and safe arrival. The next day the strike did stop all flights to and from Europe. We were glad to get home ahead of the strike.

We had a busy fall semester with the usual tight schedules, demanding committee meetings and several writing projects. We decided to take a trip to Florida in January 1982 in our motor home and make the Florida conference camp and retirement center near Lakeland our home for four weeks. On the way, we stopped at a cemetery at Zephyr Hills, Fl. to locate the burial plot of my grandfather, Joseph Baker, a Civil War veteran. To my knowledge, I was the first in our family to visit his burial place.

I needed to complete a writing project so I would spend each forenoon at the typewriter. In the afternoons we would spend visiting with a number of long time friends at the retirement center, or making trips to nearby cities or entertainment centers. The weather was beautiful, the fellowship with Free Methodist couples, widows and widowers, who had come from a number of northern states, was both exciting and inspiring.

On our way home we stopped at Orlando, FL to visit a distant cousin of the Silver branch of the Baker lineage. She gave me several items that belonged to several Silver ancestors, as well as family data. We then followed the Atlantic coast to Savannah, GA. We then swung inland to Ashland, NC, and stopped at a small town east of Knoxville, TN. We arrived home in the middle of the next afternoon. We enjoyed our visit to Florida. Now back to work in the classroom.

We mixed our summer with classes in June and short trips in our motor home. One trip was a two-week stay on our lot in Lake Tansi Village near Crossville, TN. The rest of the family came for a few days. Burt and Jeanie lived near Ann Arbor, MI. Ralph and Nellie still lived at Greenville, IL. David was manager of a factory just seven miles from us. He and Mary lived near Danville, KY.

The family's big event was the marriage of our oldest granddaughter, Karen Kae Kester to Mark Crites on December 18, 1982 at the Free Methodist Church in Greenville, IL. I participated in the wedding ceremony, along with Mark's brother, Lewis Narowetz. Since then, the couple has made their home in Greenville.

Early in 1983, Thomas Nelson Publishers asked me to assist Bob Sanford, the editor of the New King James Version, to prepare a set of maps. During January and February, Bob came to Wilmore several times to work with me on the map project. When completed, this set of maps became a standard part of the New King James Version. I helped Bob on several other projects.

After teaching classes that spring semester, I felt a surge of fulfillment. I had taught at Asbury Seminary for thirty years. I had never been seriously ill during that time and felt I might teach until almost my seventy-first birthday. We set 1987 as my retirement year. A developing problem was an increasing deafness in my left ear. A hearing aid helped me greatly.

In June, my brother Ray and wife, Ellen, came for a short visit. He had been chosen a lay delegate to represent the Northern Baptist churches of Wisconsin at the national convention in Cleveland, OH. It happened I had consented to speak several times that weekend at Springfield, OH where my oldest brother, Harold and his wife, Ethel, lived. We decided to travel together with Maria and me leading the way in our motor home. Harold and Ethel had an apartment with their daughter, Lila, and husband Ken Carson. They had not seen Ray and Ellen for quite some time, so the short visit was great.

When we returned to Wilmore, we hired a seminary student to repair our deck by putting new supports under it and building a roof over it. I spent most of the summer writing Sunday school lessons on selected Psalms.

Our eighth and last grandchild, Marianne Livingston was born October 6th, to our son David and Mary, at one of the oldest hospitals in central Kentucky at Danville, KY. The place is famous because a frontier doctor performed the first successful operation on the abdomen of a human.

In the fall, we went to visit Burt and family in Ann Arbor, MI. Their daughters were becoming very involved in figure skating, but not without a serious accident. The oldest daughter, Debby (10), had a fall on the ice rink and broke a shinbone, but had healed enough by autumn to win a silver medal. Cyndy (8) won a gold medal and four year old Laura was just learning how to skate.

One of the pressing tasks of 1984, besides teaching, was deciding how to close out several off-campus responsibilities I had. At the spring meeting of the directors of the Israel-American Institute of Holy Land Studies, I made several requests. As chairman of the Committee of Associated Schools, that gave academic advice to the Board of Directors, I requested that the coming year be the final year of my fifteen years of chairmanship. I made the same request to the Board of Directors, except my tenure would be twenty-five years.

The decision to make these requests was difficult, because I had helped establish the Institute in Jerusalem in the fall of 1959, serving as the first Field Director of the Institute. During the twenty-five years of its existence, the Institute had grown from about fifteen short-term students to several dozen working toward a Masters degree, and several hundred students who came in groups from various colleges and Universities for three weeks of intensive study in Israel. The Institute had also expanded from having about a dozen supporting schools to nearly one hundred institutions, some located in a dozen or more countries other than the United States.

In the fall of 1984, Nellie and Ralph's second daughter, Sharma, was a freshman at Central Junior College in McPherson, Kansas. Their ten-year-old son, Ken, was good at swimming.

Within the family, during 1985, changes were happening. Burt was operating a store in Ann Arbor, specializing in oak furniture and repairing and refinishing older furniture. Nellie's boy, Ken, was winning blue and red ribbons in swimming contests. Dave became manager of a manufacturing plant owned by Hoover Universal in Georgetown, KY. The job required a fifty mile round trip each work day, but he enjoyed his work. In November, Maria had trouble in her left eye that Doctor William Wood of Lexington said was due to bleeding blood vessels in the retina of the eye. He gave her a laser treatment to cure the problem.

At the beginning of the fall semester, the seminary's staff introduced to the faculty the marvels of a new technology, a computer. The seminary provided one for the faculty to use. I was so impressed that in December I bought a used Kapro II portable computer. I began learning in earnest how to make it lighten my writing load. I found it to be very helpful.

I taught a class during January, 1986, in February Maria's left eye began hurting and Doctor Wood had to use another laser treatment to stop weak blood vessels from leaking in the retina. From then on, throughout the year, we made sure we were near an expert doctor, in case the eye problem reoccurred.

In the spring of 1986, our son-in-law, Ralph, received an invitation from Seattle Pacific University to become the Associate Dean of Continuing Education of the University. Ralph had enjoyed his ten years at Greenville College in Greenville, IL, but he felt this offer was a step upward so he accepted the invitation. In June, we traveled to Greenville to help them pack up for the long trip west. Most belongings were shipped by truck. Ralph and Nellie found a house to rent in Renton not far from Seattle. Nellie had a job at Renton Technical College.

Our first great grandchild, Dustin Allen Kester, was born on July 31st, to granddaughter Sharma Kester in Seattle, WA.

In November, we decided to purchase three super saver tickets to Seattle to visit Nellie and family at Christmas time. We took our granddaughter, Cyndy Livingston, age nine, with us and had a great time getting acquainted with the great northwest. We marveled at the grandeur of Mt. Rainier. I had the privilege of baptizing Dustin. We returned December 27th and enjoyed a few days with Burt and family who came to Wilmore to pick up Cyndy. Together we motored to Dave and Mary's place thirty miles away to celebrate a late Christmas.

Dave also changed jobs, during 1986. His company, Johnson Controls, made him manager of a factory in Murfeesboro, TN. The factory made seats for a Nissan assembly plant, which produced the Sentra and pick-up trucks. He was unable to sell his home near Danville, so he drove two hundred miles Monday morning to his job and returned home Friday evening.

During the fall of 1986, Maria and I decided I should take one more trip to Israel in January 1987, with a group of four students from Asbury Seminary and seventy-five other students and faculty from all over the United States and Canada. We all went for a three-week, intensive course at the Israel-American Institute of Holy Land Studies in Jerusalem. We succeeded in organizing such a group and bought a round-trip ticket on the Swiss Airlines and began the tour on December 31, 1986.

I took Swiss Air to their hub airport at Zurich, Switzerland and transferred to a plane to Tel Aviv, Israel, where I arrived about noon on New Year's Day. The Israeli agents were very thorough in examining the luggage and items in pockets and small cases. The process took about an hour. I then boarded a bus to Jerusalem. I had already visited the city a half a dozen times. I was surprised at the improvements and new buildings I saw everywhere.

In time a taxi driver, who could not understand English, got me fairly close to the Institute. I was happy to greet old acquaintances and note that the Asbury Seminary students had already arrived. I was soon assigned to a cot in a room with several other occupants. Almost eighty students and faculty were excited about being in Israel and eager to begin their studies and tours. Due to the enlarged enrollment of the Institute, several nearby buildings had been rented for classes and equipment.

This trip was the first one I had taken to Israel in the wintertime, but the weather was more like springtime. It rained often and briefly, but when sunshine prevailed, I was amazed at the lack of haze in the atmosphere. I could see the Mediterranean Sea and distant hills. A short distance to the north of Jerusalem, one could see the snow-covered Mount Herman. The temperature was moderate; quite a contrast to the stifling heat of summertime.

The first week was a series of intensive classes about the geography of the land and the cultural variety in Israel and the West Bank. Professors who had lived in the land for some time led walking tours of various areas of Jerusalem. The students from Asbury Seminary stayed close to me and I told them personal stories about what the students saw. The week of classes was followed by two weeks of touring in several buses the length and breadth of Israel and the West Bank. At several places where I had excavated, I was permitted to explain to the tour groups my experiences at the site and how one could reconstruct its history by a study of the layers of debris and the shape and decoration of pottery found in each layer. We would eat and stay overnight at Youth Hostels that were plentiful in Israel.

There were no problems with terrorism at that time, so we traveled with safety. I met several old friends in Jerusalem whom I had not seen for a long time. It was an exciting trip. There were a lot of green grass and shrubs and many wild flowers, one of which was a flowering almond bush that was illustrated in Jeremiah 1:11, 12.

This, my last trip to Israel, was spiritually enriching. I boarded a Swiss Air plane very early in the morning on January 23rd. I changed planes again in Zurich and in New York and was in the airport at Cincinnati by early evening. The plane I was supposed to take to Lexington, KY had engine problems and canceled its flight. I was given a free room at a nearby hotel. I got a plane to Lexington the next morning and was soon greeted by my lovely wife. We were thankful for traveling mercies.

As I began classes, early in February, I was humbled as I realized that this was the last semester I would function as a professor at ATS. Naturally Maria and I, and our family, began to think how best to celebrate the conclusion of thirty-four years of tenure at the seminary. We also realized that 1987 would bring the conclusion of fifty years since we had graduated from Wessington Springs College, fifty years of marriage and fifty years of unbroken ministry, as a pastor and as a professor.

We began to plan how best to celebrate all these events. We soon learned that the student body and the faculty of the seminary were also thinking how best to recognize and honor three faculty members who were retiring from service at the May Commencement.

The chapel committee of the seminary was the first to act. Custom dictated that every retiree should preach to the student body before the end of the semester. I was chosen to present my retirement sermon at the 11:00 a.m. chapel service on March 26th. I chose as the scriptural text Ezekiel 3:16-23 under the title, "What a heavy Burden". The theme was the Lord's requirement that his messengers are responsible for warning people of the consequences of sin and the wonders of the Lord's redemptive acts. Each messenger is held accountable before the Lord, for obeying his commands.

The Junior, Middler and Senior classes of the student body were the next to act. They arranged for a banquet and ceremony on the evening of March 26th to be devoted to honoring the three retirees. These faculty were: Dr. J.T. Seamands, a missionary to India who became Professor of Christian Missions in 1961, Dr. Herbert Byrne who became Professor of Christian Education in 1967, and myself who became professor of Old Testament in 1953. I was older than the other two by only a few months. Many students, faculty and staff were present for the occasion.

The ceremony was entitled, "A Celebration of Gifts" and was made up of "Words of Thanks" by selected students and the presentation of a plaque to each professor and our responses to their kind words. President McKenna also made remarks. It was a service to be remembered.

Beginning May 8th, the senior class invited the retirees and their spouses to a special banquet. They honored the retirees with words of appreciation and memories of personal encounters with each.

The faculty and administration of the seminary followed with a retirement dinner on the evening of May 19th at the Stevens-Pike Dining Room of the Seminary. Three generations of our children were present. After a delicious banquet and a musical selection, a faculty person gave a media presentation of the life of each retiree. Several other faculty persons gave verbal tributes in honor of each retiree. Each retiree gave a brief response. The faculty wives also gave a gift to the wife of each professor. After President McKenna gave a tribute to the three retirees, he presented a specially made armchair to each. The chair was made of oak and was black enameled. On the top panel was the seminary's seal in gold.

On May 23rd, our extended family joined Maria and me in the celebration of the 50th anniversary of the three aspects of our lives together. In 1937, we could not afford to have our wedding in a church, so we decided we would renew our vows at the altar of the Free Methodist Church in Wilmore, KY. Dr. Arthur Brown, pastor of the church, and Dr. David McKenna, president of ATS, conducted the ceremony. Maria's sister, Tillie Radamacher, had been her Maid of Honor and was able to come from her home in Hubertus, WI to stand beside her. My brother, Ralph of Mason City, IA had been my Best Man and was present to stand beside me. The event was very special for us also, because three generations of our extended family were present. A number of our friends in Wilmore honored us with their presence. A reception followed in the church fellowship hall.

We had arranged for a dinner at the seminary dining room that evening with family and close friends present. It was a joyful time. That day was also our son David's birthday, so on a signal to the waiters, a large decorated cake was set at David's plate. In the center of the cake, an artist had formed a realistic racecar. David dearly loved driving his racing car at races. It was a memorable day.

The next day was the 64th Baccalaureate and Commencement of Asbury Theological Seminary. Because I had the longest tenure of the three retirees, the administration designated me the Marshal of the academic processional at both services. It was a thrill to lead the students, faculty, staff and administrative officers to their seats at the beginning and the exit at the end of each of these services. The seminary gymnasium was packed with several thousand parents and relatives of the students.

Near the conclusion of the afternoon Commencement, President McKenna had the retirees and their spouses escorted to the platform. Each of us was presented to the audience, which responded with thunderous applause. Each of us were declared to now have the honored title, "Emeritus," It is interesting to look back over thirty-four years of tenure as a professor at ATS. Many changes had taken place.

When we returned to Wilmore, KY in 1953, there were about 200 students and a dozen and a half professors. When I retired, there were over 800 students and almost 50 professors. The curriculum was mainly centered on the Bachelor of Divinity degree. The degree name was soon changed to Master of Divinity and Master of Missions and Master of Christian Education degrees were soon added. The seminary obtained accreditation with the American Theological Society in 1960, and the enrollment began to increase steadily. A Master of Theology degree (which required one more year of study beyond the Master of Divinity degree) was added to the curriculum. Next came a Doctor of Ministry degree, then a Doctor of Missions degree.

Scarcely a dozen buildings graced the Asbury campus in 1953, but in 1987 nearly 50 structures could be found on the campus, and Asbury was increasingly becoming known throughout the world as the leading Wesleyan oriented training center of effective spiritual pastors, educators and missionaries. These men and women were scattered throughout most countries of the world. We felt it was a great honor to be involved in their career training and in their spiritual development. We are happy to say that the dedication and passion of these students impacted our spiritual growth also.

Of special interest to me as a professor have been the advances that occurred in methods and equipment for teaching. The required courses tended to have enrollments of a hundred or more students and some classrooms were fairly large. However, the instructor had no microphone connected to speakers to help the voice of the professor to carry clearly to all students. The emphasis was on speaking loudly, which often produced a raspy voice. The installation of a communication system in the larger classrooms was a great help. In 1985, the computer age was birthed on the campus. We were fascinated by what these mysterious machines could do for us. Unfortunately, I retired too soon to experience the leap into extended learning offered via the Internet. I have marveled at what this learning method has done to education.

In 1953, the equipment for providing lecture notes for the students was basically limited to making copies of typewritten pages on a pan of special jelly. The result was a barely readable text. The use of visual material to illustrate aspects of the lecture was limited to 2" by 2" slides projected by a machine with a beam of light much too dim to provide a clear picture for a large class.

The invention of the overhead projector was a true blessing. Images of all kinds could be shown on a screen, using plastic sheets on which pictures, charts, diagrams could be printed or drawn. The professor could write notes on the sheet to enliven his spoken words. This device was truly a blessing. It became even a greater blessing when the experts in the visual aid department united the spoken word with the overhead projector and the computer.

Two career goals consumed the interest of the students and faculty: missions and the pastorate. Since the seminary from its beginning was oriented toward the United Methodist Church, though always staunchly independent, the majority of the students belonged to that denomination. Increasingly, the United Methodist students were admitted into more and more conferences. They soon became senior pastors of major churches, and also district superintendents. The same was true of the Free Methodist and Wesleyan students.

Students from other denominations flooded into the seminary and went out to become prominent pastors. A remarkable feature was the marked increase of students coming from various universities. They were led to Christ by evangelical student organizations. Few had any church background and almost no biblical knowledge. By attending special "make-up" courses they soon matched the other students and graduated to become effective ministers.

Another specialty was training students for missionary ministry. Besides students who were offspring of active missionary families, there were many who related themselves to independent missionary organizations such as World Gospel Missions and the Oriental Missionary Society. The graduates of the Seminary also included students who were natives of almost every continent. Most of them returned to their home churches and soon were filling top positions in churches and schools.

The administration moved to strengthen its mission's curriculum by establishing the E. Stanley Jones School of Missions in 1983. Besides a Masters of Missions degree, it offered a Doctor of Missions program that drew a significant number of students.

Through out the 34 years of our tenure, the spiritual level of the faculty and student-body was remarkable. Prayer was prominent in this feature of the seminary. The three presidents under whom I served: McPheeters, Stanger and McKenna, were role models. Each made prayer a focal part of their personal lives and actively supported prayer activities among the faculty and students. Prayer groups large and small were set up to function on a weekly and monthly schedule. Classes were opened with a brief time of prayers, and small groups, often led by a faculty member, met on a regular basis. The two chapel services each week were marked by spiritual aliveness.

During the years, two revivals swept the Asbury College and Seminary campuses and spread out to touch many local churches. The most effective revival was the one that occurred in 1970. The student bodies of both institutions were deeply affected by this event and many lives were transformed.

The most remarkable outreach of this revival was through a spontaneous creation of an annual youth affair in Wilmore called

Ichthus. Sparked by a seminary professor, Dr. Bob Lyon, and put together by students, this youth gathering met on an April weekend at the Wilmore Holiness Camp Ground. Contemporary Christian music and lively youth speakers attracted many young people from many states. In recent years, the attendance has reached 22,000. Several years ago, Ichthus purchased a farm of 100 acres. A portion of the farm was given to the City of Wilmore for a family oriented park. The remainder of the land has been used to provide parking for the tents, trailers, campers, vans and motor homes that pour into the grounds during the three-day event.

Thankfulness fills our hearts as we remember the years of ministry at Asbury Theological Seminary. When we came to the seminary, it was small and struggling to exist. When I retired from its faculty, the seminary's enrollment placed it among the ten largest in the nation. Its overall enrollment averages between 1,500 and 2,000 per year. It is humbling to realize we have lived and served the seminary during this period of its growth.

CHAPTER 10

HEALTH ENEMIES—CANCER AND DIABETES

Were my teaching responsibilities over just because I was retired? Not quite. Earlier in the year our son-in-law, Dr. Ralph Kester had invited us to go to Seattle Pacific University. I accepted his invitation to teach several courses in the Summer School session, and had to be in Seattle by the middle of July 1987.

At the end of May 1987, we decided to trade our Titan motor home for another new motor home. It was much smaller and was mounted on a Toyota small truck chassis. It drove like a dream. We had exciting plans to make a series of trips during our retirement. This was our first trip to Seattle and back and it would reveal whether it was reliable on the road. The only trouble was we found too late that we had loaded the vehicle too heavily for its size.

Our first stop along the way to Seattle was McPherson, KS. The alumni of our alma mater, Wessington Springs College (aka WSC), were holding a reunion on the campus of Central College of Kansas June 25th-28th. WSC ceased to exist in 1968, and its records were transferred to its sister institution, Central College. For that reason, the alumni of WSC met there.

We had been alumni for fifty years but during those years we had rarely met most of our classmates of the 1930's. We looked forward to meeting them again, as well as other alumni. We started the trip with hopes for a good trip, but along the way to McPherson, we got an instrument reading that the oil level in the transmission was getting low. We added oil but worried from there on that we had bought a "lemon."

We arrived safely at McPherson and had a wonderful time catching up on news about each other. A total of about 400 were in attendance. Included among that group were other members of our family. My brother Ralph, my sister Dorothy and our son Burton are alumni. Burt was unable to be there but the spouses of Ralph and Dorothy were present.

We ate together and enjoyed group gatherings. I had the privilege of thanking the couple that had organized and led a prayer meeting for me when I had a serious attack of pneumonia in the fall of 1934. For the first time in fifty years the four of us, who dated often during the last year of school, were together again for the weekend.

We visited the archives in the library where WSC materials were kept. Maria enjoyed seeing the quilt on which one square of cloth had her name. She had sewed her name into the cloth fifty-one years before.

The highlights of the reunion were the two worship services held on Sunday in the local Free Methodist Church. An alumnus preached in the morning and the music was provided by a hastily organized choir made up of WSC schoolmates. Both Maria and I sang in that choir.

Refreshed and excited, we left McPherson the next morning, June 29th, for Denver, CO where we spent the July 4th weekend with Buel and Flora Andrus who lived in a suburb called Golden. This couple rented several rooms of the house we bought in 1954 in Wilmore. They were students of Asbury College and had a small boy. We agreed to let them continue to rent the rooms until they graduated and moved to new jobs. We had become like "parents" of a son and daughter.

It was a beautiful day and I-70 had moderate traffic. However, the elevation gradually rose as we drove west. When we stopped for gasoline, we also checked the oil level in the transmission. We were concerned when we had to add oil several times. We prayed we could make it to Golden, CO. In mid afternoon, we entered Denver and were driving on the inner lane. To our surprise, a car passing us on the right honked, and we discovered that Flora was driving the car. Both of us stopped at a gasoline station. The incident seemed like an answer to prayer, for we did not know exactly how to get to Flora's home. We also had noticed that the transmission was not acting properly. As we climbed the slope to the Andrus home, we noted the transmission clearly was not acting right.

Buel Andrus was an engineer and knew how to identify car problems and how to solve them. He suggested we drive the vehicle to a Toyota garage in Denver the next morning. This we did and the mechanics there told us the transmission was in serious trouble. It needed to be replaced. Since the motor home was still under warranty, the mechanic contacted the national headquarters of Toyota in California. Happily, the company honored the warranty and instructed the mechanic to obtain a new and larger transmission from Toyota's district warehouse in Kansas City.

The mechanic was concerned because the July 4th holiday was only a few days away. Already several of their office staff had gone on vacation. After learning that the warehouse had the proper transmission on hand, the mechanic requested that the transmission be sent by airfreight to Denver. The mechanic expected the item to arrive the next day. The transmission did not arrive as planned.

Two days later, the transmission still had not arrived. The local mechanics had removed the faulty transmission from our motor home and were ready to install the new one soon after its arrival. During the afternoon, the mechanic discovered that many of the warehouse personnel had indeed gone on vacation. A substitute clerk in the warehouse finally admitted that he sent the transmission by motor freight instead of airfreight. I hope that the ordered item would arrive in Denver on July 3rd. It did not arrive that day and probably would not arrive until Monday. We might as well relax and enjoy the July 4th fireworks and our friends.

Monday forenoon the garage informed us the transmission had arrived and they would install it immediately, along with a transmission oil-cooling system. The next day the mechanics had completed the job and we went to drive the motor home to the Andrus home. A while later, I noticed that Buel was inspecting the motor area, and being curious I inquired what he was checking out. He informed me he had worked with cars a long time and had developed the habit of inspecting the work of other mechanics. He said he had discovered that poor work was often done.

Then he said, "I think we have a problem here. He pointed out to me the spot that lacked a bolt. "If you give me permission," he said, "I will call the garage and inform them of the problem." I quickly said "yes." and he soon had a mechanic on the phone. The man was amazed and doubted that the mistake could have happened. He asked Buel to bring the vehicle back to the garage. After the mechanic inspected the transmission mounting to the rest of the power train, he reacted with amazement. He called the mechanic who was in charge of the job and angrily reprimanded him. The red-faced mechanic quickly got a bolt and put it in place. Clearly, Buel's alertness saved us another expensive repair bill. As it was, Toyota paid the entire three thousand dollar bill for replacing the transmission.

On July 10th, Maria and I were on our way to Seattle. Late in the afternoon, we arrived in Salt Lake City and did some sightseeing. Then we found a campground just north of the city and spent a peaceful night. This was the first time we had traveled in this part of Idaho and Oregon. The mountains and scenic views kept us in a state of awe. We managed to cross Idaho and into the mountains in eastern Oregon where we camped overnight at Baker City.

We soon came to an impressive decline in elevation. To the north toward Pendleton was a breathtaking panorama of extensive grain fields. We went down that hill very slowly. Beyond Pendleton, we came to another marvel, the gorge of the Columbia River. We crossed into the state of Washington north of Hamilton, OR into the famous apple country around Yakima. Going over a mountain range, we noticed we were getting low on gas and looked without success for a service station. The tank was almost empty when we arrived at Ellensburg. We vowed to watch our gas gauge more closely in the future.

We found the Cascade mountain system very scenic and our anticipation of arriving at Nellie and Ralph's home was gripping us. Leaving I-90, we found our way along crooked state roads through well-kept suburbs of Seattle, to the city of Renton. Shortly we were hugging members of our family, including our first great-grandson. We were four generations in one home. I found this hard to believe, since my great-grandfather was born in 1798, my grandfather was born in 1836, my father was born in 1876 and I was born in 1916. My grandparents had died before I was born.

Ralph was in charge of the summer school program at Seattle Pacific University with an enrollment of over three thousand, most of the students were public school teachers. Many of the students were in graduate level studies. The classes of the second term started the next Monday and I had two classes in Old Testament studies. One class met for three hours each forenoon and the other class, Hebrew Grammar, for three hours each afternoon for five days. This class was connected with an extension campus of Fuller Theological Seminary in Seattle. The term lasted for two weeks. Maria and I lived in an apartment on the SPU campus during this time.

In the evenings, Ralph and Nellie took us sightseeing in Seattle and neighboring suburbs. One weekend trip was to Mt. St. Helens to view the aftermath of the volcano that blew off the top of the mountain and destroyed the forest for many miles around. Another trip was to the smaller twin summits of Mt. Rainier. Our niece, Sally Livingston, had come by plane from San Francisco and together we enjoyed the fantastic snow-covered peak of that famous mountain.

On August 5th, Maria and I boarded the ferry, Princess Margarite, to Victoria, Canada, for some sightseeing, especially the Bourchert Gardens. We took another ferry to Vancouver where we spent several days touring the city and its parks. We returned to Seattle by bus on August 7th. This was our 50th anniversary honeymoon trip, though the actual date of the wedding had been on August 12th. On that date, Nellie and Ralph took us to a fancy restaurant on top of a hotel next to the Sea-Tac airport. The waiters and waitresses gave us special attention, provided music and sang for us. We had a great time celebrating.

We started home August 17th. The highlight of the trip was a five-hour stop at Timber Lake, SD (about 600 people) where we were married fifty years before. We went to the courthouse and viewed the record of our marriage license. We then went to the small house on the west edge of the town where Maria and her family had lived. A widow lived in the house and very graciously listened to our story and took us to the living room in which the wedding ceremony took place. We felt like kissing on the spot where we had stood.

We continued on to the northwestern corner of Wisconsin where my brothers, Ray and Ralph and their spouses lived. Their homes were in the Voyager Village, near Webster. They had arranged for a family reunion that Sunday and 35 of our nephews and nieces, along with my sister Dorothy and her husband, were present. We had a happy time together.

We continued on to the homes of Maria's sister, Fanny at West Bend, WI and her sister, Tillie, near Hubertus, WI. Our next stop was at Ann Arbor, MI to visit our son Burt's family, then on to hot and dry Wilmore, KY. We had traveled about 6,000 miles and the RV worked beautifully after its repair in Denver.

Starting in late April and going throughout the summer, Maria had a continual bout with hives. After returning home, we went to a doctor, an allergist, who gave Maria a series of tests. Soon the culprits were found. Milk products and corn were found guilty. Maria eliminated these foods and the hives disappeared.

The crisis event happened In the middle of November. Maria noticed some swelling and some pain in her left breast. We went to a doctor for a mammogram. She had regular mammogram exams since her cancer episode in 1973, but this one showed something not detected by the previous mammograms.

Dr. Eastland did a biopsy on the 23rd and a cancer nodule the size of a peanut was found. The next day a radical mastectomy operation removed the left breast and several lymph nodes in her left armpit. Tests showed they did not contain cancer cells. That was great news for it put Maria in the 85% to 90% possibility of survival. She must have regular check-ups for ten years before she could have 100% likelihood of living through the ordeal. She came home on December 1st, and by taking it easy she rapidly recovered. A year of joyous celebration and travel ended with pain and anxiety. Our families came to observe Christmas 1987 with us and that was a great comfort.

Early in January 1988, I met a deadline for writing study notes for the Wesley Study Bible. The notes were on the books of Jeremiah and Lamentations to be published by the Thomas Nelson Inc., of Nashville, TN. A week later, our doctor told me I had a mild case of diabetes, a disease that is common in the Livingston family. Dad had a severe case of diabetes and several of my siblings had the disease. I kept on writing, using my computer. By mid-February, I completed thirteen Sunday school lessons for the Light and Life Press.

A few days later Maria and I motored to the southern tip of Texas to visit two weeks with my brother Ralph and his wife. They spent their winters in a trailer home at a "snow bird' village at Weslaco. We had a wonderful time that included several trips into Mexico.

In May and June I wrote commentaries on the books of Esther, Nahum, Jonah, and Daniel for the Asbury Bible Commentary. Zonderan Publishers scheduled this book for publication the next year.

On July 9th, Maria and I headed our mini-motor home toward Seattle. The temperature through the mid-western states was an intense 100+ degrees. The air-conditioner in the cab of the motor home barely kept us comfortable, but we arrived OK at the end of five days.

Nellie and Ralph had purchased a home and were remodeling their kitchen, so I got into that project. We went sightseeing on Whidbey Island and other areas north of Seattle.

During the depression years of the early thirties, many families in the mid-west moved to Oregon. Families in and around Timber Lake, SD, neighbors and classmates of Maria, were among those who made that move. Every summer they had a reunion in one of the parks in McMinnville, OR that was the meeting place for 1988. Maria's best friend during high school was Mrs. Marguerite Roghair who lived with her husband in McMinnville. She took us around to all the transplanted Timber Lake people who were at the reunion. Many of them Maria had not seen for over fifty years. We had a great time together. The next day we did some sightseeing, going to the beach, and to various frontier towns. We returned to Renton on a beautiful Sunday.

We started home the first week of September by way of the fantastic Glazier National Park in Montana. By stopping several times, we made it up the steep highway to the summit and down the east side. At the bottom of the mountain, a sign indicated a park for RV's and campers. After buying a place for the night, we went east several miles to a highway junction. We decided to eat at an authentic western cafe. Maria would not buy a buffalo hamburger, but I found mine to be dry but tasty.

The next day we traveled on US # 2 for miles and miles through a dry and almost empty prairie. Every now and then there were cattle grazing. The towns were small and rustic. A railroad track ran parallel to the highway and a few times, we tried to race with the trains, but we dared not try to match their speed. In eastern Montana, the rather small Missouri River flowed in the same direction we were going. There were some prosperous farms in the valley, many irrigated by the river's water.

In North Dakota, we spent several hours touring here and there in the Theodore Roosevelt National Park. The park had plenty of treeless hills, cliffs and ravines. The scenery gave one a wild-west feeling. We camped that night in a primitive camping site near a small town. The air was chilly in the morning. The flat countryside along I-94 reminded us much of SD. On the fourth day, we crossed the Wisconsin line, and soon stopped at a rest home for elderly people at Barron and visited with my oldest sister, Vera. We arrived at Ray and Ellen's home in the Village at dusk. On September 10th we attended the 50th wedding anniversary of Ray and Ellen. It was held at the First Baptist Church in Eau Claire, WI where they had attended for many years. Late that afternoon, we arrived at the home of Maria's sister, Tillie, near Milwaukee, WI.

We could not stay long, for an Old Testament professor had resigned at the seminary and the administration needed me to teach a class during the fall semester.

After we arrived in Wilmore, a letter from the publisher reported they were celebrating the tenth anniversary of printing the New International Version. Because I had worked on the General Editorial Committee of the Old Testament of that version, they asked me to appear twice on channel 27 in Lexington. I gave the TV station two interviews. The first one was 2 1/2 minutes long and was broadcast on the noon and evening news on November 28th. The second interview was 30 minutes long and was broadcast on December 10th. Imagine it, I got on TV!

Between these interviews, the mother of Burt's wife, Jeanie, died in Memphis, TN. We drove to Memphis to attend the funeral and stopped at our son, Dave's home, in Lexington, TN, going and returning. Two days later was my second interview recording and after I arrived home, I mentioned that I was having pains in my upper right abdomen. I began having severe nausea and vomiting, but assumed I had the flu, which was sweeping through Wilmore.

Early Sunday morning, December 11th, the pains were almost unbearable, so we checked in at the emergency room at Humana hospital in Lexington. After several hours of testing, the doctors decided I had an infected gall bladder and began loading me with antibiotics. A surgeon operated on me Monday afternoon and removed one gallstone the size of a golf ball. The pain disappeared and on December 17th Maria brought me home. That was the first time I had been in a hospital bed since my bout with pneumonia in 1934. We rejoiced that I healed rapidly, though I had to be careful for six months. We were able to entertain the families of our children with a happy 1988 Christmas celebration.

During the fall of 1988, Maria and I began planning a mission trip to the Far East. We learned that the Free Methodist College in Kaohsiung, Taiwan needed temporary faculty assistance. We made contact with the president of the school and worked out a three-week schedule for an intensive course in Old Testament history.

On March 8 1989, we boarded a Delta airlines plane to Portland, OR where we transferred to a plane to Taipei, Taiwan. A former student, Dr. Bixler, and his wife met us at the airport, kept us overnight and sent us by train to Kaohsiung, located near the south tip of the island. We were housed in an apartment on the upper floor of the modern administration building, which was also the dormitory for students who came from all over southern Taiwan. Since we ate in the college dining room, we quickly became acquainted with the students.

There were about two-dozen students in my class. Some were pastors of churches in and near the city. The class period was three hours long each afternoon for four days of each of the three weeks. A Chinese pastor of a nearby church served as my interpreter at each of the classes. Maria spent a number of hours helping in the college library. On weekends, both of us were kept busy speaking to various Christian groups in the city and in nearby towns. Maria spoke to female students and to women's groups in the churches where I preached. We got to see quite a bit of the south end of Taiwan.

One evening, the president of the college took us to an elaborate Chinese wedding. First, there was a nine-course meal that consisted of excellent food. There was a large crowd seated at tables, and remained seated during the ceremony. Then the bride and groom went from table to table, thanking each person for coming to the wedding. The event was fascinating.

On one Sunday, I was scheduled to preach an Easter sermon at a church whose pastor had been one of my students. The congregation of several hundred met in an office building. The Chinese pastor and family lived on the third floor and the congregation worshipped on the second floor. I was informed that a baptismal event would follow the service. We had noticed when we entered the building we had passed through a large room having only one feature, a large cement tank about five feet by ten feet in size and three feet in depth. It was half filled with water.

After the worship service, everyone moved to the first floor and surrounded the tank. The pastor and I quickly went to his apartment and changed into everyday clothes, for we had to enter the tank to conduct the baptisms of a middle-aged man, a teenage boy, and four teenage girls. For the Chinese Christians, a person being baptized was publicly declaring a complete break with polytheism and a serious commitment to Jesus Christ as their personal Savior. Parents were silent during each ceremony but greeted their children with joy when each one came up from the water. I read the ritual in English and the pastor read it in Chinese and we joined in baptizing each person. This was a very impressive moment.

Since Chinese churches have their services in the afternoon or evening, I preached as many as three times each Sunday, both in Kaohsiung and in neighboring villages.

When Maria and I boarded the bus to Taipei, we were pleased to see a number of the students standing outside the bus, singing a hymn for us. Since we had visited this college in Kaohsiung in March of 1964, we were happy to see the new building and enlarged student body that graced the campus in a crowded city.

We stopped at Taichung to lecture at another Christian college for several days. Some of the teachers had been my students. Dr. and Mrs. Bixler met us at the bus station in Taipei and took us to their apartment. They kept us busy speaking at various churches and student groups at the university where they taught classes.

When we had made up the schedule for the trip, we had noted that we had to change planes in Seoul, South Korea. The Oriental Missionary Society operated a college and seminary there and the president had been one of my former students. We had contacted him and received an invitation to visit his school and lecture to various classes, faculty groups and a gathering of leaders and pastors of Christian churches in Seoul. The institute had several hundred students who were attentive and friendly.

We wished we could have stayed longer, but we left by plane on April 8th and flew non-stop to Portland, OR, where Nellie and Ralph met us at the airport and took us to their home in Seattle for a few days of rest. On April 12th, we took another Delta plane from Seattle and arrived in Kentucky that evening. It had been springtime in Taiwan, South Korea, and Seattle and in Kentucky. At each place we marveled at the wealth of gorgeous flowers and trees. We regarded the trip as one of the high points in our ministry.

After a few days of rest, we headed our motor home to Burt's home near Ann Arbor, MI. We watched their three daughters, Debby, Cyndy, and Laura win medals and ribbons at a regional skating contest.

Our next trip was to Lexington, TN, where Dave and Mary were moving into a new house, by a lake, that Dave had designed and had directed the building process. He was enjoying his new management job at Johnson Controls largest manufacturing plant. I divided my time fishing from the edge of their back yard and helping with the painting of the rooms of the house. David Jr. and Marianne enjoyed taking us out in their new boat. Marianne took me out on the lake on a small Sea-Do boat. She made it turn tight curves and bounce over waves. One boat ride like that was enough for me!

On July 8 1989, Maria and I flew out to Seattle, where I agreed to teach two classes in the second session of the summer school program of Seattle Pacific University. We stayed in an apartment on campus during the two-week session.

During this time the Free Methodist Church held their General Conference on the campus. We met old friends; some were members of several of the churches we had pastored in Wisconsin and Iowa. We were also able to greet missionaries and native pastors who had come from a number of countries to the Conference.

We saw our grandson, Kenny Kester swim in several swim meets. He was becoming an expert swimmer. We celebrated my seventy-third birthday, and great-grandson, Dustin's, third birthday and later celebrated Maria and my 52nd wedding anniversary. Our stay was climaxed by a weekend visit to the west and north sides of the Olympic Peninsula. What a thrill to see the huge waves of the Pacific Ocean pound the beaches. We returned home by plane on Aug. 29th.

As in 1987 and 1988, the first two-thirds of 1989 were filled with memorable events. In each case, the last several months were marked by serious operations and deep anxiety.

On September 10th, Maria had her six-month check-up and the doctor found a lump in her right breast. After several tests, a biopsy confirmed that cancer was involved. This was her third bout with the dreaded disease. On September 21st, a mastectomy was done and she was in Humana hospital in Lexington, KY. Her surgeon contacted a radiologist and a chemotherapist. The next day, Maria began three and a half weeks of radiation. There were seventeen chemotherapy treatments by injections.

Before the chemotherapy treatments began on October 20th, Maria also had to have a fourth laser operation on her left eye. The ordeal was very difficult for all of us, especially for Maria. Her faith in God and her spiritual strength was a challenge to all of us to hold steady. Her cancer specialist was a kindly man and his nurses gave Maria tender attention as they administered the chemotherapy drugs intravenously. This regimen went well into the next year.

In spite of the chemotherapy, Maria was strong enough for the children and most of the grandchildren to come for a happy Thanksgiving dinner. When Karen and Mark came to the house, Maria and I were on the front porch and as they approached, suddenly Nellie jumped from behind Mark crying, "Surprise! Surprise!" She had flown from Seattle to Lexington, KY where she was met. We had a great weekend together. Maria said all this was the best pill she had ever taken. The episode did her a lot of good.

Maria handled the fourteen treatments of chemotherapy in January 1990 better than she did the sessions in November and December; she slept better and had less stomach upset. One plus was that she was not losing her hair. We had followed advice and had purchased a wig of gray hair. She never had to use it. The nurses thought this was unusual.

Maria's schedule of IV therapy and pills continued through April. Her doctor forbade Maria to go to public gatherings, because her immunity level was low and there was danger she could come down with the flu, which could be fatal. Maria's strength gained steadily during the rest of the year and we stayed close to home. As they could, our children came to see us.

One aspect of Maria's long period of chemotherapy was the attention the families in our church gave us. Frequently, one family or another would bring us our evening meal. We decided that if you have to get sick, Wilmore is a great place to have it happen. The people here know how to pray for the sick and to brighten your days with meals and brief visits.

In August 1990, Maria was well enough for us to take a plane to Renton, WA to visit Nellie and Ralph. Their son, Kenny was rapidly becoming an expert swimmer, winning many prizes in swimming contests. He also served as a lifeguard at the Good Will games held near Seattle. While we were at Renton, Burt, Jeanie and girls drove to Renton. Burt taught classes in the last session of summer school at Seattle Pacific University. We then surprised Burt and Jeanie with a 25th anniversary trip to the Olympic Peninsula, though the date of their wedding was in April.

Other changes in our families were Debby's entrance into the University of Michigan as a freshman, and Dave's new job as Vice President of Factory Operations for High Tech, Inc. His new headquarters were at Columbus, MS where a large factory was located. He was also responsible for several other factories, including one in Mexico. Dave drove weekly to a house he bought in Columbus but returned on Friday evenings to Lexington, TN.

I completed several writing projects during the year and in the fall semester I stepped into the classroom again, at the request of the dean of the seminary. This time I taught a class in biblical archaeology and as a special project I took the students to the Bethel Academy site south of Wilmore.

We excavated on Saturdays or Mondays, depending on the weather. We searched along the north foundation wall, hoping to find evidence of a front porch to the structure. We found some artifacts, but no foundation for a porch came to light.

As usual, members of our family helped us celebrate Thanksgiving and the Christmas holidays. We felt joy and a spiritual uplift as we gathered. The young grandchildren behaved wonderfully and the older grandchildren played games. The adults caught up on recent events.

While in Kansas for Christmas, Rodney Leonard and Sharma Kester decided to be married by his father at Kinsley, KS, on December 27, 1990. Nellie and Ralph promised to have a formal wedding ceremony in Renton that summer so that all family members and friends could share the joy of their wedding.

In February 1991, Ken Kester won the Washington state championship in the 500 meter free style race.

Ralph, our son-in-laws, mother died June 17th and her funeral was June 20th, in Portland OR.

In May Sharma got her AA degree from Bellevue Community College, Bellevue, WA in Secretarial Office work. Rod and Sharma rented a house near Renton and both settled into the routine of full-time jobs and they became active in a Nazarene church. Rodney legally adopted Dustin who rapidly became attached to his father. During the spring, the family was engaged in planning for the ceremony, with June 22nd in mind. The event was scheduled in the Renton Nazarene church with the pastor of the church and me conducting the ceremony. Maria, Laura and I flew out on June 19th and David, Mary and family flew out on the 21st and rented a van while in Renton. Rod's parents, his sister and family drove to Renton. Everything went smoothly, and as the couple recessed I thought, what an example of the redeeming power of God's grace. The next week I taught a course at the summer school session at SPU.

Our second great-grandchild, Jennifer Maria Crites, was born on July 15, 1991, to our granddaughter of Karen and Mark, in Greenville, IL.

During the fall, I continued my research activity and we took short trips in our motor home. I had another health problem in the fall. I had noticed difficulty of seeing clearly in my right eye and went to our eye physician. He said my problem was macular degeneration and thought an operation might help. A study of how to correct this problem was being financed by a certain organization to see if certain operations could cure this degeneration. He asked my permission to conduct that operation on my eye at no cost to me. I agreed and a two-hour operation on my right eye was performed. It failed to help my problem.

On December 19, 1991, I arose from bed to find I had blurred vision in my right eye. We went immediately to the doctor's office. He said the retina had detached and I needed an emergency operation to re-attach it. That afternoon a three-hour operation to put the retina back in place was performed. The doctor said I would be legally blind in that eye the rest of my life. I continued to have peripheral vision.

Our third great-grandchild, Justin Michael Leonard was born on February 6, 1992, to our granddaughter Sharma and Rod, in Renton, WA.

In mid-February of 1992, Maria and I flew to Seattle, where I baptized two great-grandchildren: Jennifer Marie, daughter of our granddaughter Karen and Mark Crites of Greenville, IL and Justin

Michael, son of our granddaughter Sharma and Rod Leonard of Renton, WA at the Renton Methodist Church. The event took place in the presence of four generations on both Nellie and Ralph's families. What a thrill for all of us. We spent a couple of weeks there and got to watch our grandson, Ken swim in the regional and State Championship competitions. His last swim, a 400 meter relay where he was the last swimmer, at the state level won the State Championship for his school by one point.

In April, we drove our motor home to Ann Arbor, MI to watch our figure skating granddaughters win medals in a skating contest. Debby had been teaching her sisters the fine points of the sport. In mid-July, we drove to Greenville, IL to celebrate Jennifer's first birthday with a number of Mark's family. Our grandson, Kenny Kester flew from Seattle to be present also.

The foregoing is the plus side, now for the minus side. During the summer, Maria had concern about an "aging spot" on the lower, right side of her face. In June, a dermatologist had said it looked OK but on August 1st, the spot began to bleed. A Plastic Surgeon recommended surgery; he did a biopsy and reported the problem was melanoma skin cancer. The doctor removed an area of skin three inches in diameter at his office that day. Skin was taken from the front of Maria's left shoulder and grafted to her face. Maria went home later in the afternoon. The wound healed very quickly with a minimum of pain. The surgery was so expertly done that I had to look closely to detect the area of the skin implant. As a precaution, the doctor had us apply a special ointment to several dark spots on her face. The procedure was a success.

The year 1993 was like the previous year in that a health crisis was followed by a wonderful recovery. For a number of years, Maria had problems with arthritis in her left hip. All winter and spring, pain in this hip increased to a severe level. Four doctors agreed she needed a complete hip replacement. A successful replacement was done on June 4th. Maria suffered much pain after the operation. I stayed with her in the hospital room day and night. After a week, she came home.

Within a month, she was using a walker and then a four-pronged cane. By the end of August, she put the cane in the closet and was able to walk normally. The hip remained tender for several months more, but the old pains were gone.

Maria then decided another long-lasting ailment should be treated. Both of her big-toe nails were thick and ingrown. I had worked on these toes for many years. In late September, she had a surgeon completely remove both nails in his office. They healed slowly, but hurt no more.

To celebrate her relief from pain, we took our motor home out several times to enjoy the beauty of the autumn colors. We also made a plane trip to Seattle to spend a two-week Thanksgiving visit to Nellie and Ralph's home in Renton. We were happy to visit also with Sharma, Rod, Dustin, and Justin. Ralph had recently been promoted to Dean of the Division of Continuing Education at SPU. Nellie now worked in the office of Pacific Metal Company.

Besides caring for Maria, I had kept busy all year doing research and writing articles about Bethel Academy, where I had supervised archaeological work during the late sixties, all the seventies and most of the eighties. In 1994, we would help celebrate the 200th year since that school had opened its doors to students by publishing these articles.

Almost by accident, I had discovered that my grandfather, Thomas M. Livingston had taken part in the Civil War battle at Perryville, KY. The date was October 8, 1862. Grandfather fought as a private in the 86th Illinois Infantry in the early phases of the battle, but not in the main battle. He was not hurt.

Skimming through a book on the Civil War battles west of the Mississippi River, I discovered that my other grandfather, Joseph Baker, was a sergeant in the 2nd Colorado Cavalry during the battle of Westport, now Kansas City, MO, on October 23, 1864. He also was not hurt during the battle. Both battles were bloody and were important Union victories.

We finished 1993 by having great times with our families when we were able to get together on Labor Day, Thanksgiving Day and Christmas. It was not possible for all of us to get together on each of these holidays. By various combinations, we renewed our family ties and rejoiced that the Lord had been good to us.

A special project dominated the events of 1994. The Wilmore Free Methodist Church was facing a crisis. The growth of the congregation was packing the sanctuary, Sunday school space and the parking lot was too small. No property near the church could be purchased to solve the problem of expansion. I was a member of a Long Range Planning committee that concluded the present church must be sold and a site located on which to build a new church complex. The church members had agreed to the proposal in January, and a Building Committee was formed, of which I was the vice chairman.

A search of Wilmore and vicinity centered attention on a hilltop west of the city that belonged to Asbury College. About ten acres were available for purchase. There was an average of three meetings a month of the Building Committee all through the year. Working on the committee took most of my time in the evenings and on the weekends, so that other projects had to be put aside. Many problems had to be solved. Asbury Seminary agreed to buy the church property and to rent Estes Chapel and some class rooms to the congregation until June 1996. Details of the land purchase must be worked out with Asbury College. We must search for an architect, and a building contractor. Decisions must be made concerning the size, shape and cost of the new building. Local and state building codes and laws must be researched and complied with. Months slipped by, as these matters were clarified and basic decisions made. It was obvious that the project would cost a lot of money. I was deeply involved in all that happened and often listened with appreciation to the suggestions of Maria and other members of the family.

In October, a surprise came to the committee. A retired couple, Eugene and June Lintemuth, not connected to the Free Methodist Church, but close friends of many members of the church, were spending the summer in their home in the Upper Peninsula of Michigan. They were interested in the location of the future Free Methodist Church and were not happy with the land the church was about to purchase from the College. After much prayer, the couple drove the long distance to Wilmore to contact Dr. Clyde Van Valin about the possibility of the church purchasing land from a Mr. Zorneger who owned property on the north edge of Wilmore.

The Long Range Planning committee had contacted Mr. Zorneger several times, but had repeatedly received a refusal to sell. Mr. Lintemuth felt he knew Mr. Zorneger well enough he could persuade the man to agree to sell a plot of land to the church. Besides, Mr. Lintemuth felt that in his prayer times he had received an assurance from the Lord that Mr. Zorneger could change his mind and sell a plot of land. Eugene, Dr. Van Valin and another minister traveled to Cincinnati to see Mr. Zorneger and his attorney. They returned with the assurance that the proposal would be given careful thought. In a few days, the trio returned to see Mr. Zorneger with more specific details about the church plans. They found Mr. Zorneger open to the possibility of selling a plot 400 feet by 900 feet, but needed more details.

When the Free Methodist congregation learned of the new developments, there was almost immediate approval. More people than the members of the building committee realized, had misgivings about buying the college land. Prayer meetings were held to discern the will of the Lord in the matter. Everything went smoothly and on November 21st, Mr. Zorneger signed a contract to sell 8.25 acres on the east side of State Route # 29 to the Church. Everyone in the church felt this turn of events was a definite answer to prayer, and the building committee focused its attention to placing the new church complex on the newly purchased land.

Fortunately, not all my spare time was taken up by committee work. Members of our family came to visit us on special occasions, such as Easter, Memorial Day, Labor Day, and Christmas.

One special occasion was the graduation of our granddaughter, Deborah Livingston, from the University of Michigan with a Bachelor of Science degree. We had the pleasure of being at this event in Ann Arbor. She was intensely interested in nature and she soon had a job leading youth groups of various ages on nature hikes in and around Ann Arbor. Her ice skating interests also helped her to become a coach of children who wanted to learn skating techniques.

One of the highlights of the summer was a visit of Beryl and Betty Johnson. He was the son of my oldest sister, Vera, and we had not seen the couple for years. We had a wonderful time renewing our friendship.

For a change, Maria had no health crisis during 1994, though she was bothered with arthritis in her left knee that produced bothersome pain. She was able to go with me to Springfield, OH on Aug 14th to visit my niece, Lila, and her husband, Ken. The visit also had another happy purpose. Lila's son, Gary, had become a born-again Christian and wanted me to baptize him at the United Methodist Church in Port William, near Wilmington, OH where he and his wife, Pam, attended. I did this baptism at the Sunday morning worship service and his pastor then admitted him to membership in the church.

Our fourth great-grandchild Austin Lee Leonard was born on October 27, to our granddaughter Sharma and Rod in Renton, WA.

Our other major trip was a flight by plane to Seattle on November 21st. We enjoyed the bright lights of the big city and a special Christmas display of lights throughout the two weeks, including Thanksgiving with Nellie and Ralph and their family. The highlight of the trip was a visit to the Warm Beach Christian Camp and Conference (Free Methodist) Center near Stanwood, WA. The place also had a retirement community and everything was decorated with thousands of lights and displays. Thus, the year 1994 ended on a high level of excitement.

The next year, 1995, had both high points and low points. One of the high points was the evidence of the building committee's hard work. The surveying and clearing of the church site proceeded rapidly. There were many large trees and much brush on the plot and the church men worked on weekends to cut down and move them to the back of the plot. Chainsaws and tractors made it possible for the bulldozers to move soil about so the contractors could lay foundations and set up the walls. Everyone in the congregation was excited to see their prayers answered.

At the same time, a low point in Maria's health developed during the winter and on April 21st, her right hip was replaced with a metal joint. The ordeal was extremely painful. I stayed in the hospital with her and after a week brought her home. Her recovery was slow but steady and at the end of the summer, she no longer needed her cane. We were thankful her problem could be cured. At the same time, Dr. Cronin kept a careful check to make sure cancer was not involved. It was not.

As for myself, I became increasingly aware that I needed a hearing aid in my other ear. After obtaining one in June, I felt I was in a new world. I could hear sounds and people about me much more clearly.

Maria and I found we needed to make another decision. We were using our motor home less and less, because Maria found it difficult to get in and out of it. Reluctantly, we advertised and soon found a young family with children who wanted to buy it. On June 28th, we felt a pang of loss as we saw the motor home leave the yard. Our enjoyable trips in it were over. We must now rely on our car or commercial planes for travel.

During July, we had a flood of company and we enjoyed every minute with family and friends. Dave and Mary were here over the July 4th holiday, Ron and Judy Highhouse of New York dropped by for a few days, although it was out of their way to Florida. We deeply appreciated their love and affection. Nellie and Ralph arrived by rental car for a short visit as they had been in Indianapolis for a meeting that Ralph attended. Maria and I flew to Seattle August 22nd to return on Labor Day.

During the summer, a correspondence developed with a Dr. and Mrs. James D. Kornwolf of the College of William and Mary, Williamsburg, VA. On October 13th, the couple arrived in Lexington, KY and asked me to meet them at the home of Mr. and Mrs. Rash, owners of Chaumiere du Prairie in Jessamine County about seven miles from our home.

Mr. and Mrs. Rash graciously gave us a tour of the place. The Kornwolfs were planning to write a history and description of the beginnings of Chaumiere du Prairie, My correspondence with the Kornwolfs continued for about a year.

The big occasion centered about the Thanksgiving Holiday. Maria's eightieth birthday was November 19th. Ralph and Nellie and family came on the 17th to plan the celebration to be held on Sunday night after church on the 19th. Our friends from the church came to wish Maria Happy Birthday.

Four generations of our family gathered at our home on Thursday the 23rd for Thanksgiving. Then on the next day, we had a photographer come to the house and take professional pictures of all of us and of each family group. Only one person, a grandson-in-law, Rod Leonard, was missing, as he could not get released from work. That evening the family also had a surprise for Maria, a public birthday celebration at Besson Inn, on ATS's campus. She was thrilled beyond words with both occasions.

We went with Dave, Mary and family to Ann Arbor, MI to spend Christmas with Burt, Jeanie and family. We were happy that the week was filled with joy and fun for all. The year ended on a high, positive note.

During the first week of January 1996, we rested and packed our car for a trip to Florida. Our dear friends, Ron and Judy Highhouse, had invited us to use their doublewide home for three weeks in January. The home is located in Barefoot Bay, a retirement village about fifteen miles south of Melbourne, on the Atlantic coast.

Judy's parents also spent their winters in a double wide home, so we often visited back and forth while we were there. We were also aware that other acquaintances lived in Kissimmee. Two of these people were Dr.

and Mrs. Jack Tremaine. For many years, he was the Professor of Music at ATS. We went to see them on January 20th, and had a wonderful time with them.

According to schedule, we made contact with Mrs. Mildred McGowan who was living at the Good Samaritan Retirement Village four miles south of Kissimmee. She was a member of the Free Methodist Church in Marion, IA when we pastored that church in 1939-41. Over the years we kept in contact with each other, but had only gotten together a few times. Another native of Marion, IA also lived in the village, and he insisted he take the four of us to enjoy a dinner and horse show called, "Arabian Nights" in nearby Orlando. While we ate a delicious dinner in a raised area, we watched a fantastic display of beautiful horses, with acrobats doing amazing stunts on them.

On Sunday January 21st, we went to Lakeland, FL, sixty miles west, to worship at the Lighthouse Retirement Village where Free Methodist "snow birds" from up north spent their winters. Mrs. McGowan was surprised when the pastor began the announcements by introducing Maria and me as his professor and wife at ATS. We quickly noted that the pastor, two missionaries, the guest speaker and a dozen and half other worshippers, most had been my students. Six had attended Wessington Springs College with us in the 1930's. We had not seen one of these couples in 58 years. After dinner, we returned to Kissimmee and attended the evening service at the Community Church in the Good Samaritan Village. Jack Tremaine was the organist.

On Monday January 22nd, Mr. Harnish drove us to Orlando to visit Epcot Center. Mildred had her own electric wheel chair so Mr. Harnish rented three more and together we toured the Center. We visited several displays of foreign countries. We ate at a Norwegian restaurant where I ate "lefse,'" a thin, potato pancake. The morsels released vivid memories of eating, as a boy, this food at the homes of our Norwegian neighbors in northwest Wisconsin. The day was long and tiring but was well worth the time and energy spent there.

The next morning Mr. Harnish took us to the Cypress Gardens, about forty miles west. We did our sightseeing from our comfortable electric scooters. We rode through a series of flower-filled gardens. One building was especially interesting. The glass building was a butterfly house. We finished the day watching a breath-taking water skiing show and took a boat ride through the canal system. We were ready to return to the Village by the time the sun was seeking the Western horizon.

Two things we enjoyed about Florida: the fine tasting grapefruit and oranges, which we bought from a nearby orchard, and secondly, the fresh vegetables we bought at a roadside stand.

On the afternoon of the 31st, we headed for Light and Life Village near Lakeland. We wanted to stay a few days at the home of Jon and Dorothy Carlton. Jon had been a classmate and close friend at Wessington Springs College. We visited a number of other friends and I also managed to play golf several times.

We intended to start home on February 2nd, but the night before, an ice and snowstorm swept across northern Alabama, Georgia and Tennessee. We kept in touch by phone with our daughter-in-law, Mary, of Lexington TN. Later, she said it appeared to be safe to start for home. We left on Sunday morning and followed I-75 through Georgia. About fifty miles north of Atlanta, ice began to show up between the lanes and then between the tire tracks in the road. Snow and ice were on the trees and bushes along the road. Toward the end of the day, we decided to stop at Adairsville, GA for a motel room. The entire parking lot was covered with ice. The temperature got down to five degrees above zero (almost unheard of in Georgia) and the heater in the motel room was not quite up to the challenge.

Our big worry was road conditions along I-75, so we stopped at the Welcome Center at the border. We were informed we should take I-24 to Nashville then I-65 north. Fortunately, at Eagle Mountain, just west of Chattanooga, I-24 had just been cleared so we had no more trouble, for there was no ice or snow in northern Tennessee or in Kentucky. That kind of weather condition does not happen often.

Coming home, we found the church's building committee still had much work to do. As chairman of the church's Board of Trustees, it was my responsibility to sign a sizeable loan contract on February 13th.

In the middle of March, Maria and I got on I-75 again to go to Burt's family in Ann Arbor, MI. Burt and Jeanie's three girls were in an important ice skating contest. They came away from the contest with each one carrying a handful of metals and ribbons.

We had heard much about the annual Tulip Festival in the middle of May at Holland, MI. We decided to return to Michigan and with Burt's family spent several days at Holland. This was a special event for

Maria, since she was born in the Netherlands. The people of the small city scrubbed their streets and put on a dazzling parade. Maria felt very proud of her people.

In Wilmore, the new church was rapidly nearing completion. The first public worship service was held in the sanctuary on June 31st, and the building was dedicated October 20th. One of the highlights of the event was the dedication of a round, stain-glass window, with an artistically arranged set of symbols of the Trinity. On each side was a longer window. Burt and Dave, and Nellie had paid for the windows in our honor. During the service, our sons shared in presenting a short biography prepared by our daughter. We felt highly honored.

The year ended with another plane trip to Seattle to visit our family there during the Thanksgiving season. Our other families came to Wilmore to celebrate with us Christmas and the New Year's holiday. We were especially thankful that neither of us had a serious health problem during the year.

Nineteen ninety-seven did not start well. A dark spot on Maria's lower, back right cheek did not look good. On February 29th, her doctor removed the beginnings of basal skin cancer at a hospital in Richmond, KY. Maria went home the same day and it healed quickly.

Maria had continuing pain in her lower back and in her legs. CAT scans and MRI pictures showed no cancer tumors in her back and pelvis. There was evidence of arthritis accretions pressing on the spinal column, so the doctor ordered physical therapy and pain management.

In April Maria's left eye began to bleed in the retina and her eye doctor did the fourth laser treatment to stop the bleeding. The result was almost total blindness in that eye.

The late winter and early spring months were uneventful, just filled with preparing a garden and doing research. Several doctors were keeping a close watch on Maria's back pains that were relentless. The most interesting of several short trips was to Gainesville, GA to the Free Methodist district annual conference on May 9th and 10th. After the conference, we drove north to Helen, GA a unique town made to look like a Bavarian, German village. The place was filled with tourists. Earlier in the spring, we had noticed an advertisement of a bed and breakfast place called "The Dutch Cottage" and had made reservations for the two nights. We discovered the owners were Dutch people who had spent their teenage years in the same area of Iowa, as did Maria. We enjoyed our visit and sightseeing trips in the area that is the southern foothills of the Appalachian mountain region.

During the spring, Cyndy was very busy at Kalamazoo College in ice skating activities along with her studies. She skated twice in the National Collegiate Figure Skating contests. She won the bronze medal at the junior level and 14th at the senior level. She also was a professional figure skating instructor for the Kalamazoo Figure Skating Club.

On June 2nd-7th, we drove to Dave and Mary's home in Lexington, TN and enjoyed some wonderful fishing at the lake that borders their property.

Sharma's family came from Kansas City, KS to spend the Fourth of July week with us. We took them to many areas around us, and the annual fireworks just outside of Wilmore.

The extended family gathered at Dave and Mary's home for a reunion and the celebration of our sixtieth wedding celebration on August 12th. The young people especially loved the boating on the lake and learning to drive a Sea-Doo.

The next week we motored to Ann Arbor, MI because our granddaughter, Cyndy, was due to leave for the Netherlands for a fall semester of study at Leiden University, in Leiden. This event was arranged as a Junior Year Abroad program through Kalamazoo College. The situation became tense because two days before she was to leave, she could not find her passport anywhere in the house. She tried to get a duplicate passport but there was not time to get one from the government. Would she have to forfeit a cheap airplane ticket by missing her tour group in New York? Fortunately, a last minute search of the house located the passport beneath her bed. She met her plane on time and arrived in the Netherlands on schedule. She had an exciting four months in the Netherlands and met some of her cousins while there. Part of her lab work was doing research in cancer with a Dutch student.

Cyndy's sister, Debby, also made a trip to Europe. She flew to the Netherlands on December 13th to travel around there and in Western Europe with Cyndy. They came home with excitement about their adventures.

In Dave's family, David Jr. went with a high school group to London, Paris and Madrid, Spain. His sister, Marianne, declared she ought to be next. At that time, she was on her high school dance team and active in dance competition.

Our fifth great-grandchild, Jessica Anne Marie Leonard was born on September 11th, to our granddaughter Sharma and Rod, in Kansas City, KS. Ralph had flown from Seattle to be there the week before in case Sharma had to go in during the day, as Rod would not be able to get home in time, also to take care of the boys while she was in the hospital. Nellie flew out on the Sunday after she was born and stayed for a week. Her three brothers were happy to have a sister. In the middle of October, we went to Kansas City so that I could help along with Jessica's other grandfather baptize her at the Antioch Nazarene Church.

In November, we flew to Seattle to be with Nellie and Ralph during the Thanksgiving week. We spent the Christmas holidays in Wilmore with our two sons and their families.

During 1997, I had spent a great deal of time gathering data for a booklet entitled "The Descendants of Joseph and Minnie Andrews Baker."

A cousin, Mrs. Veneta Mistretta, put the information in proper computer format and published it with her own printer. The Bakers were my mother's parents, so all the Livingston descendants were included. Other descendents of the Bakers purchased a number of the booklets.

We began 1998 with a sense of loss. Our long time friend, Dr. George A. Turner died in Greenville, IL. In 1936-37, he was the professor of both Maria and me in several classes at Wessington Springs College in SD. When we came to Wilmore to begin studies at Asbury (1945-48), we discovered he was a professor there. When we returned to Wilmore, we became colleagues on the faculty of the Seminary for over two decades. We were very close friends.

In March, Marianne's turn to travel abroad became possible. She joined a high school group that visited London, Paris and Madrid. Her dancing team also did well during the spring. The team won the National Championship of her school level at Myrtle Beach, NC. In September, she became a member of the High School team. Her brother, David Jr. also did well in school. He is the scholar type and was one of thirteen students in the state selected as a Governor's Scholar in Engineering. He spent a month during June/July on the campus of the University of Tennessee in Knoxville, TN.

David Sr. is the traveler of the family. During 1998, he was the Chief Operations Officer of a manufacturing company in Grand Rapids, Mi. He flew back and forth to work and to factories in the U.S., France and Brazil. Mary was able to go with him occasionally.

Other grandchildren were also keeping busy. In Burt's family, Debby was coaching about thirty children how to ice skate and also was serving as a teacher's assistant in lower grades in public schools in Ann Arbor. Cyndy was a senior in Kalamazoo College and spent the summer as an intern in cancer research at the University of Michigan. She also did some coaching of young ice skaters. Laura was a senior in high school and a member of a precision ice skating team in Dearborn, MI. The team went to an international competition in Copenhagen, Denmark and also a national competition in San Diego, CA. The team won third in each event. Laura was also a member of the Huron High School mixed choir. The choir was so good it was invited to sing at the Austrian Music Festival in Vienna. Burt went along as a chaperone.

Ken Kester was a junior at Central Washington University at Ellensburg, WA where he worked at the local swimming pool, and during the summer served as a lifeguard on a beach at Lake Washington. Jennifer Crites was in first grade at Greenville, IL. Mark and Karen were busy at their jobs. Sharma and Ron bought a home on the western side of Kansas City, KS and were busy getting settled. Sharma started homeschooling the two older boys. Between that and the two youngest children, it kept her busy.

Our entire family met at Dave's home in TN for Christmas. The going was rough in Tennessee because of an ice storm. Nellie, Ralph and Ken flew from Seattle to Kansas City, rented a car and drove to Sharma's where they spent the night. The next morning they added Dustin to their group and drove through a snowstorm to Karen and Mark's house in Greenville, IL. The next day Sharma and her family arrived in Greenville and the three cars headed for TN on snow and ice covered roads. I was with Burt in his car and Jeanie was driving our car with Maria. Near Bucksnort, TN, the car slipped on the ice and bumped into the railing at the side of I-40. Fortunately, Jeanie had a cell phone and notified the State Police that the car was disabled along side of the highway. She also called Dave's home, and Dave, Mark Crites and Ron Leonard immediately went to Jeanie and Maria's aid.

Burt and I learned of the accident when we got to Dave's home. We learned the right, front end of the car was damaged, but seat belts had kept Maria and Jeanie from serious injury. The men found that the car could still be driven and soon everyone was back at Dave's place. We had a good Christmas and an uneventful trip home. Thank God for his mercies.

Maria started 1999 with a major operation. Extensive tests in January showed that Maria was physically able to come through a major back surgery successfully. On February 22nd, two doctors with several assistants performed a six-hour surgery on her lower back. They removed a number of bony spurs from the edges of several lumbar vertebrae, and removed the remains of worn cartilage and placed a paste of ground bone between them. To hold the vertebrae in place while the bone paste fused them, straps and screws made of titanium metal were attached to the vertebrae.

I asked her that afternoon how she felt as the nurses prepared her for the operation. With a smile, she replied she had no fear, but that a song, "God is so good, He is so good to me" kept filling her mind. I rejoiced with her and was pleased to bring her home by the end of the week. The terrible pains she had in the calves and feet were gone, for which we were thankful. However, several months of healing and therapy still had to take place.

During this crisis, our children were wonderful to us. Burton came to be with us before and after the surgery. David could not get free from his work until the weekend, when he drove 450 miles to be with us at the hospital for five hours. He then drove back to Grand Rapids, MI, because he had to fly to eastern France to work with several factories belonging to Autocam Corp. of which he was Chief Operations Officer. Nellie flew from Seattle Sunday evening to be with us for a week. Because Maria could not sleep in a bed, she spent day and night in a motorized, reclining chair, except for brief periods of walking around the house, using a walker.

We were glad that at the end of May, Maria was able to travel. On May 27th, our granddaughter, Laura drove to our home, transferred to our car and went with us to Lexington, TN to attend the graduation ceremony of David Livingston, Jr. at the local high school. Laura returned to Ann Arbor, MI, to await our arrival for her Huron High School graduation on June 10th. David Jr. wanted to be present too, so he drove to our home and went with us to Ann Arbor. The two cousins were thrilled they could be at each other's graduation.

Cyndy Livingston's graduation from Kalamazoo College came next, on June 12th. All of us drove to Kalamazoo and enjoyed the elaborate ceremony that was conducted on the spacious outdoor plaza. Cyndy looked excited as she marched with others in the processional. The sun was so hot we had to watch the affair from a dormitory porch.

On June 17th, my brother, Ralph, arrived from Mason City, IA to visit for a few days. We had a great time remembering our younger days. He returned home by way of Toledo, OH to visit his daughter Carol.

On July 2nd, Maria and I drove to Anderson, IN to spend some time at the General Conference of the Free Methodist Church of North America meeting there for two weeks. At a special dinner, The Commission on Higher Education gave plaques of appreciation to professors and administrators who served for twenty-five or more years in schools of higher education. I had served two years as dean at Wessington Springs College and thirty-four years at Asbury Theological Seminary. I was given a plaque honoring those thirty-six years of service. We met many friends at the conference and enjoyed observing the delegates to the conference in action. After a few days, we drove back to Kentucky. The plaque has a special place in my office.

Late in August, several of our grandchildren moved to schools of higher education. David Jr. entered the school of engineering at Vanderbilt University in Nashville, TN. He was fortunate to receive a handsome scholarship to help toward tuition for four years. He lived in the dormitory at the University.

Laura entered the Wayne County Community College at Detroit, the school at which her parents have taught for over two decades. She studied to be a Registered Nurse.

Her sister Cyndy took a job as a tutor of biology students, who were in academic trouble, at the same Community College. The older sister, Deb, took a job with a tourist agency that emphasized environmental trips. She, with her sisters, continued to coach ice skating students.

Burt's and Dave's families came at Christmas time to bring cheer to our home. Except for Maria's surgery in February the year passed by on a happy, positive note. God had been so good!

Livingston Family 1995
Front l-r, Maria, Herbert
Back l-r, Burton, Nellie, David

CHAPTER 11

Maria's Pain Filled Years

The year 2000 started as almost a copy of 1999.

After a series of tests to determine the source of pain in Maria's groin and also in the upper abdomen, several doctors decided that an inflamed gall bladder was causing Maria's trouble. On February 15th, the pain became so severe we took her to the emergency room at St Josephs Hospital in Lexington. On the 17th, the surgeon found an inflamed appendix and removed both of them during the same operation. Two days later, I brought Maria home from the hospital. The pain soon disappeared and Maria recovered quickly.

Early in the year Nellie and Ralph informed us that they were planning on retiring early, and would be willing to move to Wilmore at the end of July and live with us as they were concerned about our health. Nellie and Ralph suggested they would live in our basement apartment and take on the heavy work about the property. They would help care for Maria, and be closer to their two daughters. We were thrilled and expressed joy that they were willing to come help us.

On March 11th, Maria and I drove to Ann Arbor, MI to be on hand the next day at the Detroit airport to see Cyndy and Laura off to Europe. They were members of the Dearborn, MI precision ice skating team, which again was representing the United States Figure Skating Association at a skating contest. A week later, they returned with bronze metals.

Another great-grandchild, Kelly Ann Crites was born on March 24th, to our granddaughter Karen and Mark in Greenville, IL. Her sister Jennifer was excited to have a baby to play with.

Early in May, Maria began to have a sharp pain in her right leg. On the 8th, a doctor ordered a bone scan to determine the cause. The right hip seemed to be the culprit, but Maria already had had a hip replacement there. No more could be done to help the situation. On the 24th, Nellie arrived by plane from Seattle for a few days to attend a reunion of all the grade school kids that had attended there over the years.

The student couple that rented the apartment was moving away at the end of June, which would give us a month to remodel the apartment. We agreed to the proposal and hired carpenters to do some major changes. We were feeling our shortcomings, for we were approaching our middle eighties. Nellie and Ralph gave a lot of their furniture to their children and put their home in Renton on the market. They would hire a truck to move many personal items to Wilmore. Their son-in-law, Mark Crites, would use his vacation to fly with his family to Seattle and drive the rental truck across the country with Karen and Kelly with him. Ralph, Nellie and Jennifer would follow by car.

On July 28th, the caravan from Seattle arrived at our house. The next day Sharma and family arrived, for another important occasion was to happen on Sunday. I had the honor of baptizing our great-granddaughter, Kelly Ann at the Wilmore Free Methodist Church.

The first week of August was marked by a flurry of activity. The truck was unloaded onto the patio and in the apartment, boxes were everywhere, some partially emptied. Carpenters and plumbers were completing the remodeled bathroom. Then a shocking event happened on the morning of the Sunday the 6th.

Nellie had been working very hard and came down with the flu. She did not recover right away. On the 5th our granddaughter Laura came down to visit before she started her classes in Nursing. On Sunday, Ralph, Laura and I thought we would let Nellie sleep in, and Maria said she would stay home, so we went to church. Early in the service, an usher came to us and said Maria had called and that we should come, right home, as something was wrong with Nellie. We hurried home, wondering what was the problem.

Maria took us to Nellie's bedroom, saying she could not get Nellie to wake up. Efforts to wake her up were unsuccessful. Immediately, Ralph called 911 and requested an ambulance. I took her blood sugar count and it was very low. The ambulance arrived quickly and emergency medical technicians checked Nellie's vital signs and strapped her on a gurney. During this time, several policemen and firemen arrived to help get Nellie to the ambulance. We told the driver to take Nellie to St. Joseph Hospital in Lexington. Ralph rode with the driver and I followed in our car. A short time later, Laura and Maria arrived at the hospital.

Nellie was still in a coma when we arrived at the emergency room of the hospital. Nurses immediately began to try to get Nellie fully awake. Her eyes were open and she tried to talk but could not. Blood samples were taken and IV lines were attached to her arms. They feared Nellie had had a stroke, but could find no evidence for it. However, after about two hours, she responded to the nurse's request to move her fingers and toes on her right side. She did both, but her only sounds were groans and her eyes seemed to see nothing. She was taken to the Intensive Care Unit, where she was given special attention. Several specialists carefully examined her and found she had pneumonia, hypertension and low sugar count. A while later her temperature rose to 106 and the left side of her brain started to swell. The IV tubes multiplied and nurses gave her special care.

Laura and Maria returned home late in the afternoon, but Ralph and I stayed. After dinner, we visited Nellie's bedside for a few minutes and each of us prayed an earnest petition that the Lord would be merciful to her. Just before we left the hospital, a doctor told us Nellie was in critical condition. The next twenty-four hours would tell whether she would pull through. I remember vividly a sense of shock as I looked at Nellie's blank face just before we left. Everyone in our extended family, church congregation and their friends and the church in Seattle had been kept up-to-date on Nellie's condition. We were uplifted by the realization that many people were praying for her recovery.

The next day we went to the hospital with anxious hearts, but smiling nurses greeted us in the intensive care unit telling us that Nellie had come out of her coma. When we entered her room, her eyes searched our faces but did not seem to recognize us. She could not voice our names. As each of us hugged her, she seemed to understand what we were saying. We were allowed only a short visit, so we went home and returned later that afternoon.

Laura decided to give Nellie a sweatshirt with the word, Kentucky, printed on it. That evening Nellie was more alert, and seemed to recognize us. She repeated the name of each one, and when she saw the sweatshirt, she smiled at Laura as she received it. The nurses were optimistic about Nellie's recovery, but indicated the pneumonia was still severe. She would be in ICU for several more days.

On Friday, Nellie's lungs were clear and she was transferred to a private room. Action in her arms and legs had greatly improved, raising questions about how severe her stroke had been. Nellie was having trouble with low blood sugar and tests were made to determine what medicines were best for her. She was taken off one of her pills. Finally, on the 13th, Nellie was released to come home. Much healing had to take place yet. Words were not coming easily to her mind, but she improved daily. Several weeks went by before she could help Ralph unpack boxes and put household items in their proper places. We were thankful she was gaining strength daily.

In August, Ken graduated from Central Washington University, in Ellensburg, WA with a bachelor's degree in biology.

During September, Maria's right eye was becoming more and more blurred. On November 9th, an eye surgeon removed a cataract and inserted a replacement. Maria was able to return home after the operation, with a patch over the eye to protect it.

Several of the family celebrated Thanksgiving with us, but twenty-four of our extended family came for a Christmas celebration. We all had a great time playing games, laughing and talking.

Maria continued to gain strength but had no relief from pain in her thighs. Most pain medicines upset her stomach, so ice packs were used often when the pain became too severe. Ralph and Nellie continued to refurbish the apartment into an attractive dwelling. One big plus for me was that I didn't have to shovel snow from the sidewalk and driveway. They took over the driving task whenever we went to Lexington and beyond. The big plus for Maria was that they prepared the noon and evening meals and joined us at the table to eat.

In 2001, my basic task was doing research for the family memoirs. I found that my habit of keeping most of our college diaries and letters was a gold mine of information. The pastoral documents and mutual memories of ministering together at our several appointments and graduate school experiences were exciting to discuss. Our children gave us insights about their experiences at school and at the churches we served over the years. Putting all this information into a narrative format was challenging and rewarding.

In January, Ralph was given a job at Asbury College, in their new Master's Degree program teaching Research and Development one night a week.

On the morning of March 30th, Maria awoke to find her left eye was swollen shut. We went to her eye specialist's office in Lexington and one of his assistants diagnosed the problem as shingles, because the left side of Maria's face was tingling with pain. The left eye was treated to protect it from damage by the shingles, and special medicine was given to lessen the pain. Maria continued to have pain on her face for several months.

At the beginning of June our great-granddaughter, Jennifer Crites came to stay with Ralph and Nellie for two weeks. Grandpa and Grandma took her to many interesting sites nearby and saw to it that she got to ride a horse. Jennifer also attended Vacation Bible School for one of those weeks.

That same month, Maria's leg pains came to a climax in her left knee. The pain became so intense we took her to the emergency room at St. Joseph's Hospital in Lexington. For nine days, she went through a series of tests, with the doctors having differing opinions about the cause of her pain. The procedures suggested by some doctors seemed to do little to solve the problem. Finally, a sports doctor gave injections into the left knee that seemed to help. We took Maria home and went to this doctor several times for more injections, but the pain did not fully go away. We chose not to have an operation on the knee.

In July, our great-grandson, Dustin Leonard came to visit with his grandparents, for two weeks. They took him to a number of historic places in central Kentucky, such as Daniel Boone's village of Boonsboro. A rebuilt fortress is located close to the original settlement. He was also taken to the site of the Battle of Perryville, near Perryville, KY. Here a key victory over a Confederate army took place in October 1862. Another place they went to was the Kentucky Horse Park a few miles north of Lexington. He has developed a serious interest in the history of the United States.

During this time, several events affected our lives. The first of these events shook the foundations of our nation severely and involved many other nations as well. We remember well how we felt when we turned on the TV about ten o'clock in the forenoon of September 11th. Repeated pictures showed a large commercial plane crashing into one of the towers of the World Trade Center in New York City. Soon the scene appeared of another commercial plane crashing into the other tower. Huge billows of smoke poured from the towers and in a short time both towers collapsed. Another plane crashed into the Pentagon.

Even as our emotions were in turmoil, watching these crashes and trying to comprehend the enormous loss of life involved in each crash. Another drama over western Pennsylvania came to a climax and reporters pieced together the story of how passengers learned from e-mails and their hand held radios about the crashes in New York City and in Washington. The westward bound plane had suddenly veered sharply left from its path and seemed to head toward the eastern cities. We soon learned that several male passengers had assaulted the pilot cabin where several hijackers had killed the American pilots and taken control of the plane. These passengers wrestled with the hijackers and within minutes the plane crashed into a pasture on a farm.

This series of events were unbelievable, yet they had happened. Our eyes were fixed to the TV screen hour after hour. The scenes of the crashes dominated every waking minute. The airlines shut down their flights and everyone, in the government and in our nation as a whole, were gripped with shock and awe. Slowly the crashed buildings were examined and mangled bodies came to view. It was soon learned that all the men who had taken control of the four planes were of Middle Eastern origin. They were motivated by hate-filled leaders to severely damage the United States. This event and its aftermath created uncertainty in our family about how an important event close to our hearts was going to come to a successful conclusion.

Early in the year, I had been asked to conduct the wedding ceremony of a young couple in the Catskill Mountains of New York state on October 6th. The bride-to-be had close ties to Maria and me. Sarah Highhouse is the daughter of a Ron and Judy who had been teenagers related to the United Methodist Church of Callicoon, NY, one of the four churches I served as pastor. Over the years, we bonded so that they became as a "son" and "daughter" to us. We kept in close touch with each other and they taught their son Jeff and daughter to always call us "grandpa and grandma."

Forty years later, I was scheduled to join Sarah and Bradley Field in marriage at the Free Methodist Church in Liberty, NY. Early in August, Sarah had obtained for me a plane ticket to Newburg, NY and return to Lexington, Ky. Would I be able to fly there to conduct their ceremony? Would the planes be back to scheduled flights before October 6th? We held our breaths and prayed. By the end of September, Delta Airlines was on schedule again, so I planned to leave for Newburg and had no difficulties passing through the screening process and arriving on time. Ron was at the airport to meet me. After some stops to do some shopping, we drove through the mountains viewing a marvelous scene of fall colors on the trees. As we approached their home near Callicoon, the roads and the contour of the hills became familiar.

Arriving at their home, Sarah and her Mom hugged me and I met for the first time the groom, Bradley, his parents and sister. They are fine Christian people. Brad and Sarah had graduated with engineering degrees from Messiah College, near Harrisburg, PA. The couple already had jobs in Connecticut. The ladies, particularly, were very busy preparing for the big occasion that would happen on Saturday. I took a few moments to rest and chat with the various friends of the family that stopped by. The next forenoon Ron and I went to Liberty, NY to talk to the Free Methodist pastor about the upcoming wedding ceremony. Everything at the church was ready for the wedding.

On the day of the wedding, all the ladies were busy preparing themselves and soon after lunch, Jeff Highhouse and his lady friend took me to the Liberty Free Methodist Church. The pastor and I joined in conducting the ceremony. My part was to lead the bride and groom through the exchanging of vows and rings. Then I gave a fifteen-minute homily about the meaning of the vows and led them in their commitment to each other. Then I presented them to the congregation as Mr. and Mrs. Bradley Field. A pianist, a violinist and a soloist from Messiah College provided music. Ron invited everyone to travel about fifteen miles to a lakeside pavilion for an evening meal and fellowship. The next morning I attended worship service at the Liberty Free Methodist Church.

Monday morning Ron and Judy took me to Newburg, NY to meet my plane. Our granddaughter, Cyndy was visiting with her fiancée, a student at the Culinary Institute of America at Hyde Park, NY. We had arranged by phone to meet them at a restaurant near the airport for lunch. The trip home was uneventful.

In September, pain developed in the colon area and Maria's cancer doctor made a careful examination and decided diverticulitis was the cause of this pain. The treatments and medicines he prescribed slowly cleared up the inflammation. By the holiday season, Maria was feeling much better but had to use her walker whenever she moved about.

In the late spring months of 2002, an invitation came to me from Tyndale House Publishers to join their project of enhancing their New Living Translation by providing the public with a study Bible edition. They invited me to provide introductory observations, a time line of the historical events and a topical outline of Jeremiah. They also wanted study notes on every verse of the book and theme articles. I was given a year to complete the assignment. I regarded the proposal as a major challenge and accepted the invitation. During the remaining six months of the year, I spent many hours doing research for this task.

Ken Kester decided to begin classes in teacher training so he could be certified to teach in the public schools of Washington State, and continue coaching children who liked to swim. Karen and Sharma's families kept busy at their jobs and the task of rearing children.

A number of the family came in for Thanksgiving. Everyone assisted in the preparation of meals and had a great time chatting and bringing events in their lives up-to-date. The same was true of the Christmas gathering.

Health wise we had a fairly good year in 2002. Oh yes, there was a colonoscopy on January 9th, and a CT scan of Maria's legs on January 14th. The first one showed a few benign polyps that were removed. As to the second one, a foot doctor found ingrown nails on her big toes and after several treatments the doctor decided Maria had gout. In a few days, the pain in the legs disappeared.

I worked steadily on study notes on each verse of the book of Jeremiah, until I finished the project in October. It amounted to about 60,000 words. The editors at Tyndale Publishers had the job of trimming what I had written into proper format. The projected publishing date was set at late 2007.

During an afternoon, Ralph, Nellie and I were downstairs doing various tasks and Maria was alone on the main floor of our home. Nellie came to my office and told me Maria was calling for help. We all rushed upstairs and found Maria on the floor by the open front door unable to get up. She said her left leg was hurting. Nellie dialed 911 while Ralph lifted Maria to a chair. She could not stand by herself. The ambulance came and technicians placed her in the ambulance. I rode with the driver and Nellie followed in our car.

On the way to St. Joseph Hospital, the technicians in the ambulance learned that the hospital's emergency room was overloaded with patients and requested that we go to the Central Baptist Hospital. It was becoming dark and rain was still falling. The emergency room was busy but not crowded. Soon an x-ray was taken of the left thigh and we were told the film showed the femur bone was fractured alongside the steel spike of the hip replacement. We contacted our hip surgeon's office and were told he was out of town but a back-up surgeon would look at the leg. These doctors did not do their work at Central Baptist hospital, so they requested that we transfer Maria to St. Joseph Hospital East.

The rain was still coming down as the ambulance took Maria across to the eastern side of Lexington. Nellie was behind the ambulance barely able to keep it in sight until we all arrived safely. Maria was placed in a private room about midnight, and immediately a person with a portable x-ray machine took another image of Maria's left thigh. Nurses hovered over Maria for at least an hour. I was permitted to stay in her room on a sofa bed and Nellie headed home. Neither Maria nor I were able to get much sleep. The hip doctor arrived the next morning and informed us no serious damage was done to the femur bone.

The next day Maria was released to return home to heal. The doctor ordered Maria to use a wheelchair for at least three months. Ralph built a ramp to fit the two steps of our front porch. After three months, Maria's leg had healed so well that she was allowed to use a walker in the house and a wheelchair outside.

In early August, we were happy to host my brother Ray, ninety years of age, and one of his sons, Roger. They stayed only a few days but what a time of sharing memories of growing up on a farm in northwestern WI and interacting through the years. At the same time our great-grandson, Justin Leonard was here visiting his grandma and grandpa. Ralph and Nellie took Justin and Roger around to different places of interest.

The other aspect of our family excitement was the soon arrival of Maria's and my sixty-fifth anniversary on August 12th. Burt, Nellie and Dave and their spouses had for some time been planning a public celebration of this event at the Christian Ministry Center at our church. The date of the occasion was for the afternoon of August 18th. Everyone was hoping and praying that Maria would be strong enough to be present at the celebration. The day and night before, she had a high fever and was physically weak. At about two o'clock in the morning, the fever broke and she was able to sleep. Happily, she was able to attend the celebration and enjoy it. Several weeks passed before she felt strong again.

Family and friends came from seven states to join a number of church members and friends from the community. The story of our life together was projected in pictures as a narrative was read. About a dozen of our relatives and friends gave short testimonies of how we had affected their lives. Several musical numbers were sung and refreshments were served.

We were glad we could welcome some of the extended family for Thanksgiving and Christmas reunions. It was interesting to see how the grandchildren and great-grandchildren were growing up!

In Burt and Jeanie's family, the two older daughters, Deb and Cyndy were busy at their jobs and continuing their graduate studies. Deb's interest was Middle or High School teaching. Cyndy was excited about genetic counseling. The youngest daughter, Laura, was finishing her nurse's training.

Nellie and Ralph's oldest daughter, Karen and Mark's two daughters, Jennifer, in sixth grade and doing great, Kelly Ann (2) liked to run; jump and chatter, making everyone laugh. They still lived in Greenville, IL. There second daughter, Sharma and Rod's family remained in Kansas City, KS. Rod and Sharma kept busy in their Nazarene church with music and mission studies. Dustin (18) was the president of the youth group. Justin (13), Austin (8) and Jessica (4) kept everyone busy. Their son Ken remained in the Seattle area busy training eager swimming students and serving as a lifeguard.

Dave and Mary were enjoying their home on a lake at Lexington, TN but Dave was becoming tired of retirement and was thinking about returning to factory management. David Jr. was coming to the end of his engineering major, and Marianne graduated from the High School and enrolled in the University of Tennessee at Martin, TN. She was enrolled in a civil engineering program.

January 2003 started with fairly nice winter weather. We were happy to have two of Maria's relatives, offspring of Maria's oldest sister Lucy, from Hastings, MN for a dinner. A son, Don Robinson and his wife Lois and his sister, Rita, and husband John Cahill. We had known them as children and had met them briefly at the funeral of Maria and Lucy's mother. We had a happy time getting re-acquainted and hearing about their brothers and sisters in MN and WI. They continued their vacation in the southern states. Their visit had a down side. They brought bitterly cold air with them. They were glad to go south and we were glad the almost zero weather did not last long.

The big family event in February was Laura becoming a registered nurse and starting work at the Children's Hospital connected with the University of Michigan. She had earned the highest grade average of anyone in her class.

Not at all matching that event was a severe ice storm that swept through central Kentucky. Electric power was shut off for three days. A neighbor graciously took Maria and me into their home until the power supply was restored. Their electric line had not been damaged. Ralph and Nellie stayed at the house to make sure the water pipes did not break. They kept warm by the fireplace in their apartment.

My brother Ray, almost 91, died at Chippewa Falls, WI at the end of April and I flew to Eau Claire, WI for his funeral. He was buried with his wife Ellen, beside our father and mother in a cemetery near Eau Claire. I spoke briefly at his memorial service. Of interest was the fact the milk processing and delivery dairy where Ray had worked for over three decades had become the funeral home where the service was held.

Ray and Ellen had seven children and they were all at the service with their spouses and children. Most of them I had not seen for many years and some I had not seen at all. What a joy to meet and visit with them during and after the reception following the service. My sister Dorothy and her husband Fay were living at Cumberland, WI. They were at the service with several of their children. Dorothy and I were the only ones living of eight children of our parents. She was in her eighties. The flight home stopped for several hours at Detroit so our son Burt and his wife Jeanie came to the airport and ate lunch with me.

At the same time, Maria was having trouble with her right eye. Her ophthalmologist confirmed that she had become legally blind in both eyes. He referred her to a low vision specialist who said she needed special glasses and special gadgets to help see a bit better. She did so but she remained unable to read normal print size and unable to pursue her craft projects. She had long been an expert in crochet work and embroidery projects. She was very disappointed.

On May 8, Ralph and Nellie took Maria and me by car to Nashville, TN to attend the graduation ceremony of David Jr. at Vanderbilt University the next day. David Sr., Mary and Marianne were there also to see David Jr. receive his bachelor's degree in civil engineering. It was very hot in the building so we were taken to an air-conditioned room from which we could watch the proceedings.

After the event, Dave Sr. and Mary led us to the garage where they showed David Jr. his graduation gift, a new Honda car. We next attended a meeting of engineering faculty and graduates held under a tent. The faculty honored each graduate for his/her achievements as a student. We all went to a nice restaurant for a celebration dinner. After having a great time together, we drove to the Dave and Mary's home.

A month later, I presented my resignation as supervisor of correspondence courses in O. T. History and Psalms, for ministers seeking ordination in the Free Methodist Church of North America. A Certificate of Appreciation, signed by the bishops of the denomination, was presented to me.

In September, David Jr. enrolled in the Master of Science in engineering program at Vanderbilt University. Marianne entered her sophomore year at the University of Tennessee. She switched her major to home decoration.

In Burt's family, Deb started her teacher's certificate program at Eastern Michigan University in nearby Ypsilanti, MI. Cyndy was accepted by Sarah Lawrence College in Yonkers, NY. She planned to pursue a master's degree in genetic counseling.

Ralph continues to teach at the college and Nellie stays at home and takes care of us.

In November, an important package arrived from Tyndale House Publishers. An editor sent me 113 pages of the introduction and study notes I had previously written and sent to them on Jeremiah last year. The editor asked me to revise my work according to suggestions made in the manuscript. I was also to fly to Atlanta, GA to meet several editors at a convention where they were advertising Tyndale books. I made the trip, talked to the editors and returned to plunge into an intense effort to complete the project.

The stress of spending too many hours at the computer caught up with me on the evening of December 20th. I went to bed and soon afterward experienced an unusually fast and uneven heart beat. I told Maria about the condition and she phoned Ralph and Nellie. They quickly came upstairs and called 911. The medic confirmed my condition and took me by ambulance to the emergency room at St Joseph Hospital. Doctors soon told us I had an episode of arterial fibrillation of the heart. They put me in a room and treated me with medications. Maria stayed with me the first night.

Dave drove to Lexington and stayed with me Sunday night. Burt drove from Ann Arbor and stayed with me Monday night and took me home Tuesday noon. I was feeling none the worse for what had happened, as I had felt no pain or shortness of breath. I got orders to slow down on the revision project. In a few days, many others of the extended family came to celebrate Christmas with us. Ken Kester flew from Seattle on Wednesday to be with us until Saturday.

Maria's health was a bit better during 2003, with the exception of an attack of gout in her right foot, but medicine soon brought the disease under control. The pain in her thighs never seemed to go away; applications of a pain relief gel seemed to help. In December, she had prickly pain on the surface of her abdomen, but a neurologist diagnosed the problem as neuropathy caused by diabetes and prescribed a medicine that slowly cleared it up.

In the autumn of 2003, our son-in-law Ralph, serving as chairman of a church committee, asked me to prepare and present eight lectures on Church History in Brief on Wednesday nights. Each lecture was to cover 500 years up to the present. I have loved reading widely in church history, so I agreed to do so.

As January 2004 became a reality, I decided to put the editorial work on the study notes on hold and carefully match my energy level to the church history course. I greatly enjoyed the course that continued until the middle of April. Afterwards, I returned to the editorial task that I completed toward the end of June.

Our seventh great-grandchild, Krista Lee Anne Leonard was born on February 2nd, to granddaughter Sharma and Rod in Kansas City, KS. Nellie went to their home for three weeks to help in case Krista came during the day and Rod could not get home in time to take Sharma to the hospital. She was able to spend a week with the baby.

During the winter and early spring months, our granddaughter, Cyndy, was preparing for a June wedding to Michael Murray. Combining this preparation with her studies at Sarah Lawrence College in Yonkers, NY was not easy, but in May, things were going well. She had asked me to take a major role in their wedding ceremony on June 6th in Ann Arbor, MI.

On May 23rd, events would be happening in granddaughter, Sharma's family. Krista Lee Anne would be dedicated and oldest son, Dustin, would graduate from a Christian High School in Kansas City, KS. Maria and I wanted to be present at these events. A schedule of travel was worked out. We felt riding in a car that long would be too difficult for Maria, instead, on May 22nd, Maria and I flew to Kansas City. Ralph and Nellie drove their car to Greenville, IL where they picked up their daughter Karen and her two daughters, Jennifer and Kelly, and arrived at the Leonard home the day before we arrived.

The next morning, Sunday, we all went to the Antioch Nazarene Church where I assisted in the dedication/baptism ceremony for Krista. She was about three months old. We went to a restaurant for dinner and spent some time in a city park. At 3:00 p.m. we were at the gym of the Christian High School. A big moment came when Dustin's name was called and he marched across the platform to receive his diploma. We met his girlfriend who would also enroll in Mid-America Nazarene University in nearby Olathe for the fall semester. We enjoyed the party afterwards at Sharma's home.

On Monday, Nellie and her family left by car to return home by way of Greenville, IL to leave off Karen and girls. We visited with the Leonard family during the day, getting better acquainted with the great-grandchildren. On Tuesday, we boarded a plane that took us to Detroit, MI where we were met by Jeanie and Cyndy and taken to their home.

During the next week, various members of Jeanne's family arrived and they joined the rest of us helping Cyndy with a number of small tasks in preparation for her wedding. Cyndy was rushing back and forth to stores in Ann Arbor, taking care of clothes and events connected with the coming wedding. I helped Burt lay bricks for a new patio, whereas Maria was busy in the house.

Early in the first week of June, Cyndy took Maria and me to the First United Methodist Church to meet its pastor, Dr. Jack Harnish. Jack was in several of my Old Testament classes at ATS during the early 1960's. We had a great time recalling memories and reviewing the procedures of the coming wedding of Cyndy and Mike.

On the afternoon of the 5th, Burt took Maria and me to a hotel across the street from the UM church. He wanted us to rest and be removed from the excitement of the arrival of many of Cyndy and Mike's relatives. Most of the relatives took up residence in motels. Burt made it a point to eat breakfast with us. On Friday evening, the Murray family honored the wedding party and families with a delicious dinner. It was exciting getting acquainted with the Murray family.

On Saturday afternoon, everyone was arriving at the church and preparing for the big event. I spent an hour with the pastor chatting and reviewing the procedures of the wedding ceremony. The groom, best man and his companions were present and we had a friendly time getting acquainted. Finally, at five o'clock, the church organist began playing melodies and the men entered the sanctuary and took their places. The co-maids of honor, Deb and Laura, marched up the aisle to the altar, followed by several bridesmaids: Mike's sister and our granddaughter, Marianne. The flower girl, our great-granddaughter, Kelly Ann Crites followed the other girls, doing her part perfectly. Ken Kester and David, Jr. were the ushers seating the guests.

Dr. Harnish began and ended the ceremony with prayers and saw to it that the ceremony proceeded properly. I took care of the other phases of the ceremony, including a homily. After the vows were repeated, the rings placed on the proper fingers, I declared the couple was man and wife. The pastor introduced them to the audience. The organist played a lively march and the newly married couple moved down the aisle. The congregation then gathered on the front steps of the church and greeted the newly-weds.

The day concluded with a wonderful feast at the hotel where we were staying. The newly married couple took center stage, where Burt served as master of ceremonies. After the meal, everyone enjoyed dancing for several hours. The next morning, Burt met us for breakfast and then helped us pack our belongings. Later in the morning, Ralph and Nellie arrived and after packing everything in the trunk, we left for Wilmore. Our great granddaughter, Jennifer Crites, came with us and spent ten days with grandma and grandpa Kester. Jennifer helped in the Vacation Bible School and made trips with her grandparents to various sites in central Kentucky.

A new development for me was confirmation by a diabetic doctor that my insulin shots should be done four times a day. The procedure is much easier to use and I am slowly learning how to eat correctly.

While we were at Cyndy's wedding, Burt suggested I replace my power Mac system with a new Mac laptop. Early in July, Burt phoned that he had found a good laptop, plus a printer. In less than a week, two boxes appeared on our front porch. My challenging task was to learn how to use them.

The way we celebrated our sixty-seventh anniversary was interesting. When we were at the Diabetic Center in the spring, we were asked to donate to a health cause. For every dollar donated, a ticket would be put in a box and within a week a drawing would determine the winner of a prize. I rarely give such donations, but put ten dollars toward the project. After the drawing, I found out that I was the winner of the first prize. This prize had two gifts, a night stay at the Super Eight Motel in Nicholasville, KY and a coupon for a first-class meal at a restaurant. We decided to use the coupon for the night at the motel on August 11th. Our stay ended on our anniversary day.

Fortunately, Dave and his family stopped at our place, Aug 15th-17th, on their way home from a sports car race in Mansfield, Ohio. Dave's wife, Mary, and son, David Jr. know Mac computers and taught me a lot about my new machine.

Maria had been bothered with a small growth on her left cheek. She had already experienced an operation on a melanoma lesion and a basal cancer lesion on her right cheek. She went to her Plastic Surgeon on September 14th. The growth was removed and tested. Happily, this lesion was benign.

Maria was beginning to have problems with her hip replacements. In each hip, joints sounded as if they were popping in and out of their sockets. Maria's hip specialist said she was too old to have any more such surgeries. The only helpful procedure would be methods of pain management. This news did not make us happy.

We were happy to have Burt and Laura with us over the weekend of October 22nd-24th. They decided to obtain my Christmas present ahead of time and I soon had a new scanner connected to the computer. They showed me how to use the scanner to copy pictures and documents onto the computer. Slowly I am learning new ways to use the machine.

Concerned about Maria's tremors and the pain in her legs, Ralph and Nellie attended a conference on aging held by the University of Kentucky. They heard about the expertise of a Dr. Nancy Stiles at the Cardinal Hill Rehabilitation Hospital in Lexington. Obtaining an appointment on November 12th, Maria was interviewed and tested. The doctor recommended a series of therapy sessions in the hospital's warm water exercise pool and an appointment with a specialist about the tremors. Several therapists also interviewed Maria. The pool therapy began after Christmas and lasted for two months.

Some of our family came to Wilmore and celebrated Thanksgiving with us. At Christmas time everyone in our extended family, a total of twenty-six from five states and four generations, gathered at our home. Ken Kester brought Jenn Sitts, his girlfriend, to introduce her to the family. What a great time we had together, but it was marred somewhat by Cyndy becoming ill with the flu for several days. We had cold weather and some snow, so the weather contributed an old fashioned feel to the occasion. Overall, 2004 has been a good year.

In 2005, Maria improved as the months passed by. Her low point was during the winter. In January, she had just gone through a bout with urinary inflammation and she was feeling quite weak. For three months, St. Joseph Home Care sent a nurse and a physical therapist to our home. Her strength came back quite well. We obtained a wheelchair and a walker with a folding seat and four wheels. Increasingly, she was able to get around, but could not walk by herself.

In September, a dark spot developed in front of Maria's right ear. Biopsy samples determined the problem was basal cancer. She had her sixth cancer operation. A laboratory nearby kept testing flesh samples sent by the doctor until no more cancer cells were found. The wound healed quickly. In spite of it all, family members came to celebrate her 90th birthday, November 19th, along with Thanksgiving.

Ken Kester finished his course work for a teacher's certificate in December and began substituting for the Kent, WA school district.

My big project for 2005 was the production of our family memoirs. It was being improved with the help of editors within the family. We were putting together documents and pictures to back up and illustrate the narrative. Three appendices were being shaped to add more information to the book. After the main body of the family memoirs is completed, the appendices will be attached.

A big event in December was the graduation of our granddaughter, Marianne, from the branch of the University of Tennessee located in Martin, TN. Maria, myself, Nellie and Ralph traveled down to watch Marianne receive her bachelor's degree.

Members of the extended family came to Wilmore to join us in celebrating the birth of Jesus at Christmas time. The year 2005 ended on a high note of joy.

The year 2006 began with concern about Maria having physical problems so a physical therapist came from the Good Samaritan Hospital in Lexington to help her regain strength enough to move about with a wheelchair or her walker.

At about the same time, our three children decided to hire trained lady care givers through an organization in Lexington called Comfort Keepers. They would select and provide a lady to come to our house for six hours a day Monday through Saturday. The hired ladies would care for Maria's needs and make it possible for me to complete some projects, including our Memoirs. Nellie and Ralph would continue preparing our noon and evening meals and eat with us. These ladies were Christians and related to Maria very well throughout the remaining years of her life.

In April, we learned that our granddaughter, Cyndy, was assigned by the hospital where she works in New Jersey to attend a conference in Louisville, KY. She drove to our home a few days ahead of the conference to visit with us on the 5th-7th and after the conference on the 9th. She is excited about her job as a genetic counselor. Her husband, Mike, is a chef at a country club near their home in Yonkers, NY.

My eye doctor in Lexington, informed me in April, I had a cataract in my left eye. An eye surgeon replaced the defective cataract with a new lens May 16th with excellent results.

During the spring and summer, two important events occurred in our extended family; two grandchildren were to be married. Our youngest granddaughter, Marianne, was married to Jessie Goff at her parent's home. Jessie's pastor and I were in charge of the ceremony conducted in their yard near the shore of a beautiful lake. The date was May 26th.

On July 27th, an important milestone in my lifetime happened. On that date, I had my ninetieth birthday. However, due to circumstances, the extended family and community celebrated the occasion on July 22nd.

The other important event was the marriage of a grandson, Ken Kester, to Jenn Sitts on August 5th. I assisted Jenn's pastor in the marriage ceremony that was held at a small buffalo ranch that overlooks the bay of Puget Sound. The view was spectacular and located in the southeastern corner of the Olympic Peninsula not far from Tacoma. A number of our family flew out for the wedding, except Maria who was physically unable to travel that far. Ron and Judy Highhouse came and stayed with Maria. Ken and Jen live in Puyallup east of Tacoma. Ken was a teacher in a nearby Middle School and Jennifer has a responsible position in the planning department of Gig Harbor a few miles north of Tacoma.

During the last three months of 2006, Maria and I spent several mornings each week at the local retirement community, called Wesley Village. We took part in weekly physical therapy exercises. The physical movements were intense for one-half hour. After each session, we spent about twenty minutes on a machine called "Nustep" that gave us a good workout.

No others of the family were here Thanksgiving Day so Nellie, Ralph, Maria and I ate dinner at a restaurant. However, Dave Sr. and his family were here for several days after Thanksgiving. Karen and her family were here from December 22nd to the 28th for Christmas. Dave Sr. and his family came on Thursday after Christmas and stayed until after New Years.

On January 3, 2007, our granddaughters, Deb and Laura, arrived to visit a few days. Burt and Jeanie came from Ann Arbor, MI to spend about a week with us. We wished other members of our extended family could have come, but circumstances prevented that from happening.

Our seventh great-grandchild, Ryan Craig Goff was born on February 16th, to granddaughter Marianne and Jessie in Jackson, TN.

During the winter and spring, my big project was centered on genealogy. A nephew, David Richard Livingston, has retired and now lives in Cedar Park, Texas. He has spent years working with computers and offered to assist me in completing our family tree research. During the first five months, I sorted through files of family information in three drawers of the file cabinet. These files contained my thirty-year accumulation of data about the Baker, Andrews, Silver, Johnson and Livingston families. Articles of information were cut out and sheets torn from various publications, organized, copied and sent to him. There were close to 1,000 pages in the collection. I finished in late May. One of the first of David's achievements was the discovery of where great-grandfather and mother, Thomas C. and Nancy (Polly), Livingston spent the last years of their lives, died and were buried.

Family Bible records stated they had died and were buried in Cass County, IN, but officials there could not find records that this was so. I had requested information from officials in DeWitt County about Livingstons there and received information on a few of them, including Calvin, son of Thomas C, but nothing about his parents. David's search revealed a document that stated great-grandmother, Polly (i.e. Nancy) Livingston died at age 64 in July 1859. Another document revealed that Thomas C. died March 15, 1875, age about 80. His actual age would have been 77 years. David R is working on the family tree data.

The summer months were hot but Maria and I enjoyed life together. In July, I began having discomfort in my right chest area so Ralph took me to the hospital. Tests showed I had arterial fibrillation; as a result, I was diagnosed with congestive heart failure and had fluid in my lungs. They gave me a special drug to get rid of a lot of the fluid. Ten days later Nellie had to take me back in to go through the same procedure.

During this time I also found out I had a problem with my blood being too thick, so my family doctor put me on a medicine for that and told me to come to the Medical Center at least once a month to have my blood tested and the dosage adjusted as needed. The goal was to prevent the blood from getting too thick and cause a heart attack or a stroke, or to become too thin and cause internal bleeding. Either condition could be fatal.

In August, Maria and I celebrated our seventieth anniversary with Burt and Jeanie in MI.

Ken and Jenn Kester came for Christmas and announced she was with child, to be born in August. We were all thrilled.

Throughout 2008, lady caregivers came to the house to be with Maria except for Sunday and national holidays. Maria was unable to walk. She needed daily leg exercises to keep her mobile and needed help in many activities. There have been a variety of these ladies. All of them became Maria's friends, as they were kind, thoughtful and protective.

Because they took care of Maria twelve hours a day, I was free to indulge in a series of projects.

Our ninth great-grandchild, Owen Magnus Kester was born on August 25th, to our grandson Ken and Jenn in Tacoma, WA.

During the autumn, I sorted through all my sermon outlines and written speeches and inserted each one in a plastic document preserver and organized them according to when I first composed and preached each sermon and put them into a notebook. Each notebook was labeled according to each church I pastured, each school I taught at and many places in the USA and in other countries. Many of these sermons were preached a number of times in various churches. This data is noted on the back of most of the productions. I have eight notebooks full of such sermons and speeches. They are placed in the archives of the seminary library.

I have also stripped my home office of my books and have given them to several different missions organizations to be placed in Bible schools and seminaries in various mission fields.

Maria's health declined as her Alzheimer disease caused hallucinations, and her strength failed steadily. Maria could no longer see things or people with enough detail, to read normal print or recognize her friends. It was difficult for Maria to adjust to these handicaps, but she always has been a woman of tough courage and deep faith in the goodness and mercies of her heavenly Father. I often read articles to her from newspapers and magazines. She enjoyed attending church and greeting her many friends. Many of them told her they are inspired as they observed her sweet, positive attitude while she suffered through the years.

As a family, we decided on November 6th to take her to the Royal Manor Nursing Home in Nicholasville, eight miles from our home. The Manor's nurses and assistants gave her excellent care. Since she was blind, they had to help her a great deal. Nellie took me to visit her about two hours every other afternoon. She recognized our voices and could respond to us. We placed our CD player on a dresser beside her and often played music on it, I would converse with her and read devotional passages. The nurses would place her in a wheel chair and I would push her around the main floor and explain what I saw. During the holiday season, many of our extended family would come to our home. Small groups of them would visit her and she enjoyed hearing who they were and would talk to them briefly.

Marianne was proud of her Masters of Arts degree from the University of Tennessee. Her mother, Mary, had an abdominal operation and healed quickly. Dave and Mary's son, David Jr., continued to work on the construction of a 22 floor building in Nashville, TN.

Burton and Jeanie still taught at the Wayne County Community College. They say they enjoy teaching so much they will put off retiring as long as they can. Their oldest daughter, Deb, was blessed with a remarkable opportunity. For several years, she had befriended a deaf lady and learned to communicate with her by using sign language. They became interested in Gallaudet University for the Deaf in Washington D.C. Both decided to apply to the graduate section of this school for advanced degrees. When they went to interview officers for admittance to graduate studies, they used sign language instead of speech.

The officials were so impressed that within a short time they admitted Deb's friend to a four-year doctoral program in psychology for the deaf. Deb was admitted to a four-year doctoral program in audiology. Both were given grants to pay the tuition and board and room for four years. They could room together and eat meals at the graduate dormitory. They moved to the university the third week in August.

Cyndy and her husband have continued to enjoy their jobs. Laura, the youngest and a registered nurse, was promoted to the pediatric intensive care unit at the children hospital at the University of Michigan.

Nellie and Ralph have continued to live here and help us a great deal. Their children and families have remained busy and doing well. Karen and her family were able to visit us several times including the holidays of 2008. Sharma and her family in Kansas City were too far away to visit us.

In 2009, the winter and early spring months were dominated by Maria's steady decline. Our sons came to see her when they could and Nellie visited her every time she took me in to see Maria. Pastors and friends came to see her often. As the weeks went by, she was less and less able to respond to them and to me. She preferred to stay in bed.

Of concern to the nurses and us was a sore that developed on her lower back, and refused to heal. In April, Maria was barely able to talk, and the sore was becoming so bad that the nurses asked our permission to transfer her to St. Josephs Hospital on the 23rd. We granted the request and I stayed overnight with her. Several doctors gave her a series of tests, and on April 27th, we were informed that the ulcer on her back was incurable, though it was not cancer.

The doctors recommended that Maria be transferred to the Hospice Health Care Center on the same floor of the hospital. Maria was unable to understand what was happening, so Nellie and I made the decision to move her to Hospice. Two doctors made arrangements with Hospice and soon Maria was moved. The nurses and assistants were outstanding in their treatment of Maria. The pain caused by the ulcer was intense, so they gave her adequate pain medicine to keep her calm and were on call at any time. Nellie and I decided to take turns being with her twenty-four hours each day from twelve noon to twelve noon. There was a foldout bed in the room on which we could get some sleep during the night. Burt or Dave stopped several times. After the first week, Maria no longer responded to their greetings. A doctor told us she would be able to hear our voices until the time of her death, so we each talked to her with encouraging words and prayer. Maria died at 6:30 p.m. Wednesday, May 20th.

Maria's body was taken to Betts and West Funeral Home in Nicholasville. We had a problem, because that Monday was Memorial Day. The Blue Grass Memorial Gardens, where we have lots, would not permit burials between noon Saturday and 8:00 a.m. on Tuesday. Because our extended family had to return home before Tuesday, we decided to have a family funeral service and burial just before noon on Saturday with a Memorial service Sunday evening. Because Maria was the last charter member of the Wilmore Free Methodist Church, it was decided to have the service at 6:00 p.m. in the church.

The senior pastor, Dr. Diddle, led the service. Our son, Burton, read a series of tributes written by members of his family and the pastors read the rest of the family tributes and a few of the members of the church. One member of the congregation, who had known Maria for many years, gave a verbal tribute. Dr. Dean Cook a former pastor gave a heart-felt message. I greatly appreciated the service. I found it difficult to say goodbye to my family as they departed on Monday.

On June 2nd, Burt came down to take me to his home where I spent over two months. Often after going to bed, for an hour or two, memories of my nearly seventy-two years of living with Maria would flash through my mind. They were good memories, but that did not prevent a deep sadness that she was no longer by my side. Little by little, the intensity of that sadness eased.

When I returned home early in August, the pain was still deep within me. Nellie and Ralph watched over me with love and concern. I kept busy by moving items from my study downstairs to the porch room upstairs, and continued my writing projects. I was learning a new aspect of life without Maria. I found that being thankful for all the positive episodes that mark marriage balanced the effect of experiencing the pain of not having her near me.

Early in November, I flew by plane to Washington D.C. where I joined Burt for a short visit with Deb, who was in the middle of the third year of working toward a doctor's degree. Burt rented a car and we, including Deb, picked up Jeanie at the airport, and drove to Philadelphia. Cyndy drove from Yonkers, NY to be present also. Burt and Jeanie's youngest daughter, Laura, was a member of the Detroit Derby Girls, who were to play the New York Gotham Girls the evening of November 13th. Detroit lost the game. The occasion was the National Roller Derby Tournament held in the Pennsylvania Convention Center November 13th-15th. The Detroit Derby Girls won the game they played on the 14th. We were able to watch two other games. We then went back to the Baltimore/Washington DC airport to fly to Detroit and on to Burt and Jeanie's home.

I visited with Burt and Jeanie for three weeks. Burt took me by car to Lebanon, OH where we met and ate dinner with Nellie and Ralph at the Golden Lamb restaurant and I returned to Wilmore that evening.

The holiday season was difficult for me, because I was facing my first Thanksgiving and Christmas without Maria.

Late in 2009, long term friends, in fact "adopted family", Ron and Judy Highhouse of Callicoon, NY, asked me to spend some time with them at their winter home in Sebastian, FL. I spent ten wonderful days in January 2010 with them. Then on March 24th I flew to Detroit, MI and spent three weeks with Burt and Jeanie. On most days I did a lot of reading and spent, on the average, of three to four hours on my laptop computer. My writing project was centered on this book.

On May 20th, Nellie and I obtained a fresh bouquet of artificial flowers and replaced those that been at Maria's grave since Christmas. As we were by her gravesite, I remembered keenly our over seventy years together as man and wife.

On May 27th Ralph, Nellie and I drove up to Greenville, IL to attend their granddaughter Jennifer Crites' high school graduation. Sharma and four of her children also came. Her son Justin also graduated from home schooling so we had a family program at the city park for him.

In the first week of June, Burt drove to Wilmore to take me to his home near Ann Arbor, MI. for most of the summer. The weather was pleasant in Michigan and I enjoyed going to classes in Detroit that Burt taught several days each week. I went shopping quite often with Burt or Jeanie in both Ann Arbor and Plymouth, and visited often with their youngest daughter Laura who is a registered nurse. She is employed at a Children's Hospital connected with the University of Michigan.

Our tenth great grandchild, Casen Ryker Goff was born on June 28, to our granddaughter Marianne and Jessie in Jackson, TN. Two days later, he was rushed to Vanderbilt Children's Hospital in Nashville, TN. On July 1st, he had surgery to remove part of his intestines. Two weeks later, he got to go home and has been growing like a weed.

In August Burt, Jeanie and I drove to New York City to spend 10 days with their daughter Cyndy and husband Mike. While there I received a call from Nellie telling me that my sister Dorothy's husband Fay had passed away. That was on Wednesday and Friday I flew from of New York City to Minneapolis, MN where my nephew picked me up and took me to Cumberland, WI to Dorothy's home. I spent four days with my sister and her family, some I had not seen in a long time. On Tuesday, Dorothy and her daughter Sharon took me back to the Minneapolis airport to fly down to Burt's home in MI.

Laura is a member of the Detroit Roller Derby Girls. This team ranked high in the Mid-West Conference. Laura's team qualified to enter a regional Derby contest in Green Bay, WI. On September 10th Burt, Jeanie and I drove from Ann Arbor to Green Bay to cheer on Laura's team during the contest.

There was ten days between this contest and the National Championship contest in which Dave's son David, Jr. would be in a car race at the Road America track near Sheboygan, WI. I wanted to be present at that race also. We knew Dave, Mary and David would be driving the trailer with the racecar from Lexington, TN to WI. Burt and Jeanie took me by car to where we could join them at the north end of I-65 near Gary, IN. I spent that entire week with them at the racetrack.

The days of the races were very noisy, for there was a continual sequence of races from early morning until 6:00 p.m. each day. There were several hundred race cars of different types in the races. David Jr. placed high enough in his first race to qualify to race in the # 17 spot in the championship race of his car's type. In that final race of about thirty cars, David moved up to ninth place, but one half mile from the finish line, David's car began to sputter and he had to turn off the track. Dave discovered that a wire had disconnected from the distributor cap. He was very disappointed.

The next day Dave put me on an air flight from Milwaukee, WI going to Louisville, KY where Ralph and Nellie met me and brought me home. I had had enough travel for the summer! On November 21st Dave drove up to Wilmore and picked me up and took me home with him to spend the week of Thanksgiving with his family. From then until the end of 2010, I divided my days between reading, and finishing this book on my computer.

Herbert and Maria's 70th Anniversary

Burt Livingston's Family
L-r: Laura, Deborah, Cyndy and Michael Murray, Jeanie and
Burt

Ralph and Nellie Kester

Crites Family
Front l-r: Jennifer, Kelly
Back l-r: Mark, Karen

Leonard Family
Front l-r: Sharma, Krista
Back l-r: Austin, Dustin, Justin, Rod and Jessica

Ken Kester Family
L-r: Jenn, Owen, Ken

David Livingston's Family
Front l-r: Jessie, Ryan, Marianne and Casen Goff
Back l-r: David, Sr, David, Jr, and Mary

APPENDIX A

ARCHAEOLOGICAL PROJECTS

KIBBUTZ RAMAT RAHEL 1959

My interest in biblical archaeology was quickened in a class on the subject taught at Asbury Theological Seminary in 1946. As a pastor, I had read some articles on the subject but was primarily concerned about the salvation message of the Scriptures. The seminary class helped me see that knowledge of the culture of the biblical people was also important.

During the time (August to the end of December 1959) that Burt and I were in Israel, I was the Director of the newly established Israel-American Institute of Holy Land Studies in Jerusalem. (See chapter 7 of the Memoirs). One of the courses was on archaeology led by Dr. Ruth Amiran. She arranged for our students to do some excavating at Ramat Rahel about three miles south of Jerusalem, starting August 17. Dr. Yohanan Aharoni supervised the excavation. Both of these scholars were top archaeologists in Israel and professors at the Hebrew University in Jerusalem. Twenty-five local men worked at the site.

Our small student body was divided into two groups. The students worked on alternate days at the excavation site two mornings a week. The work period started at 7:00 a.m. and ended at 3:00 p.m. for two weeks. I led one group on Mondays and Wednesdays. Burt worked with a group of students on Tuesdays and Thursdays. We made a round trip to the dig on a city bus for twelve cents.

The site covered a small area on a hilltop (in Hebrew, Ramat means hill-top) and in the popular mind, it is regarded as the place where Jacob's wife, Rachel, gave birth to Benjamin (Gen 36:16-19). From the hilltop, one has a full view of Bethlehem, about one mile to the south.

Dr. Aharoni had chosen this site as a digging project for his class in archaeology at Hebrew University located in Jerusalem. Some remains of walls were visible and he believed the remains of an important building should be uncovered. The digging had already begun when our students joined the project. The soil was dry and hard and our tools were small picks, trowels and brushes. Each of us had a container into which we would place the artifacts we brought to light. A university student, who was experienced in the methods of excavation, showed a team of several of our students where and how to dig, how to recognize artifacts and how to keep records of what we did. The digging was hard work and the temperature quickly rose to mid-ninety degrees. At the end of the working period, our backs and hands were sore. We were hungry and thirsty and appreciated the cooler temperature in the stone school building.

The most important building uncovered at this dig belonged to the royal palace of the Kingdom of Judah during the reign of King Jehoiakim. (See Jeremiah 22:13, 14).

Let me quote from two letters written to Maria. One letter is dated August 18, 1959.

> "Yesterday, I became an archaeologist! Seven hours of digging with a pick the size of a tack hammer and a small broom and trowel did it! All of us went out to Ramat Rachel, two miles south of Jerusalem, for an orientation lecture and four plus myself stayed to dig. We were working in Byzantine (Christian) rubble and fallen, stonewalls, dating from AD 300-600, and found several baskets of pottery pieces and a few pieces of green glass. Some plaster was on stone-walls. There were about 25 other men working at the dig. The sun was powerfully hot but a breeze was blowing which helped.—we walked ½ mile to a bus and were at school at 3:45 p.m. It cost twelve cents for the round trip. Burt went out with me on Wednesday.

The other letter is dated August 19, 1959.

"Yesterday, (actually today) I went out to the "dig" with my group, and worked quite hard. My job was cleaning out an old well into which much broken pottery and other junk had been dumped from about AD 100 to 699. (During the last three hundred years of this period, Christians lived in this area). My most interesting finds were part of an upper stone mill grinder which was flat and ridged on the bottom and had been worked back and forth by hand; a well preserved narrow neck of a flask with two handles intact and its bottom; and a small loom weight used on a weaving frame. We found many pieces of broken pottery, mostly from AD 100-200. We found the spout of a small lamp. Burt seemed to enjoy the work too, and his ear cleared right up."

We professors and the students felt we had a helpful "hands on" introduction to the scheduled archaeological class and the various trips that took us to a number of famous sites where "digs" had been carried out over the years.

Et-TEL—Ai 1966

In early January of 1966, Dr. Joseph Callaway of Southern Baptist Seminary in Louisville, KY sent a letter to Dr. George Turner, a professor at Asbury Theological Seminary in Wilmore, KY. Dr. Callaway enclosed a copy of his 1964 excavation at et-Tell (biblical Ai). He suggested that Asbury Seminary join an excavation of the same site that summer and send a faculty member or two to aid in supervising a new area on the site he was planning to open. Their work would be published in the report of the excavation.

The fee charged for each person provided by the seminary would be three thousand ($3,000) dollars. Room and board would be provided by the funds supporting the "dig", but travel expenses would be the responsibility of the person or persons who accept a place on the staff that would number about eighteen. A number of artifacts found during the summer would be given to the seminary. The excavation began on June 6 and ended on July 29.

Dr. Turner felt he could not spend the summer away from Wilmore so he asked the other faculty of the Biblical courses whether anyone would like to join the excavation. He would provide the $3,000. Immediately I felt an urge to respond to the opportunity. Maria and I, as well as many others, prayed about the matter. I would have to get a fellow faculty member to teach several courses assigned to me during summer school. Dr. Turner volunteered to teach the classes. A student, Loal Ames, wanted to go also and Dr. Callaway accepted both of us. Reference to this project is found in Chapter 9 of the Memoirs.

Loal and I left Cincinnati on June 1 and arrived in Jerusalem on June 4. We took a taxi to Deir Dibwan, fourteen miles to the northeast. Deir Dibwan is an Arab village of stone houses a quarter of mile from the excavation site.

We spent two days getting settled in two stone buildings Dr. Callaway had rented. We began work on et-Tell on the early morning of June 6. The daily schedule for the summer would start with get up time at 4:30 a.m. followed by breakfast, and a hike up the slope to the "dig" site. We started work at 5:00. We wore jackets because it was cool. The sun was soon shining on us, so within two hours the jackets came off. We stopped for a second breakfast at 8:30 a.m. and worked from 9:30 until 11:45 when we had a fifteen-minute lemonade break. We quit at 1:45 p.m., washed ourselves at the headquarters house and ate a delicious dinner prepared by a male, Arab cook at 2:00 p.m. From 3:00 till 4:00 was rest time. After 4:00 p.m., we helped sort pottery pieces or other needed tasks. By 6:00 it was dark. We ate dinner at 7:00 and at 9:30 lights were out.

On Saturdays, the staff ate breakfast at 4:30 a.m. and worked from 5:00 a.m. till 9:00 a.m. We then went to Jerusalem to rest or roam the city and spend the night in a hotel. We returned to Deir Dibwan on Sunday evening to begin work on Monday morning.

Before we continue, I will provide some historical background to the site called in the Bible Ai (Gen 12:8; Josh 7:2). In modern Arabic, Ai is called et-Tell. When Edward Robinson toured the Middle East in 1838 in an effort to identify biblical sites, he chose a small ruin, Khirbet Khaiyan, at the edge of et-Tell, as the biblical Ai. In 1881, a tourist named V. Guerin selected Khirbet Khudriya, a site one mile east of Deir Dibwan, as Ai. In 1924, Dr. W. F. Albright pointed to et-Tell as the proper location.

Dr. J. Garstang of England led the first excavation in 1928 along the outer wall and the damaged stone structures at the upper western end of the site. He left limited information about his findings.

The next attempt to dig at el-Tel, in 1933-35, is known as the Rothschild Expedition supported by French funds. A lady, J. Merquet-Krause, was chosen to supervise the excavation. She produced several reports and an important controversial map of et-Tel, but her untimely death in 1936 brought the project to an end. Her map proposed a walled city of about twenty-seven acres. Many archaeologists thought the city could not possibly be that large.

In 1966, Loal Ames and I were assigned to area B. The first job for the workers was to remove topsoil that had debris from the wheat harvest. We had several Arab workers experienced in excavating a square.

Dr. Callaway wanted us to learn his method of removing the soil from the squares and collecting the artifacts in a sturdy sack. To guide the workers, sixty-penny nails were driven into the ground at each corner of the square and a strong string tied to the nails to outline the square. By using nails and a string, Dr. Callaway controlled the digging by dividing each square into five, one-meter wide strips.

Arabs who knew how to work as teams dug the strip selected. One man had a full-sized pick and began breaking up the hard ground to a depth of five centimeters. At a safe distance, another man with a hoe moved the loose soil between his legs to a man with a rubber basket. Each man would carefully search the soil for artifacts. The soil was put in a screen to further search for small artifacts, and then the soil was dumped on a pile.

If any wall was found and the content of the soil changed, digging was stopped so the soil could be carefully removed from the surface of a new stratum (layer) of soil. The team then moved to the next strip and dug it down to the same level. When the five strips had been dug to the same level, the same procedure was repeated. Each level had the debris of an older period of use or occupation. The digging stopped when solid rock appeared.

Loal and I each had a sturdy notebook with blank pages. The left page had lines for writing notations. The page to the right had small squares. On this page, we made drawings with a pencil of any walls or large artifacts, and their location in the square.

At the beginning of the second week, Dr. Callaway told Loal and me that a new site would open on a terrace down the slope from area B. The new site would be called Area G. I would be the supervisor and Loal would be my assistant.

Dr. Callaway had a reason for selecting this particular terrace. He believed, as did many other archaeologists that the French map showed walls enclosing a much larger area (27 acres) than was realistic. The belief was that the true size of the fortress was only five acres. Dr. Callaway believed the terrace on which area C and area G were located was where the original wall was hidden under the surface. Our job was to uncover this wall. The people working in area C were to bring to light the corner where the southern wall ended and the proposed wall began.

During the second week, the debris of the wheat harvest was removed and the architect laid out the nine squares we would work in. On the second day of that week, our crew of men started to dig in several squares. Soon several meter-wide walls came to light on the eastern side of the double line of squares. These narrow walls contrasted sharply with the triple walls, six meters wide that enclosed the south side of the fortress. It turned out that the walls in area G were terrace walls. Dr. Callaway was surprised.

Our Arab teams emptied all nine squares to solid rock about two meters below the surface. By the middle of July, Dr. Callaway began to take the French map seriously. On the afternoon of July 18, Dr. Callaway asked Dr. Schoonover of Southern Methodist University and me to search the parallel terrace walls that crossed the mound from south to north. We would look for large stones like the oldest walls on the site. Going back and forth along the face of the terrace walls, we found none of these large stones.

Finally, Dr. Callaway said, "Let us follow the dotted line on the French map and see what we can find." We started on the lower portion of the north side and moved along the eastern side. We quickly found large stones, some close together in a row, as shown on the map. We also found large stones forming a corner. Going south, we found the stones, as on the map. We also looked among bushes and found at the base of the terrace wall were large stones. This discovery happened several times. We decided, reluctantly that the French had made a valid map. Callaway concluded there was enough data to support an excavation of several areas along this eastern dotted line. I decided I wanted to return in 1968 to supervise any area assigned to me.

At the same time, a group of teams were excavating several areas on et-Tel; another group of teams were excavating a site one mile east of Deir Dibwan called Khirbet Khudriya. The ruins there proved to be the remains of a Christian monastery, dating from about AD 100 to about AD 600. A square stone pillar had a cross-shaped depression carved in its top. In this depression, a person could sit while being baptized. Some of us enjoyed reminding the several Baptists on the staff that evidently Christians at that early date were baptized by either poring or by sprinkling. Beautiful mosaic floors were found in many of the rooms. Crosses were either carved or painted on plastered walls or on artifacts.

During the summer, I kept a diary account of each day's work that I sent to Maria regularly. I am randomly selecting from the diary one day's text and reproducing it below.

Diary—June 13

"4:30 a.m. came early, but I had slept well. The breeze was cool enough for a jacket until 8:30 a.m., at the second breakfast break. A heavy haze obscured the Jordan Valley and hid Jerusalem from view. Clouds were in the sky. Work in my square became more interesting as we got into fallen rocks and different layers of dirt, indicating occupation levels. The pottery was Iron Age. I am keeping in fair health though I have cramps. A pill or two of Intero Vioform seems to keep everything under control. Dr. Callaway has one important problem to clear up. He discovered Saturday that his original government permit didn't cover the excavation at the Byzantine church two miles east of Deir Dibwan, so he had to go to Ammon to negotiate for a permit.

Gradually, I am picking up Arabic names for tools and pottery and numbers. I learned slowly but everyday several new words or expressions become fixed in my mind. The workers are pleasant, but slow as "molasses in January," but they do keep up a steady pace. They chatter almost constantly. Each man has his job and it is hard to get one to do something else than that to which he is assigned. They thought some jobs had a higher status than other jobs.

The Jordanian foremen were trained at the Jericho excavation and are referred to as the "Jericho men." "Their standard tools are a small pick and a small trowel.

They detect a change of soil very quickly. Some of the workers covet a chance to borrow the supervisor's trowel to clean around rocks and to clean the bottom of a stratum of soil. They have to be watched carefully for they are not experienced and tend to dig down where they are not suppose to and to gouge into the side of the square where they are not supposed to dig.

The supervisor's job is to watch the men carefully and to keep careful records of changes of soil. He sees to it that the potsherds are kept in separate baskets (guffas) and are properly tagged. The supervisor also carefully sketches all the walls and the arrangement of the large stones.

This evening, after an hour's nap, Dr. Callaway took us out to the yard, where the washed pieces of pots were arranged on grass mats, and showed us how to sort the pottery so that only the important pieces are preserved, for the artist to draw and the recorder to label with India ink.

Following supper, we sat for 20 minutes and sang old American folk songs, then prepared for the night, doing some reading and writing."

Early in July, our teams were uncovering bed rock in square after square. We had gone through four layers of occupation debris and the lower courses of the stone-walls of houses in which the first occupants of the site lived. They settled here about 3,000 BC. They lived here generation after generation until about 2,400 BC.

Some of the pottery and artifacts indicate there was a trade relationship with Egypt. Et-Tel (Ai) was possibly controlled by that country. In short, this place was the largest fortress in Palestine during the Early Bronze Age (the historian's label for this period).

The name of the people that destroyed this fortress is unknown. A severe earthquake could have destroyed this fortress, causing the occupants to flee and not return. No inscriptions were found that could give us that kind of information.

Immediately above the Early Bronze strata is a layer of soil that contains ruins of a few buildings and potsherds of the period dating from 1,200-1,000 BC, known as Iron Age I. This is the period when most of the judges lived, as recorded in the Book of Judges. Evidence in area B and in G, between the Early Bronze and Iron I ages indicates there were no settled peoples on this site for 1,200 years the inhabitants were Israelites.

The occupation stratum above the Iron Age I strata began about the time the Khirbet Khudriyah monastery was established, sometime between AD 100 and AD 200. The monks apparently tilled the soil on area G, for parts of farming tools and broken water jars used by the Byzantine monks were found in the soil. This activity ceased in the middle AD 600's. There had been no occupation or tilling of et-Tel for at least 800 years.

Again, et-Tel lay barren for over a thousand years. Arabs settled near et-Tel two centuries ago at Deir Dibwan and have farmed on et-Tel since then.

I boarded a plane at Israel's Lodd airport at 9:00 a.m., August 2, and arrived in London that evening. Several Asbury Seminary professors were studying in London, so I spent several days touring London with them. I left London August 5 and arrived in New York City at 3:10 p.m. I left for Cincinnati and arrived there at 7:00 p.m. What a relief to be home!!

Ai 1966 Area B Layout

Ai 1966 Ruins of Israelite house

Et-TEL—Ai 1968

Dr. George Turner and I joined the 1968 expedition to excavate at et-Tel and Khudriyah. The big change was that in 1967, during the Six-Day War, Israel miraculously defeated the combined armies of Egypt, Syria and the Kingdom of Jordan. The army of the latter country was driven out of the West Bank. This victory meant that Deir Dibwan was under the control of Israel's army. Dr. Callaway was able to obtain permission from Israel to continue the excavation.

By letter, Callaway originally assigned Dr. Turner as an assistant supervisor at area B. and assigned me as the supervisor of the excavation of the monastery.

In 1966, the Moslems in Deir Dibwan were unhappy that we excavated on Friday, the Muslim day of worship at their mosque. Saturday was the Jewish day of worship in Israel. Christian communities worshiped on both Saturday and Sunday. Callaway compromised by agreeing to not work on Friday and Saturday and work on Sunday through Thursday. We Christians agreed to worship on Saturday. The excavation would begin on Sunday, June 16 and end Thursday August 8, 1968.

Dr. Turner and I learned that Wheaton College, located near Chicago, was sponsoring an archaeological tour in Israel. We were able to join their group, and thus obtain cheap flight tickets.

On June10, we left New York City at 5:00 p.m. on Olympic Airlines # 412 to Athens, Greece where we spent most of two days sightseeing. We boarded a plane at 3:30 p.m. local time and in two hours, we landed at Beirut. We enjoyed roaming about the city until 8:00 a.m. when we boarded a plane to Cairo, Egypt. We viewed the Pyramids and the contents of Cairo Museum for eight hours and returned to Beirut. On the 15th, we visited Tyre and Sidon.

The flaw of this schedule was that we did not arrive at Deir Dibwan until the first day of work on the "dig". We discovered that Dr. Callaway had asked Dr. Wagner of Canada to supervise all the areas on et-Tel, especially of Area A, but found that was too much work for one man.

I discovered Dr. Callaway had also decided to open an Area H near the southeastern corner on et-Tel and wanted me to supervise it. Dr Turner was assigned as my assistant. The architect had already laid out the squares on Area H. Another man was assigned as supervisor of Khudriyah. Our daily schedule of work and meals remained the same as in 1966. There were 25 men and women from the USA and from Canada on the staff, and 120 men were hired from the community as the work force.

On Monday morning, men were assigned to work under our supervision at Area H. This area was a level strip just wide enough for two lines of five-meter squares and, a one-meter-wide strip, called a baulk, between the squares.

Along the east side was a steep drop of four meters and then a gentle slope toward the west edge of Deir Dibwan. Along the west-side of the row of squares was a line of fruit trees. The olive and fig fruit were in the early stages of growth. The local law prohibited our workers from digging around the trees, but baskets of dirt and small stones could be carried to the far side of the tree line where they could be dumped.

During the first week of work, the removal of twenty centimeters of soil revealed closely packed stones in my squares. In Dr. Turner's squares, the same level, the stone surface was thirty centimeters wide and stopped. Many smaller stones in disarray filled the space to the west edge of each square where the face of another wall came to light. This wall extended under the trees.

Along the east edge of my squares, was a line of large boulders that suggested an impressive face to our wall. A careful examination of this line of boulders, and several meters down the steep slope, clearly revealed the reality of a massive wall. Dr. Turner's team dug down several meters in his row of squares and found nothing new.

Dr. Callaway decided to split our crew in half. One group would continue to take soil and small stones away from the wall until the base of the wall was discovered. Dr. Turner would supervise this project. Dr. Callaway took the rest of the crew and me, to the southeast corner of the mound and opened another area and designated it Area K. An architect laid out a group of squares, some of which stretched to the east and some to the south. Callaway wanted us to confirm that some kind of structure formed the corner of the mound of et-Tel. Until the end of the second week, our team was busy removing the top-soil from these squares.

During the third week, the top of a wall became visible, that matched the one Dr. Turner's crew had uncovered. We found the same mixture of soil and stone and the face of another wall that matched the one Dr. Turner had found in area H. Fruit trees were not growing in our new area, so we could take the soil off the top of another wall that came to light. This wall measured five meters wide instead of the six-meter width of the inner wall of the system at the upper, western portion of et-Tel.

Part of my crew proceeded to expose a five-meter portion of the outer wall while the rest of my crew worked in the squares that formed the inner corner and the southern arm of our area. The outer wall soon came to light. We quickly learned the corner was not a ninety-degree angle, but was a curve in shape.

We also found that beyond the inner wall an unusual sequence of strata was being excavated. There was a row of stones, each about the size of a human head, and there was dark, finely textured soil. The stones appeared to form a narrow wall. Behind the stones was a layer of firmly packed, red clay. It took five weeks to dig out, draw and photograph what we were finding. The edges of these strata were seen clearly on a smooth, perpendicular surface. None of us could come up with a satisfactory theory that would explain what this series of layers pointed to. In 1969, I was unable to join the project and being involved in solving the mystery.

In 1969, Dr. Callaway had the flat area to the north of area K excavated. Before the summer work was finished, a sizeable reservoir was discovered.

In August, 1969 I received a hand-written letter from Dr. Callaway dated August 16. Here is a quote from that letter:

> "The discovery of the year was at site K! You recall the enigmatic fill of red clay in the north and west baulk of KIV. We opened KIX just a meter north, between the olive trees, and discovered a ramp of large stones set in the red clay, angling up from a flag stone paved surface to the surface of the ground. The surface reached across four squares northward to a second ramp running east to west and connecting with the city wall. It finally dawned upon us that we had an EBIII city water system—an ingeniously engineered above the ground reservoir about 25 meters wide and possibly 20 meters long, averaging over 2 meters in depth, a capacity of 1000 cu. m.
>
> Your red clay was the plaster to prevent seepage from the reservoir, and the loose stones against the city wall were to allow ventilation and an outlet for any water that might seep through. The "V" shaped, ashy layer was a cushion under the meter thickness of red clay that backed the stones of the dam to the top of the wall. The closely jointed paved bottom is also set in red clay to prevent seepage. It is quite an engineering job, and is the only known inside-the-city water system in Palestine."

Two other surprises made the 1968 summer dig exciting. The thick outer wall was measured as four meters high and was in almost perfect condition. It was built sometime between 2,800 and 2,500 B. C. The stonework was so expertly done that Egyptian craftsmen probably constructed the wall. It is one of the best-preserved, ancient walls in Palestine.

The second surprise burst upon us two days before the season of excavation ended. Dr. Wagner and I were busy drawing various items in area K. The foreman of the team cleaning loose dirt in several squares came to us, saying in an exited voice, "We have something over here you must see." We followed him and he pointed to some large rocks that he said looked like an ancient gateway. The structure was a layer of stones that was one meter wider than the wall above it. This width made the wall the same thickness as the six-meter wall at the upper western end of et-Tel.

Careful cleaning of the stones and a measurement of the gap between stones revealed a threshold of big flat stones, and several courses of large stones. The ends of these stones were lined up vertically. The resulting space was over a meter wide. This was indeed a gateway. At that time the gateway was one of the oldest gateways found anywhere in the world and the wall is the second oldest wall. The structure unearthed at Jericho is the only one older than this one.

This summer of 1968 at et-Tel was not all excitement; there was sorrow and concern as well. On Thursday evenings, we usually went to Jerusalem to pick up the mail and on to lodge at Christ's Church Hostel. On the third weekend, I received an airmail letter from Maria that contained shocking news. On June 23, Floyd my second to oldest brother had been killed by lightning on his farm near Cameron, WI. His funeral was scheduled for the day before I received the letter. When I returned to work Sunday morning, the foreman of the workers asked why I was depressed. When I told them about my brother's death, the foreman and his men expressed sympathy and treated me with kindness. Their response uplifted my spirit.

Two weeks later, an airmail letter from Maria told me that the other professor of Old Testament studies at Asbury seminary, Dr. Dennis Kinlaw, had been selected as the President of Asbury College. This act forced me to make a difficult decision. I was scheduled to have a sabbatical leave for the fall semester, so I could engage in research and a writing project. This meant that there was no one to teach Old Testament courses that fall, unless I gave up my sabbatical leave and returned to the classroom. After much prayer, I wrote an airmail letter to the Dean of the seminary, informing him I would teach classes that fall. My research could wait.

Was et-Tel really the Ai mentioned in the Old Testament? Dr. Callaway had become convinced this place was not associated with Abraham and Joshua. He suggested the biblical accounts were latter stories based on folklore.

I disagree about Abram (Abraham). Gen 12:8 says, "He moved from there to the mountain east of Bethel, and he pitched his tent with Bethel on the west and Ai on the east . . . ." Also Gen 13:3 reads, "And he went on his journey from the South as far as Bethel, to the place where his tent had been at the beginning, between Bethel and Ai." (NKJV).

The mountain ridge to the west of et-Tel fits these statements very well. The correlation of et-Tel with Joshua is different. A close look at the Book of Joshua brings out these points. Joshua 7:2 reads, "Now Joshua sent men from Jericho to Ai, which is beside Beth Aven on the east side of Bethel . . . ." Joshua 8:9 states, "Joshua therefore sent them out, and they went to lie in ambush and stayed between Bethel and Ai, on the west side of Ai . . . ." No mention is made of a mountain ridge. The first attack on Ai failed but the second attack was successful. In 8:10-29, a description of the battle and the complete destruction of the city. The people were destroyed, the city was burned and the walls and gate were destroyed, afterwards it was a ruin, an Ai.

The excavation of et-Tel proved that between 2,400 B.C. and New Testament times, only one village, an Israelite village, existed from 1,200 to 1,000 B.C, and et-Tel was not occupied again until New Testament times. Ai cannot be the location of the Ai of Joshua's time. Further search for Joshua's Ai has been attempted, but with no clear-cut success. The situation on the West Bank has been too dangerous for archaeologists to do their work. A team of archaeologists were excavating a ruin called Khirbet El Maquatir, near Bethel, hoping it is the ancient Ai.

I returned home by joining the Wheaton College Archaeological Tour on August 16 for the trip home. Stops to do sightseeing in several cities prolonged the trip so that I arrived at the Cincinnati airport the evening of August 26. My happy family welcomed their happy husband and father with joy.

Early Bronze Wall

Early Bronze Gate
(At the time of discovery, these two were the second oldest
found of their kind)

Edge of Early Bronze Reservoir
(At the time of its discovery, this reservoir was the first
found in Palestine)

Crew Starting to Dig

TEL QASILEH, 1972

Our family memoir mentions our project of taking a group of students to Israel for three weeks of study at the Israel-American Institute of Holy Land Studies. Our group joined several other groups of students to spend two weeks, June 18-30, excavating at Tell Qasileh located a few kilometers northeast of Tel Aviv.

The four-acre mound (150 by 100 meters) is on the south bank of the Yarkon River that empties into the Mediterranean Sea where the river forms a small harbor for small ships. Cedar logs from Lebanon, destined for Solomon's Temple in Jerusalem, were no doubt unloaded at this harbor.

In 1948-50, Professor Benjamin Mazar of Hebrew University supervised an excavation of a portion of the mound. Philistines built the first city about 1,200 BC. The city was abandoned by Arabs of the Mameluke period.

Amihay Mazar resumed excavation in 1971. He is the son of Benjamin Mazar. Amihay had decided to extend the project for four seasons and use his report as the basis of his PH.D. dissertation. In 1972, he selected an area of 500 square meters in the northeastern corner of the mound.

Our group was housed in an Israeli youth hostel near the site. The beds were army cots and the meals were limited varieties of Jewish, kosher menus. A bus took us to the dig at 5:00 a.m. A cool breeze was coming off the Sea but the sun boosted the temperature rapidly. The first day was spent removing brush and weeds and laying out the grid of five-meter squares. A graduate student at Hebrew University was our area supervisor.

Dean Johnson, brother of my sister Vera's husband, had come with me on the trip. He and I worked on the same square. The supervisor instructed us to remove the soil to the depth of ten centimeters with hand trowels and sift the dirt through a screen for discovery of small artifacts. This procedure was repeated with care, for the supervisor explained that walls on Tell Qasileh were usually constructed with pressed, sun-baked brick made of the local, dark soil. The best way to identify a mud brick wall is to watch for narrow white lines. These lines were composed of mortar, separating the bricks from each other. Most walls were about one meter wide.

At a depth of about thirty centimeters, Dean and I found such lines close to the south side of our square. Clearly, the wall went into the baulk, so we didn't know the width of the wall. We told the supervisor and he was excited. Perhaps an important building would come to light. Walls of other buildings being uncovered nearby had stonewalls. Our building was no doubt much older.

After removing soil for the entire length of the wall, we began digging along the inside face of the wall. We noticed a difference in soil texture and a different kind of artifacts. The upper strata had some pottery pieces of the time of King David and King Solomon. The newly found pottery pieces had decorations that pointed to a Philistine people. Wow! We had not found any of this kind of pottery at Ramat Rachel or at et-Tel.

Amihay Mazar assigned other students to work with us and a large amount of soil was screened, deposited in wheelbarrows and dumped on a nearby pile. The Philistine people made all of the artifacts used from 1,200 to 1,000 B.C. Early in the second week of excavation, several walls 1.2 meters wide were uncovered. They enclosed an area measuring 14.5 meters by 8 meters and divided the space into two rooms. The walls were covered with white plaster and survived at a height of 0.80 meter.

The larger room measured 7.2 meters by 5.65 meters. Low, plastered benches had been built at the base of three of its walls. Also in this room were two round, flat stones that served as bases for cedar pillars that supported a ceiling. They were about two meters apart.

The smaller room, 6 meters by 3.70 meters, had a wide opening on the east side of the larger room. The smaller room had a doorway in its northern wall. People on the outside could not look directly into the larger room.

I remember well the last day of our excavation assignment. The top archaeologist of Israel, Dr. Yiguel Yadin, stopped for a short visit. He and Amihay were standing near the edge of the dig, comparing drawings with the items described above. Dr. Yadin paused and made a surprising statement. "I believe we have here the remains of a Philistine temple. It is the first one found in Israel. Congratulations!" We all gasped and then began slapping each other on the back. Dr. Yadin interrupted by shaking hands with Amihay and all the students. Several Philistine temples have been found in Israel since then, but ours was the first.

We concluded our four weeks in Israel by attending classes and touring throughout the West Bank and Israel. We visited a number of archaeology sites. We were glad to board a plane and return home again.

BETHEL ACADEMY, WILMORE, KY

Dr. Howard Shipps, church history professor at Asbury Theological Seminary of Wilmore, KY, and I spent a day in the fall of 1964 at the site of Bethel Academy. With spades, we found the exact lines of the four foundation walls of the original building. We determined the outside measurements were thirty-five by eighty-six feet. I suggested that I should take the students of my class in "Archaeology in Palestine" to the site on weekends and excavate around the foundation walls. We transformed this suggestion into reality in the spring quarter of 1965. We would dig at Bethel Academy on Saturday or Monday forenoons, depending on the weather. We wanted to gain factual knowledge about the school from strata and artifacts and then compare that knowledge with written records related to the school.

The class had ten students who could choose to dig or work in a lab set up in the basement of a dormitory on the seminary campus. The young ladies in the class tended to prefer to work in the lab, but did work at the dig occasionally. The first day at the site was April 16, 1965.

The ruins of Bethel Academy is located in a farm pasture just off Handys Bend Road that connects with State Road 29 about two miles south of Wilmore. The ruins of the school are in a cluster of trees and brush in the center of the pasture.

We emphasized finding walls and artifacts the way they did it at Ramat Rachel, except we used "yards," "feet" and "inches" instead of the metric system. The first task of the students was to clear small trees, brush and weeds from the site.

The students were divided into two member teams. One team began uncovering the top of the north wall, it was labeled Wall A. The east wall was B. The south wall was C. The west wall was D. As each wall was cleaned, a search was made along the inside edge for evidence of cross walls within the structure. Some cross walls were found and the teams focused on the east end of the building. The walls of two rooms were located. The bases of double fireplaces were found in several walls that separated the rooms. A few artifacts of recent years were found in the topsoil.

During the spring quarter of 1966, the new class of students cleared the tops of walls on the west end of the building. The walls and double fireplaces were duplicates of those on the east end. A large central room was present. Long narrow "hallways" separated the central room from the two rooms at each end. Most likely stairs to upper floors were located in these halls. A capital letter was assigned to the newly located walls. See the floor plan of the building displayed below.

While working during the summer of 1966 at et-Tel, Dr. Joseph Callaway taught me his method of excavation known as the Wheeler-Kenyon procedure. I decided to apply this method to our excavation at Bethel Academy in the spring of 1967. I taught the new class of students how to lay out a grid of squares and baulks. The details of this method as applied to Bethel Academy are given in my article, "The Spade Uncovers Bethel Academy", The Asbury Theological Journal, fall 1994, Volume 49, Number 2, pages 68-70.

Most squares were sixteen feet on each side. A few were thirteen by sixteen feet. The center of the building was determined and a row of squares were laid out from east to west. The center of the squares matched the center of the building. A row of squares lay on each side of the center squares. Each square was given a Roman numeral.

Selecting a locos in alternating squares across the inside of the building, we dug through three layers of debris searching for evidence of a cellar. Instead of a cellar, we found undisturbed red clay. In each locos we dug through three layers of soil.

The top layer (strata) was two to four inches thick and was dark, humus soil. The artifacts were modern. The second layer averaged a foot thick and had many broken pieces of brick as well as undamaged brick. Broken window glass, chunks of plaster and many square nails were found in this layer. This strata would date from the time the building was dismantled, i.e. in 1820. The third strata averaged two to three inches thick and became known as the "gold strip", because it contained a number of artifacts of everyday living of the teachers and pupils who lived at the school from 1794-1804. Near the walls were loose dirt and small stones probably thrown aside as trenches were dug for the foundation stone walls. Very few artifacts were found in that dirt.

The building that housed Cokesbury College in Maryland was the model for Bethel Academy's building. We examined pictures of that college and noted that the roofline had four chimneys. The outer chimneys were close to the ends of the building and the inner chimneys were evenly spaced on either side of center. In 1970, the students searched along the wall separating the two east rooms. A baulk had to be removed to fully bring the top of the wall to light. The foundations of two fireplaces, back to back, were located at the middle of the wall. A duplicate set of fireplaces was uncovered at the west end of the foundations. We then searched each inner wall of the central room and found a fireplace in the middle of each wall. The Bethel Academy was indeed a smaller copy of the Cokesbury College building.

During the 1970's, an excavation of the back yard of the Chaumeire du Prairie property took up half of the weekends of the digging season. A brief description of that project follows this article. Since rain canceled some of our weekend work during the spring, the time of digging was shifted to the fall. During that decade, the students spent most of their time working on the area on the outside of the south and the west walls.

We were looking for evidence of supports for an entryway into the building. No stone bases for such an entryway came to light. Removing soil outside the eastern wall, we found the threshold stones for a doorway and a path paved with flat stones. We decided to follow the pathway and made an interesting discovery.

We had often wondered where and how the bricks for the main walls were made and also how the plaster was produced. About twenty feet to the southeast of the main building, four rows of stonewalls were found. They were not oriented according to the four points of the compass. The walls were pointed toward the northwest. About eighteen inches of open space separated the walls that had no end closures. A few bricks were stacked along the west side and wood ash filled the open spaces. Some lime was found mixed with the soil a few feet from the northwest ends of the walls. Some research identified the structure as the remains of a brick/lime kiln.

Thus ended our sequence of annual digs at Bethel Academy. However, in 1990, I was asked to teach one more class of Biblical

Archaeology. I asked the students to help me to make one more attempt to find the main entrance to the building. We had not excavated along the outer side of wall A because of a grouping of middle-sized trees a few feet from the wall. This time we dug between the trees near the middle of this wall. Our best effort failed to locate any stone bases for a front porch.

Another phase of research that remained a mystery was the location of survey and legal documents related to the state grant of 6000 acres of lands to support Bethel Academy. Someone suggested that the State Department of Libraries and Archives in Frankfort, KY may have these records. I made a trip to Frankfort and found that the Library had a microfilmed record of these surveys. The librarian kindly made copies of these surveys for me. She also informed me that each survey record had to be approved by the governor and those documents would be in the archives of the governor's office in the capital building. I was able to obtain printed copies of the governors' approval of each survey of land granted to Bethel Academy Trustees. All the land was located in Union County in the Western section of the state. I have not found records of the sale of these tracts of land.

The site where the ruin of Bethel Academy is located has been placed on the National Record of Historic Places.

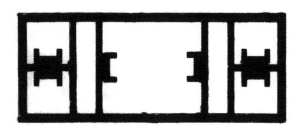

Bethel Academy Floor Plan

Bethel Academy Plaque

CHAUMIERE du PRAIRIE, JESSAMINE COUNTY, KY

In the spring of 1970, the Jessamine County Historical Society in Nicholasville, KY, seven miles from our home in Wilmore, KY invited me to speak to the members of the society. The members were interested in the archaeological project that I had been supervising at the Bethel Academy foundations near Wilmore.

After I had finished my presentation, a lady spoke to me about a newly inherited property on Catnip Hill road six miles northeast of Wilmore. She was a widow who had lived in Lexington, KY for many years but her husband had died of a serious illness. The farm she inherited soon after his death had belonged to the Steele (her maiden name) family since 1884.

The farm, called Chaumiere du Prairie, had historical significance in Kentucky, dating back to 1796; David Meade II migrated, with his family and servants, from Virginia in that year to the Blue Grass region of Kentucky in search of land on which he establish a plantation. He and his family and slaves lived on this land until his death in 1829. Soon after his death, the property was sold to a series of families until this lady had inherited it.

She decided to restore the brick home and add modern electrical and plumbing systems. When workers dug a ditch across the back yard for a water line, they found the remnants of a brick wall. The lady knew little about the history of place and decided to do some research. She learned about the Meade family and the importance of the farm during the lifetime of David Meade. She wondered if I would be willing to bring my archaeological class to her place on weekends. She showed me a map of the layout of the original buildings. I told her I would consider her request seriously.

For several months, I learned more about the importance of this farm. I was soon aware of the fact that Bethel Academy was functioning during the same time that the Meade family was setting up housekeeping. This meant that the artifacts found in the oldest layer at the Bethel building would be of the same time period as the oldest level in the back yard of Chaumiere du Prairie. A comparison of the cheap chinaware, utensils and pottery of Bethel Academy with the more elegant chinaware, utensils and pottery of Chaumiere du Prairie would be interesting.

I made a decision to dig in the backyard of Chaumiere by alternating week-end and work-days with the work at Bethel. The fall semester of 1970 for this class would be set so that on a Saturday or Monday, depending on the weather, would be at Bethel and the next weekend would be at Chaumiere. We found that this sequence was practical and the class members would learn about the equipment of a poor school and the more costly equipment of a well-to-do plantation.

The procedure of alternating weekends between Bethel and Chaumiere was satisfactory to everyone. We were impressed with the abundance of artifacts at Chaumiere. Almost every shovel filled with debris had artifacts. The artifacts were more elegant and costly than those at Bethel. Of particular interest were shards of Chinese tableware. Some of these shards came to the USA by way of England. Items from France and Germany were also found.

In most squares, each layer was from three to six inches thick and the third layer dated from the time when the Meade's lived at Chaumiere. The upper layers yielded less expensive artifacts than the back yard did.

In fact, the back yard seemed to be a place to dump garbage and broken items.

Foundations of several buildings came to light. The first one was easily located because a portion of its brick superstructure was still above ground. Because pieces of slate writing boards and broken slate pencils were in the debris, we concluded the building housed a school. The fireplace was extra large and its flames were fed by logs thrust into it from the outside, through a hole in the wall.

A cellar was found a short distance north of the school. The cellar had a stone-wall that went into the earth four feet. The contents of this cellar were different than those found in flat ground around it. Broken farm equipment had been thrown into the cellar after the small building had been destroyed.

Farther to the north, another stone foundation, possessing a fireplace on the east end of the structure was filled with a mass of ashes. Several artifacts suggested the building housed the kitchen, serving the main household. Excavation of this backyard ceased in 1979. A map of this layout can be found below.

In 1995, I received a letter from Dr. James D. Kornwolf, a professor in the Department of Art History of the College of William and Mary located in Williamsburg, VA. He had learned of my excavation at Chaumiere from an academic friend who lived in Kentucky. He was making a study of ornamental gardens in England and in America. His friend had alerted him to the fact that David Meade had developed a remarkable garden at Chaumiere. The friend had suggested a careful study of this garden.

I was aware of this garden and examined the area of its location on the Chaumiere property, but little evidence of the alleged structures remains. I had chosen to center my dig on the backyard rather than on the garden. I informed Dr. Kornwolf of this decision and sent him copies of data and pictures I had on hand. I assured him I would do everything I could to increase our mutual knowledge of the garden's history.

In the summer of 1997, Dr. and Mrs. Kornwolf motored to Lexington, KY. I met them at Chaumiere and Dr. and Mrs. Rash, (the widow who owned the property had remarried) graciously showed us the garden area and then took us by car to the cemetery on the farm where Mr. and

Mrs. David Meade were buried at the time of their death. Later, relatives had their remains transferred to a cemetery in Virginia.

The Kornwolfs wrote a detailed article about the garden, claiming that David Meade had produced the finest English style garden in the USA, dating to the first two decades of the nineteenth century. The article was entitled, "David Meade II: Pioneer of 'Le Jarden Anglais in the United States, 1774-1829'". It was published in the Journal of Garden History.16, no. 4, (1996) 254.

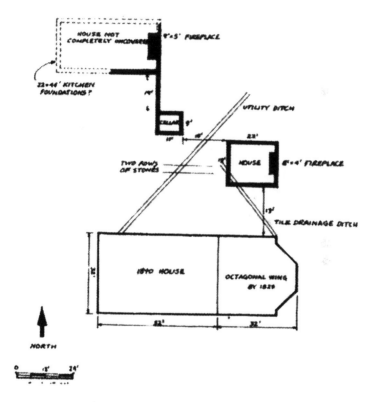

Chaumiere du Prairie excavation area.

APPENDIX B

LISTING OF WRITINGS

By Dr. G. Herbert Livingston

The Hebrew Prophetic Consciousness, Ph.D. Thesis 1953

"That Dynamic Book", Free Methodist, vol. 88, Light and Life Press, 1955.

"Kierkegaard and Jeremiah" The Seminarian Asbury Seminary, 1957.

"God's Spokesmen", Senior High Manual, vol. 1&4, Light and Life Press, 1957.

"Roots of the Church in the Old Testament", Senior High Manual, Vol. 2, Light and Life Press 1957.

GENESIS, 2 Volumes Aldersgate Biblical Series, Light and Life Press 1960

"Jonah and Obadiah" Wycliffe Bible Commentary, Moody Press, 1962

JEREMIAH, 2 volumes, Aldersgate Biblical Series, Light and Life Press, 1963

GENESIS, 13 lessons, Arnold's Commentary, Light and Life, 1964

"God's Purpose Through His People", 13 lessons, Arnold's Commentary, Light and Life Press, 1965

"Response to God's Call", 13 lessons, Arnold's Commentary, Light and Life Press, 1966

"General Introduction to the Pentateuch", volume 1, Wesley Bible Commentary, Wm. B. Eerdmans Pub. Co. 1967

"The Excavation of Et-Tell (Ai) in 1966", The Seminarian, Asbury Seminary, 1967

"The Prophets' Messages", Thirteen lessons, The Asbury Herald, Asbury Seminary, 1967

"Psalms 73 to 150", Volume 2, Wesley Bible Commentary, Wm Eerdmans Pub. Co., 1968

"The Excavation of Et-Tell (Ai) in 1968", The Seminarian, Asbury Seminary, 1968

GENESIS, Volume 1, Beacon Bible Commentary, Light and Life Press, 1969

"God's Plan and Man's Rebellion", Part I and Part II, Arnold's Commentary, Light and Life Press, 1969

"The Song of the Suffering Servant", The Seminarian, Asbury Seminary, 1970

"Old Testament Theology", The Seminary Herald, Asbury Seminary, 1971

"Prophets of Righteousness and Mercy", 13 lessons, Arnold's Commentary Light and Life Press, 1971

"Preaching from the Old Testament", The Sermon Builder, December, 1971, January,1972, March, 1972

"Guilt as Understood in the Old Testament", The Seminarian, Asbury Seminary, 1972

"Prophets of Judgment and Hope", 13 lessons, Arnold's Commentary, Light and Life Press, 1973

"The Pick and the Hoe", The Herald, Asbury Seminary, 1973

THE PENTATEUCH IN ITS CULTURAL ENVIRNMENT, Baker Book House, 1974

THE NEW INTERNATIONAL VERSION, General Editorial Committee OT, 1974-76

"Old Testament Survey", 13 lessons, Arnold's Commentary, Light and Life Press, 1974

"Biblical Authority", The Seminarian, Asbury Seminary, 1975

"Eliada, Eliadah;" "Eliakim;" "Eliam;" "Eliasaph;" "Eliashib, Eliasib;" "Elihiv;"

"Saul;" "Solomon;" "Sons of God;" "Tree of Knowledge;" "Tree of Life.", Zonderan Pictorial Encyclopedia of The Bible, 1975

"Acrostic;" "Adonijah;" "Ahaz;" "Ahaziah;" "Ai;" "Ain;" "Alliance;" "Altar;" "Amaziah;" "Anoint;" "Aphek;" "Aramaic;" "Armenia;" "Ashdod;" "Athaliah;"

"Baasha." Wycliffe Bible Encyclopedia, Volume I, Moody Press, 1975

"Structural Aspects of the Prophets' life and World," The Seminarian, Asbury Seminary, 1976

"The Relation of the Old Testament to Ancient Cultures", Volume I, THE Expositors Bible Commentary, Zondervan Pub. Co., 1979

"Origins of Life and Death", New Horizons Bible Study Series, Light and Life Press, 1980

"Judan's Later History", 13 lessons, Arnold's Commentary, Light and Life Press, 1980

"Peace With God", Studies In Conversion, Light and Life Press, 1980

Hebrew words numbered: 48, 49, 638, 685, 1580, 1846, 2191, and 2222.

Theological Wordbook Of The Old Testament, Volumes 1 and 2. 1980

NEW KING JAMES VERSION, Executive Review Committee, 1979-84

PSALMS, New Horizons Bible Study Series, Light and Life Press, 1983

"Age, Ages;" "Jerusalem;" "Primal History;" "Rabbinic Theology," Beacon Dictionary Of Theology, 1983

"Bethel Academy" and "Chaumiere du Prairie", Proceedings Of The Symposium Of The Ohio Valley, Urban Historic Archeology, Volume 1, 1983

"Bethel Academy", The Seminarian, Asbury Seminary, 1984

"Nahum Study Notes", New International Version Study Bible, 1985

"Damascus", Major Cities Of The Biblical World, 1985

"Seals and Scrolls", Illustrated Bible Life, 1987

"A Case Study of the Call of Moses", The Asbury Seminary Journal, Asbury Seminary, 1987

THE PENTATEUCH IN ITS CULTURAL ENVIRONMENT, 2nd Edition, Baker Book House, Grand Rapids MI, 1987

"The Walls of Jericho", Illustrated Bible Life, 1988

"The Life and Times of Amos", Illustrated Bible Life, 1989

"Hosea", THE Evangelical Commentary Of The Bible, 1990

Consulting Editor, Revell Bible Dictionary, 1989-1990

"Introductions to Jeremiah and Lamentations", The Wesley Study Bible, 1990

"Jeremiah and Lamentations Study Notes", The Wesley Study Bible, 1990

"Archaeology", The New Twentieth Century Encyclopedia Of Religious Knowledge, 1991

"Remnant", The Holman Bible Dictionary, 1991

"Vineyards in Ancient Israel", Illustrated Bible Life, 1991

"Esther;" Daniel;" "Jonah;" "Nahum.", The Asbury Bible Commentary, 1992

"According to the Prophet", Adult Sunday School Curriculum, 1992

"The Archive of Ebla", Archaeology and Biblical Research, 1992

"The Archive of Mari", Archaeoloogy and Biblical Research, 1992

"Why is God so Mean?" Illustrated Bible Life, 1993

"The Archive of Nippur", Bible and Spade, 1993

"The Archive of Nuzi", Bible and Spade, 1994

"The Archive of Hattusas", Bible and Spade, 1995

"The Archive of Ugarit", Bible and Spade, 1997

CREATION AND EVOLUTION, Unpublished, 1998

"Translation of Jeremiah and Lamentations", The New Living Translation, 1996-1998

Livingston Memoirs, WALKING TOGETHER THROUGH LIFE, Unpublished, 2003-2008

"Study Notes on Jeremiah and Lamentations", The New Living Translation, 2008

APPENDIX C

Though I had four years of Greek language studies in college and graduate schools, I never taught Greek to classes at any time in my career. Instead, my interest in the Hebrew language and my classes in Old Testament and archaeology was the basis of my employment as Professor of Old Testament at Asbury Theological Seminary, Wilmore, KY in 1953. For thirty-four years, I taught Hebrew classes as part of my teaching load.

In 1972, Dr. Wilber Dayton, New Testament professor at ATS, asked me if I would be interested in working on a translation team of the New International Version (a.k.a. NIV). I answered in the affirmative, so he notified the Executive Committee of the project. Soon I was hired to serve part-time on the General Editorial Committee of the Old Testament. I could do some translation of assigned Old Testament books at home and meet the full committee during semester breaks, during Christmas and Easter vacations and during the summer months at various locations.

The booklet entitled, "Holy Bible New International Version" is available from Zondervan Bible Publishers, Grand Rapids, MI. The story of how the project came into existence, how it was organized and how it was produced is presented in some detail. A few highlights of that story are summarized here.

THE NEW INTERNATIONAL VERSION

The idea of a new, modern translation developed in the Christian Reformed Church in the early 1950's. In 1962, the National Association of Evangelicals joined this church for an exploration of how to produce such a translation. In 1965 a group of evangelical scholars set up a Committee on Bible Translation to oversee a translation in modern English that would be acceptable to English speaking people in a number of countries, hence the word "international" in its title. There were fifteen scholars on this committee. The task would not be a revision of the King James Version. In 1967, The New York Bible Society decided to finance the project.

Over a hundred Old Testament and New Testament evangelical scholars were enlisted to produce the translation. For a list of these scholars, see pages 9-12 of the above mentioned booklet. The New Testament was published in1973.

Representing a number of countries and denominations, the scholars rotated their involvement in the work of various committees. For example, Dr. John Oswalt, my colleague at ATS, took my place, after I had served for several years. I continued to review completed translations of individual books. After ten years of hard work, the translations of both testaments were completed. They were published in October 1978 by Zondervan Bible Publishers. Almost everyone was surprised and pleased the sales of the NIV soon soared to hundreds of thousands of copies. In most of the years since 1978, the NIV has been the best selling Bible, often exceeding a million copies per year. I am glad I was an active member of the translation team.

One of the outstanding benefits of the NIV project was the discovery of a large number of evangelical scholars who were competent enough to do this translation task. Many of these scholars had never met before, yet they quickly became friends and completed a first rate product successfully. I was and continue to be enriched by the fellowship with a number of scholars who are Calvinists in their theology. They are genuinely Christian in their attitudes and in their relationship with me and other Wesleyan scholars.

THE NEW KING JAMES VERSION

In 1979, I was faced with another decision about engaging in a translation project that in reality was called a revision of the text of the revered King James Version (a.k.a. KJV).

The story behind this endeavor is interesting. The president of Thomas Nelson Publishing Co. Nashville, TN, Sam Moore was a

Christian immigrant from the Middle East and knew some English. In college, he became proficient in the language, but found the English of the KJV a challenge to master. In the course of time, this man became president of Thomas Nelson Inc.

The president's children had to commit to memory verses from the Bible. The children were soon complaining they found it difficult to memorize the language of the KJV. The president knew that a large percentage of his company's customers revered the KJV. It was either his customer's opinion or his children's need. He decided to probe the situation. To his surprise, he found that many of the evangelical scholars in the south shared his views. Soon a committee of New Testament scholars were preparing, in the middle 1970's, an updating of the King James Version into modern English. An encouraging response greeted the publication of a New Testament in 1979.

A small group of Old Testament scholars were formed to update that part of the Bible. In 1979, one of the committee members became too ill to function. A telephone call informed me of the situation. I was asked if I would consider coming to the Thomas Nelson office for an interview. I agreed to do so. In a few days, the interview took place and I was soon a member of the committee.

In contrast to the four major committees of the NIV project, the Thomas Nelson project had only one major editorial committee, hence, was much less costly than the production of the NIV. As a matter of fact, the task of the KJV committee was much less complex and the editors of the company did much more of the paper work. Our committee did not do a translation; it primarily did updating into modern English the KJV text. Outdated nouns, adjectives and adverbs were changed to modern terms (for example, corn was changed to grain). Pronouns "thee" and "thou" were changed to "you" and "your", and other such substitutions as necessary. The verbal system was the most radically updated, both in spelling and format. Long, technical words based on Greek or Latin origins, such as justification, sanctification, and others were replaced by shorter words or phrases based on Anglo-Saxon parentage. Verses were grouped into paragraphs instead of presented separately. One goal was to change the reading level of the KJV from its upper high school level to an eighth grade level. Our revised text was repeatedly checked to make sure the eighth grade level was achieved.

During 1998 and 1999, the committee met mostly on the company's campus, or nearby in Nashville. We ate at nearby restaurants and spent our nights in motels. I noticed the costs were high in both places. In 1980, I suggested that they take the example of the NIV and spend the summer in St. Andrews, Scotland where room and board rates were much cheaper at the university. The president of Thomas Nelson responded by contacting the university in St. Andrews and received a positive response. The costs in Scotland were so much cheaper the company decided it could afford to send the spouses of the committee members also. A new goal was to complete the revision process by early August. On the last day of this period of time, Prince Charles and Princess Dianne were married. Both were descendents of King James I. We watched the ceremony on TV and went back to our workroom and finished the Book of Malachi. We sang the Doxology.

Maria and I had scheduled three weeks for a short tour of London, a visit with Maria's relatives in the Netherlands, several days at Lake Lucerne in Switzerland, a train tour of Austria, Hungary and southern Germany. We ended the tour with a boat ride on the Rhine River. We spent most of a week with Maria's relatives. Then we boarded a plane for home. The memory of that summer remains vivid in our minds.

The publication of the NKJV was a success in the South and in other sections of the USA. In a short time, this new revision also sold over a million copies per year.

A number of evangelical scholars of Wesleyan conviction decided to produce a study Bible based on the NKJV. Beginning in 1986, Dr. A.F. Harper was chosen as General Editor of the project. His assistants were Dr. Bob Lintszenich, Associate Editor; Dr. John Oswalt, Old Testament Editor and Dr. G.L Cockerill, New Testament Editor. Scholars were assigned to prepare study notes on the contents of individual books in both testaments. I was asked to prepare notes on the books of Jeremiah and Lamentations. In 1990, the Wesley Bible was published by Thomas Nelson Inc.

THE NEW LIVING TRANSLATION

Kenneth N. Taylor had been deeply concerned that poorly educated people found the KJV too difficult to read, so they did not read the Bible. He decided to produce a Bible that anyone could easily read. Without financial support, no training in the biblical languages or guidance by a biblical school, he began writing the Scriptures as a paraphrase. Taylor ignored the fine points of proper grammar. He avoided difficult, theological words and phrases, and stressing the thought content of the biblical passages, he made much use of popular expressions and vivid verbs. The result was a Bible that shocked educated readers but was welcomed by the poorly educated masses.

Taylor published the Living New Testament in 1967 and it sold by the millions of copies. Both testaments were called The Living Bible Paraphrased and were published in 1971. The Tyndale House Publishers, Inc. was formed to print and distribute this Bible among English speaking people.

As the sons of Mr. Taylor earned college, and higher, degrees, they became involved in the administration of the printing company. The sons convinced their father it was time for the Living Bible Paraphrased (the name was changed to The Book) to be updated by qualified scholars. The goal was to produce an acceptable text that possessed a sixth grade reading level.

A Bible Translation Committee was formed with the task of creating a Bible Translation Team. The NIV and the NKJV used a word-for-word translation method that matched Hebrew, Aramaic or Greek words with equivalent English words. The scholars translating the NLT text were to be guided by a thought-for-thought method. Each thought expressed in the original text would be carefully determined and matched with equivalent thought patterns in English. To ensure that this equivalence happened, each biblical book was assigned to two or three scholars.

Each of these scholars submitted a translation to a general reviewer who evaluated the several translations. The reviewer worked with the scholars to present a proposed text to the Bible Translation Committee. This committee worked with various editors to produce a text for printing.

The New Living Translation has an introduction that explains this procedure, names the scholars assigned to the Bible Translation Team and lists the scholars assigned to each biblical Book. I was assigned with Dr. E. A. Martens to provide translations of Jeremiah and Lamentations and to review editorial changes of the text. Unlike the NIV and NKJV procedures that had frequent committee meetings, we never met together to compare notes. In 1996, the translation task was completed and the text was published.